David Heagle

The Bremen Lectures on Great Religious Questions of Today

By Various Eminent European Divines

David Heagle

The Bremen Lectures on Great Religious Questions of Today
By Various Eminent European Divines

ISBN/EAN: 9783743392496

Printed in Europe, USA, Canada, Australia, Japan

Cover: Foto ©Lupo / pixelio.de

More available books at **www.hansebooks.com**

THE

Bremen Lectures

ON

GREAT RELIGIOUS QUESTIONS OF TO-DAY

BY

Various Eminent European Divines

Translated from the Original German
BY
DAVID HEAGLE, D. D.
Professor in Theological Department of Southwestern Baptist University

A NEW AND IMPROVED EDITION

PHILADELPHIA
AMERICAN BAPTIST PUBLICATION SOCIETY
1898

PREFACE[1]

TO THE

NEW AND IMPROVED EDITION

THE striking excellence of the *Bremen Lectures*, as a defense of Christianity against the assaults of modern unbelief, has been widely recognized. A common verdict of persons who have read the book with intelligence, is—as was affirmed in the preface to a former edition—that it "would be difficult to find, at all events in English, another work wherein is included, in so brief a compass, so much of that which, with the present helps from science and thought, can, and should be, said" on the themes discussed. In other words, the lectures form an exceptionally strong and successful argument in support of the

---

[1] The "Bremen Lectures" first appeared in German, in 1868, during the same year in which they were delivered orally in the city of Bremen, under direction of the Board of Internal Missions in that place; the occasion preparing the way for them being certain disorders of an ecclesiastical nature existing in Bremen. In the first English edition, as also in the German collection, the first discourse, by Dr. Christlieb, was wanting; it not having been delivered in the original Bremen course. But it was inserted in the second English edition, to supply the place left vacant by the failure of Dr. Fabri's lecture to appear in the German collection, Dr. Fabri having been one of the speakers in the Bremen course. As presented in this book Dr. Christlieb's lecture is really a condensation of two discourses found in his *Moderne Zweifel am christlichen Glauben*, the published translation of which, carrying the author's approval, we have, with a few changes, followed in our work.

main tenets of the Christian faith, which in these times are being violently assailed by unbelief; and in accomplishing this end they make use of all the helps which the latest science and thought can offer. So it was with the production at the time when it first appeared, and since then the conditions have not materially changed. This means that in all essential respects the material of these addresses is still as fresh and as well adapted to needs of the day as when it was first published.

Accordingly it is believed that a new edition of this work will, besides meeting with an extensive welcome, be really, as was the first issue, an important contribution to current Christian apologetical literature. To make the work as acceptable as possible, the present publishers have, in this edition, introduced certain improvements. Besides furnishing a summary of each lecture and a general index, making a few corrections in the text, and altering the title-page, they have, with considerable painstaking, been able to secure the portraits of all the distinguished authors of these discourses, the faces of most of whom have been quite unfamiliar in this country. It will therefore be a real gratification to the reader to see in this new issue, at the head of each lecture, accompanied by brief biographical notes, a correct likeness of the author whose production follows.

As to the state of things in Germany which—as appearing especially in the city of Bremen—was the occasion of these lectures, it may be remarked that, while changes more or less important have occurred in both the religious faith and practice of the German people since then, still the general situation remains much the same.¹ In philosophy the reigning systems, if there are any such, would seem to be at present those of Wundt, Von Hartmann, and Lotze—especially the first. And these systems all being conceived from a Monistic point of view, and being affected more or less by either Pantheism or Materialism,² none of them can be regarded as fully in accord with Christian doctrine. Still Christian ideas have, to some extent, been appropriated by each of these schemes of thought, and especially has the philosophy of Lotze been esteemed by many of its ad-

[1] Dr. Christlieb, in his *Moderne Zweifel am christlichen Glauben*, p. 41, says of religious matters in Germany at the time when his book was written (1868, 2nd ed., 1870), that "the great mass of the educated, yet more of the half-educated classes,—the diplomatists almost without exception, the great majority of officers in the army, of the government officials, lawyers, doctors, teachers of all kinds but professed theologians, artists, manufacturers, merchants, shopkeepers, and artisans,—stand on the basis of a merely nominal rationalistic Christianity; while the lower middle class (that is, the class between those mentioned and the very poorest) carried away by the materialistic tendencies of the time, assume a more or less hostile position toward it." This is, however, true at present of only that portion of German society which resides in towns and especially in the larger cities; the vast proportion of the agriculturalists and peasantry still confess to the old faith, and in truth, have never ceased so to do. Besides, a new and better order of things has of late been gaining a progressive foothold even among townspeople and the educated. A larger attendance upon public worship in the cities is reported; increased activity obtains in church construction and in missions, foreign and domestic. Far the greater number of pulpits seem now to be dominated by an evangelical spirit, as is also the case with the theological faculties in most of the universities. Moreover, a very extensive evangelical literature has of late been produced, and at many points public lectures in defense of the old faith have been given. So taking all of these indications together, it would seem that during the last few decades, positive biblical Christianity has in Germany been making considerable advancement.

[2] Von Hartmann's philosophy is thoroughly pessimistic in its teachings.

mirers as peculiarly agreeable to the Christian view of the world. In theology there has been going forward lately quite a noticeable movement in the direction of what may be termed a more positive construction than before existed of the Christian doctrines and facts, the most prominent representative of this movement being perhaps the school of Albrecht Ritschl, who for many years prior to 1889, the year of his death, was professor of theology in the University of Göttingen. The distinction of this school is that it emphasizes the religious life, and puts the church strongly forward as the kingdom of God on earth, considering the divinity of Christ and other gospel facts as less essential to a true understanding of Christianity than these more practical elements. So also all along the line of the more practical interests of the Christian religion has there been of late throughout Germany a strong awakening, one evidence of which is the increased activity everywhere manifest in connection with Inner-Missions.

But it is especially to the serviceableness of this work in the way of meeting needs which exist particularly among Americans that attention is here invited.

1. For example, the book gives, throughout its whole extent and especially in the first lecture, by Dr. Theodor Christlieb, a full, thoroughly scriptural and therefore correct, doctrine respecting the Divine Being as he is in himself and in relation to the universe about him. More than this, the different non-scriptural conceptions of God are here also presented, and their falsity is made to appear by being held up in sharp contrast with the true or Christian view. Thus, for instance, that notion of the Deity which

just now seems to be quite in favor with not a few American scholars—the notion which represents God and the universe to be one in essence, and is therefore called Monism—is by this first discourse in the present work made to appear so erroneous and contrary to true Christian teaching that it needs only a reading of the discourse to have the untenableness of this view become apparent.[1] In like manner numerous other erroneous or unscriptural conceptions of God— such as are taught by Pantheism, or Materialism, or Rationalism, or still other isms of the day—are by this work shown up in their true light, and while any verity contained in them is readily acknowledged, their erroneous contents are also thoroughly exposed. Thus the present volume would seem to be excellently adapted to correcting false notions respecting the Supreme Being, wherever such notions may be held ; and it would, we think, be difficult to find a more correct doctrine in general touching the Deity and his relation to the universe than is, throughout and particularly in the first lecture, offered by this book.

2. Another service which the following work is capable of rendering to whomsoever may need it, is to bring out in clearest and fullest conception a correct doctrine with respect to the supernatural, or touching the relation of a truly spiritual world to a world existing under the laws of necessity or that is physical in its nature. Such a teaching is necessary in order to find place for miracles, or to make it possible that any intervention of the higher or spiritual world should occur in this lower or material order of things. The entire revelation given in the Bible, together with all

---

[1] See especially pp. 28–36, also 152–161.

the more essential facts of Hebrew and Christian history, come, it may be affirmed, under the head of the supernatural ; and therefore are to be understood only as a correct doctrine of this subject is possessed. Such a correct view both of the supernatural and of its relation to the natural may be found in this book. For that reason we esteem it to be a production of especial value, particularly in times like ours when, owing perhaps to the influence of a short-sighted natural science or of a materialistic philosophy, many persons seem to have lost, with regard to the whole realm of the supernatural, much of their faith. (*Vide* lecture on "Miracles," by Pastor Fuchs, also Lectures VI., IX., and I.)

3. Again, the whole teaching of the Bible with respect to the personality and work of Christ, his resurrection from the dead, and the atonement which he accomplished on the cross—all this is by the following production set forth with exceeding clearness and fullness, as well as substantiated by unusually strong argument. And the consequence would seem to be that if any person will inform himself touching these topics, as the knowledge is here so very ably furnished, he need not be subject either to error or ignorance as to those great matters. (*Vide* Dr. Luthardt's lecture on the "Person of Jesus Christ," Dr. Uhlhorn's on the "Resurrection of Christ as a Soteriologico-Historical Fact," and the discourse by Dr. Gess on the "Scriptural Doctrine of Atonement.")

4. Still another service of a doctrinal nature which this volume can perform, for the benefit of any who will receive it, is to furnish him clear, comprehensive, and we may per-

haps also say, thoroughly reliable views both of the written word of God as a revelation, and of the certainty of our now having, in the New Testament, at least, a revelation that is genuine, or one that can be traced up to its original inspired authors. One of the most scholarly and instructive contributions found in the book is the lecture by Dr. Constantin Tischendorf, on the "Authenticity of Our Gospels"; and this, we may observe, is his latest word on that important topic. (See also lecture by Dr. Cremer on "Reason, Conscience, and Revelation.")

5. Lastly, this production may be confidently recommended to readers, both in this country and elsewhere, because of its presenting in a wonderfully wide-reaching discourse by Dr. J. P. Lange, a most inviting, and from a scriptural point of view one would say, satisfactory conception of the "Kingdom of God as Consummated," or of the final things in the history of our world. As an illustration of the extensive sweep and deeply penetrating power of modern German thought on a religious topic, this one lecture is sufficient to give an intelligent critic some appreciative conception of the high character and worth of the book. So also the lecture by Dr. Zöckler, on the "Doctrine of Creation and Natural Science," is an unusually meritorious production; containing a vast array of facts, with judicious conclusions drawn from them. And the last discourse in the volume, the one by Pastor Disselhoff on "Christianity and Culture," has been regarded as particularly important, containing much well-selected information and numerous wise reflections on the subject considered.

So taking all these lectures together, it is not overrating their value when, as a book of information and a work in the line of Christian apologetics, they are declared to be exceedingly important. Hence they are again offered to the public with the belief and hope that in their new and improved form increased benefit will be accomplished by them.

OCTOBER, 1897.
THE TRANSLATOR.

PREFATORY NOTE

My attention was first called to the "Bremen Lectures" soon after their publication in Germany, and from the known ability and standing of the authors I was sure, before reading them, of their high character. When, therefore, at the request of my friend, the Rev. D. Heagle, who proposed to furnish the American public with a translation of them, I gave the lectures a careful perusal, I was not surprised to find them rich in thought and admirable in style— indeed, singularly worthy of being put into the English language for the benefit of American readers; for they are noble defenses of the Christian religion against fierce attacks from living adversaries; and, like all good defenses of "the faith once delivered to the saints," they deal with central facts and principles, and possess a value quite independent of controversy. Accordingly, without wishing to endorse every sentiment expressed in these Lectures, I believe it simply just to say that they are characterized by candor and breadth of view as well as by logical force and zeal for Christian truth.

The translator, a German by descent and familiar with the German language, has performed his task with fidelity and skill, giving the reader the true flavor of the original, yet modifying the structure of sentences so far as to make the English perspicuous. Such a work is a precious gift to the people of God, and, with the blessing of his grace, will do much to establish their hearts in the present truth.

Alvah Hovey.

CONTENTS.

LECTURE I.

THE BIBLICAL CONCEPTION OF GOD. 15
BY THEODOR CHRISTLIEB, D. D., UNIVERSITY PREACHER AND PROFESSOR OF THEOLOGY AT BONN.

LECTURE II.

THE DOCTRINE OF CREATION AND NATURAL SCIENCE. 65
BY OTTO ZÖCKLER, D. D., PROFESSOR AT GREIFSWALD.

LECTURE III.

REASON, CONSCIENCE, AND REVELATION. 105
BY HERMANN CREMER, D. D., PROFESSOR OF THEOLOGY AT GREIFSWALD.

LECTURE IV.

MIRACLES. 143
BY REV. M. FUCHS, PASTOR AT OPPIN, NEAR HALLE.

LECTURE V.

THE PERSON OF JESUS CHRIST. 177
BY CHR. E. LUTHARDT, D. D., PROFESSOR OF THEOLOGY AT LEIPSIC.

LECTURE VI.

THE RESURRECTION OF CHRIST, AS A SOTERIO-
LOGICO-HISTORICAL FACT. 207
BY GERHARD UHLHORN, D. D., FIRST PREACHER TO THE
(LATE) COURT OF HANOVER.

LECTURE VII.

THE SCRIPTURAL DOCTRINE OF ATONEMENT. . . . 249
BY W. F. GESS, D. D., PROFESSOR AT GOTTINGEN.

LECTURE VIII.

THE AUTHENTICITY OF OUR GOSPELS. 277
BY CONSTANTIN TISCHENDORF, D. D., PROFESSOR OF
THEOLOGY AT LEIPSIC.

LECTURE IX.

THE IDEA OF THE KINGDOM OF GOD AS CONSUM-
MATED, AND WHAT IT TELLS US REGARDING HIS-
TORICAL CHRISTIANITY. 301
BY J. P. LANGE, D. D., PROFESSOR AT BONN.

LECTURE X.

CHRISTIANITY AND CULTURE. 345
BY REV. JULIUS DISSELHOFF, PASTOR AND INSPECTOR
IN KAISERSWERTH.

LECTURE I

THE BIBLICAL CONCEPTION OF GOD

By THEODOR CHRISTLIEB, D. D.

UNIVERSITY PREACHER AND PROFESSOR OF THEOLOGY AT BONN

THEODOR CHRISTLIEB, D. D.

BIOGRAPHICAL

DR. THEODOR CHRISTLIEB was born at Birkenfeld, Würtemberg, March 7, 1833. After having studied at Tübingen (1851-55), he became pastor of the German congregation in Islington, London, N., in 1858. Here he built the first German United Church, comprehending Lutherans and Reformed. In 1865 he became town-pastor at Friedrichshafen, on Lake Constance, being invited there by the king of Würtemberg, who resided at this place during the summer. In 1868 he was made professor of practical theology and university preacher at Bonn. In 1873 he attended the Evangelical Alliance Conference in New York, and read there a paper on "The Best Methods of Counteracting Modern Infidelity," which was afterward published in a number of languages. He was also president of the West German Branch of the Evangelical Alliance, and attended the conferences at Basel (1879) and Copenhagen (1884). He was for some considerable time one of the editors of the *Allgemeine Missions zeitschrift*. His publications were quite numerous; among the more important of which may be mentioned his *Moderne Zweifel am Christlichen Glauben*, which, under the title "Modern Doubt and Christian Belief," has been translated into English, and has had a wide circulation both in this country and Great Britain. Besides being a superior scholar and teacher, Dr. Christlieb was a powerful speaker, having gifts fitting him especially for the argumentative religious lecture. He died at Bonn, August 15, 1889.

SUMMARY OF LECTURE I

RELIGION the greatest ruling power on earth—The question regarding faith now is between Christianity and nothing—The non-scriptural conceptions of God diverge into three main tendencies, as they regard the Absolute a Material Substance, an *Anima Mundi*, or the Creator of the world—Atheism is the absolute denial of any kind of θεος—Materialism defined—Pantheism described—The Deistic and Rationalistic view—The biblical conception holds fast both to God's supramundane and his intramundane character—This idea teaches, against Atheism, the existence of an eternal, unbeginning God, the Creator of all things—Against Materialism it teaches that matter is not eternal, and is in nature different from God—Against Pantheism it holds to both the antemundane and supramundane character of God, and to his difference in essence from the world—Against the Rationalistic and Deistic view the scriptural idea holds to the continued dependence of creation on God, and to his ruling presence in the world—Atheism is absolute falsehood; but it rests upon the argument of God's invisibility, a truth taught by the scriptural notion—The truth of Materialism is that God, though a Spirit, is yet substantial (not material) in his being—The truth of Pantheism is that God is omnipresent, and universally active in the world—The truth of the Deistic and Rationalistic view is that God is a Personal Being, and as the world's Creator is yet separate from it—Thus in the Biblico-Christian notion of God all the separate sparks of truth concentrate, or are focalized—Different arguments advanced for the truthfulness of this idea.—II. THE TRINITARIAN CONCEPTION OF THE DIVINE NATURE. This notion as expressed in the Apostles' Creed, and more fully defined in the Athanasian Creed—Defects of the Athanasian definition—Five lines of argument in support of the Trinitarian conception.

THE

BREMEN LECTURES.

I.

THE BIBLICAL CONCEPTION OF GOD.

BY THEODOR CHRISTLIEB, D. D.,
UNIVERSITY PREACHER AND PROFESSOR OF THEOLOGY AT BONN.

IT has been justly said, that religion is the greatest ruling power on earth. Any one who attentively considers the history of the world and its culture, in the light, not merely of surface events, but of the internal motives which determine its development, cannot fail to apprehend this truth. Even Goethe acknowledges,[1] that "the only real and the deepest theme of the world's and of man's history to which all other subjects are subordinate, is the conflict between faith and unbelief." As long as the religious question remains unsolved, there will be plenty of external "questions" on the Tiber or the Rhine, in Constantinople or in Washington. However, since the French revolution in the last part of the eighteenth century, the religious question has entered upon a fresh, and, if I am not mistaken, upon the last stage of its development. The issue, taken as a whole, lies no longer in isolated dogmatical differences between

[1] In his Abhandlungen zum westöstlichen Divan.

the various churches; even the controversy between Protestantism and Romanism has in public life become a secondary question. The question now is, *whether the Christian faith in any form shall continue to exist.* The battle of centuries between belief and unbelief is in our days tending more and more to the point where the decisive question must be put, whether the Christian religion shall be retained as the basis and rule of our civilization, or whether it must as such be wholly abandoned. "To be, or not to be; that is the question" nowadays with the Christian faith; and this question, if any, must be the last, just as two thousand years ago it was the first.

Nothing indicates this so clearly as the present shape of the controversy about the idea of God. And we may remark, that in the conflict between faith and unbelief it is the idea of God that always forms the heart's core of the matter, the vital question, the question which decides as to our view of Christianity in general, and of all particular dogmas. This controversy is not the same now that it was a hundred or two hundred years ago. At that time, if we except a few pantheists, the existence of a personal God was not generally disputed; and hence the only point for contention was God's agency in the world, whether he could work miracles, whether his providence extended to all things, whether Christ was truly divine, and the like. In the present day, however, not only is all this again called in question, but also the whole existence of God, and consequently the existence of the human spirit as a distinct essence. Formerly the issue lay between Biblical Christianity and deism; now it lies between Christianity and — nothing; between belief in God as the personal Spirit, who is Love, and the denial of God, which must be the denial of man's spiritual and moral being.

It would be an unprofitable and thankless undertaking, and one for which we have not here the time, for us to attempt regularly to refute the innumerable non-Biblical conceptions of God which have, during the history of philosophy and of false religion, appeared; moreover, our task just now is rather to set before you the Biblical conception. We will, therefore, first, only notice briefly, in the way of description, the *fundamental forms* under which all the non-Scriptural ideas of God, whether of our times or of any other, may be included; and then pass to a more extended examination of the Bible doctrine with respect to this subject. This course, while it will enable us to see, by comparison and contrast, the elements of truth and of error, which are contained in the various non-Biblical conceptions, will also help us to perceive the untenableness of these conceptions, as also to appreciate better the Biblical view and the sure foundations upon which this view rests. All views of God, not taught by the Bible, diverge into three *main tendencies*, according as they regard the Absolute as a universal *Material Substance*, as an impersonal, unconsciously working *Anima Mundi*, or as *the Creator of the world* — personal indeed, but not exercising any direct influence upon its present life. These are the distinguishing marks of the systems of materialism, pantheism, and deism; but before describing these, let us first hastily glance at atheism, as forming the most direct contrast to the Scriptural doctrine of God.

First, then, Atheism: this is the absolute denial of any kind of θεος, that is, of any Divine Being, and therefore cannot be classed among the ideas of God above mentioned. This view, that there is absolutely no God at all, was so much detested by the ancient Greeks, that they considered atheism synonymous with wickedness; it exists, as a principle, although not strictly carried out, in Buddhism; and after having for ages appeared only quite sporadically, it first assumed the character of a system — if indeed it be worthy of the name — in the train of French materialism. La Mettrie, for instance, pronounced the belief in the existence of a God to be as groundless as it was unprofitable; and during the "reign of terror" under the Convention, when the "Hebertists" laid it down as a principle, "that the King of Heaven must be dethroned just as the kings of the earth," this atheistic tendency, as is well known, penetrated the mass of the French people. Let no one imagine that the tendency is as yet extinct; nay, quite recently all doubt as to even the growing power of atheism has been removed by the blasphemous "Manifestos" of the Commune and the International, as well as by the openly avowed aims of many of our Socialist Unions. Of late, too, some of our own literati and poets have been *un*-German enough to try to transplant this tendency into our German soil; and there are also philosophers — as, e. g., Feuerbach — who come forward as its advocates.

Now of atheism it has been said, not without good reason, that it never really existed as a full conviction in any human breast, and that there is always an underlying self-deception whenever any one professes to be a pure atheist. That a person, in a fanatical over-estimation of reason, should imagine himself able to know and investigate everything, and curtly deny whatever is beyond his knowledge; or that, in the pride which refuses to acknowledge either sin or its Avenger, he should believe himself all-sufficient, in base dependence on the world of sense, denying everything that does not belong to it, and thus persuading himself that no God exists, — this, after all, is conceivable enough. But that one should, consciously and conscientiously, make this idle notion his *permanent* conviction, and that he should not, when denying the Christian's God, venerate aught else as the Divine Power, this is difficult to believe, even apart from the fact that, notwithstanding all the trouble which atheists have taken to discover but one nation utterly devoid of religious consciousness, we have found, down to the present day, *in all nations*, even the most degraded, some conception or other of a Higher Being, and a feeling of dependence on supernatural powers, and consequently some kind of religious exercise. Cicero's question (De Nat. Deorum, I. 16) still holds good — " What people is there, or what race of men, which has not, even without traditional teaching, some presentiment of the existence of Gods?" But it is not our intention to discuss the being or the non-being of a God in this place; so, we proceed to a description, —

Secondly, of Materialism; which is but the twin-brother of atheism. These two forms of the denial of God must necessarily be simultaneous; for he who denies God's existence is unable to maintain the spiritual personality of man. Historically, materialism either precedes or closely follows atheism. The two play into each other's hands, and, in fact, amount to the same thing. For the latter must ultimately believe in the eternity of matter, and, just like materialism, must make matter its God. Between materialism and pantheism, however, a distinction must be drawn. Pantheism considers God as the Soul of the world, and material nature as his body only. Materialism merges God in matter; for, according to it, *nothing at all exists but matter, — there is no such thing as a separate spiritual existence.* All that exists is material; and that which is called spirit, or spiritual life, is nothing but a function of the life of the body, a necessary product of sensuous perception, and of the nutritive matter absorbed by us, but pre-eminently of the action of the cerebral muscles. Materialism may well be called the gospel of the flesh; it is the absolute deification of matter and of the creature, traces of which pervade the whole history of mankind from Babel and Sodom onwards; nay, from the tasting of the forbidden fruit in Paradise down to our own days. Every false belief, and every act of unbelief, like that of Thomas, involves a disposition to sensualism and materialism. Every apostasy from the living God, who is a Spirit, necessitates a tendency in the opposite direction to the deification of the flesh, though it may not always go so far.

Hence unbelief has constantly, from time to time, landed in materialism. We find it in the Buddhism of ancient India; in Greece, among the atomists and the sophists, the Epicureans and the sceptics; also in the middle ages, when the Roman church clearly betrayed her tendency to the worship of matter; and again in the seventeenth and eighteenth centuries, as the ultimate result of the long-protracted doubts as to revelation. In our own days, the materialistic view has obtained a wide-spread acceptation, owing to the fact that many natural philosophers assume the entirely material descent of mankind, and make out that the ancestors of our race, just like other mammals, originally sprang from the primeval slime. In Germany, too, the influence of this school has been no slight one during the last decades; L. Feuerbach, C. Vogt, J. Moleschott, Büchner, Czolbe, &c., having been, and still being, the chief heralds of this peculiar wisdom.

Thirdly, we more particularly describe Pantheism. This system of unbelieving thought derives its name from the motto ἒν καὶ πᾶν, i. e., "One and All," which was first brought into vogue by the Greek philosopher Xenophanes. According to pantheism, God is the universe itself; *beyond* and *outside* the world he does not exist, but only *in* the world. He is the soul, the reason, and the spirit of the world, and all nature is his body. In reality, God is everything, and besides him there is nothing. Thus, making God the soul of the world, pantheism is distinguished, on the one hand, from materialism, according to which God and nature are immediately identical; and, on the other hand, from theism, that is, from the belief in a self-conscious, personal God, who created the world and guides even its most minute details. For the main point of pantheistic belief is, that this soul of the world is *not a personal, self-conscious Being*, who appears in his *totality* in any one phenomenon or at any one moment, so as to comprehend himself or become comprehensible for us, but that it is only the one ever same essence which, filling everything and shaping everything, lives and moves in all existing things, and is revealed in all that is visible, yet is itself never seen. Goethe has depicted it in the oft-quoted words, —

> "I rise and fall on the waves of life,
> I move to and fro in action's strife;
> Birth and the grave, — an eternal sea, —
> A web that changes alternately, —
> A life which must ever glow and burn,
> On the whirring loom of life, in turn
> All these I weave, and the Godhead see
> Clad in a robe of vitality." [1]

The father of occidental pantheism was the Jew Spinoza (1632–1677). "I have," says he, "opinions as to God and nature entirely different from those which mod-

[1] Faust, erster Theil.

ern Christians are wont to vindicate. To my mind God is the immanent (that is, the intramundane), and not the transcendent (that is, the supramundane) Cause of all things; that is, the totality of finite objects is posited in the *essence* of God, and not in his *will*. Nature, considered *per se*, is one with the essence of God." He also makes out that " God does not act in pursuance of a purpose, but only according to the *necessity* of his nature;" which expresses the fundamental view of every form of pantheism. Even Hegel's conception of God, as the absolute Idea or the absolute Spirit which, in eternal self-movement, proceeds from itself and becomes nature, and then again reverting to itself, becomes a self-conscious spirit, is, in truth, only another name for the same thing. For Spinoza himself distinguishes between nature "begetting" and "begotten" (*natura naturans et naturata*). The latter is the ever-varying phenomenal world, the former the intermittent bourn from which these phenomena take rise, and into which they sink again.

Fourthly, the Deistic and Rationalistic View. In many respects this view is the antithesis of the pantheistic. According to pantheism, God exists only *in* the world as its soul; according to deism, he exists only *above* the world as a personal Spirit: by pantheism, God and the world are regarded as absolutely inseparable; by deism, as absolutely severed, and as not merely different, but divided one from the other. God is for the deist a *personal* Being, who, after creating the world by his will, now acts towards it like an artificer with a finished machine, which mechanically pursues its natural course according to the laws laid down for it, and no longer requires the immediate assistance or interference of its maker. Thus, while, on the one hand, the being, personality, and supramundane nature of the Deity (hence the vague and awkward term " deism "), and the creation of the world by him, are acknowledged, on the other, any *continuous active presence of God in the world, and any living interposition in its affairs, are denied.* Hence there can be no special providence; miracles are an impossibility; in fact, every particular manifestation of God must be denied, — all supernatural elements in the Christian belief, even those involved in the person and work of Christ, must be excluded, and everything in Scripture bearing on these points must be explained away by a reference to natural causes.

In all essentials, then, deism coincides entirely with what was formerly denominated *"naturalism;"* [1] for it pronounces the laws of nature to be adequate to the continuous existence of the world, and natural religion to be the only essential form of belief, even in connection with Christianity. It likewise agrees in principle with what is called *rationalism*, the essence of which consists in the position that reason is not merely the formal, but also the material, principle of religion, and supreme arbiter over the whole substance of the Christian faith. At the present time, both in German and English theology, the rationalistic principle has but few representatives, but reckons a proportionately larger number among Swiss (Zurich), French (Strasburg), and Dutch (Leyden and Gröningen) theologians; while the great body of educated laymen, and especially of the students of modern natural science, are confessedly under its influence.

[1] At the present day, in Germany, naturalism and materialism are used as nearly synonymous terms for the theory which derives from the operation of the laws of nature only, not merely the continuance, but the very existence and even the origin, of the world; whilst in England, for instance, "naturalism" still retains its original meaning, and is defined as "the denial of any divine rule and providence extending to individuals." (Cf., e. g., *Pearson on Infidelity.*)

These, then, are the principal non-Biblical conceptions of God, especially as current in the present day. Let us now turn to that view of the divine nature which is given us in the Christian Scriptures. This we shall find to be alone fundamentally true and scientifically tenable. And the truth of the Scriptural conception of God is apparent from this, that *while it excludes all that in the various other conceptions must be recognized as false and negative, it combines in a living unity all their scattered elements of positive truth.* We have a twofold problem to solve: first, to exhibit in general terms the fundamental Scriptural conception of the divine nature, i. e., Biblical theism, and establish the truth of its various principles; and then briefly to justify its full development in the Christian doctrine of the Trinity as the deepest, highest, most perfect presentation of the idea of God.

I. Biblical Theism.

The teaching of Scripture concerning God is based on the theistic conception, that, namely, which holds fast at once his supramundane and his intramundane character; the one in virtue of his nature and essence, the other of his will and power. For while theism, on the one hand, regards the *Theos* (God) as a personal Being, and so as essentially distinct from the whole created universe and from man, it is no less careful, on the other hand, to present him as the ever-living and working One in his immediate personal relationship to man and the universe by the doctrine of a universal Divine Providence. This view of the divine nature is virtually expressed in the first verse of the Bible: *In the beginning God created the heavens and the earth,* and in the fundamental article of the Apostles' Creed: *I believe in God, the Father Almighty, Maker of heaven and earth.* Now permit me hastily to show you how this and other definitions of Holy Scripture exclude what is false in the several non-Biblical conceptions of God which we described.

And first, against *atheism*, which we need scarcely mention, Scripture here, as everywhere, teaches an eternally existing un-beginning God, from whose creative activity heaven, and earth, and time itself took their beginning, — an absolute self-existent One, who saith, I AM THAT I AM, having in himself the ground of his own being, — the unchangeable, ever-living One, who "hath life in himself, and therefore hath given to the Son to have life in himself" (John 5:26); "who is, and who was, and who is to come" (Rev. 1:4, 8).

Against *materialism*, we find a protest in the first sentence of the Bible. *Matter is not eternal.* It had a beginning along with time; heaven and earth were created in that beginning. Matter, therefore, cannot itself be God, but came into existence through an act of his will. And he is distinguished from it not only by priority of existence, but also by difference of nature. "*God is a Spirit*" (John 4:24), that is, a *thinking Being*, e. g., "*Thy thoughts are very deep*" (Ps. 92:6); and "*of his wise thinking there is no end*" (literal rendering of Ps. 147:5).

In like manner we find in those first words of Scripture a protest against *pantheism*, with its confusion of God and the world, and its assumption of the identity of essence in both. God is both antemundane and supramundane, and as to his essence distinct and separate from the world, and existing independently of it: "*In the beginning God created heaven and earth.*" God IS — is absolutely and without beginning; the world is brought into existence, and is dependent on its Creator, not he on it. Moreover, it comes into existence *through* him, but not *from* him. Every theory of emanation which would make the world, in whatever form, old Indian or modern pantheistic, an efflux from the Divine Essence, is from the first excluded by the word "created," which simply expresses the fact that the world's origin is derived not from the essence, but from the will of its Creator; that its production was not a necessity, but a free act on God's part, who is, therefore, to be distinguished and separated from the world as a living, thinking, willing, and *personal* Being. Throughout Scripture God speaks as a person — I — who does not, as Hegel thought, attain to self-consciousness in the human spirit, but has possessed it independently from the beginning. So little, according to Scripture, is God from us, that we are rather from him. He is not a mere Idea, but Personality itself, absolute Freedom, and the highest Self-consciousness, — the prototype of all other self-consciousness, all other personality, — that which alone and eternally IS, which we are always becoming, who is before and above all, and from whom our own personality is derived (Gen. 2:7; Eph. 4:6).

Finally, against the false *deistic* and *rationalistic* separation between God and the world, Holy Scripture makes like protest in the same opening sentence, which declares the dependence of the world in both its parts (heaven and earth) on the will of Him who called it into being. The same is also indicated in the divine names most commonly used in Scripture, expressive of divine power and might (*Elohim, El, Eloah*), as well as of lordship and dominion (*Adon, Adonai*), and indicating at once the essential unity of God in opposition to polytheism (Deut. 6:4), and his fullness of living energies: hence the plural form of the divine name *Elohim*, used ordinarily when reference is made to the Divine Activity in the creation, preservation, and providential government of the world in general. God (it tells us) makes himself seen and felt by us, both in the universe as a whole and in its smallest details, as the absolutely simple and yet complex Life. He is, therefore, in the highest sense the living One and the living Agency, which not only created the world, but also continuously upholds and maintains it: who, " upholding all things by the word of his power" (Heb. 1:3), and in his omnipresence pervading everything, " giveth to all life, and breath, and all things" (Acts 17:25). So much, too, is he needed by the world at every moment of its existence, that all life would cease were his influence withdrawn: " Thou hidest thy face, they are troubled ; thou takest away their breath, they die, and return to their dust" (Ps. 104:29). Whereas deism asserts that the Creator has withdrawn himself from his work, and is now far removed from the world, the Scriptures say, " He is *not far* from every one of us ; for in him we live, and move, and have our being" (Acts 17:27, 28). All these and other attributes follow, still more clearly, from the name *Jehovah*. In fact, this name is in itself a complete refutation of deism. The latter asserts that God worked on one occasion only, — in the creation, — and that since then the world has spontaneously followed its own course; but Christ says, " My Father *worketh hitherto*, and I work: the Son can do nothing of himself, but what he seeth the Father do ; for what things soever he doeth, these also doeth the Son likewise (John 5:17, 19). The Scriptures teach us that God can work miracles (Luke 1:37) ; that he has revealed himself in special, supernatural modes (Heb. 1:1, ff) ; and that even now, by means of his Spirit, he makes himself recognized, felt, and enjoyed. In short, they tell us of God as One who in a thousand ways every moment places himself in mutual relationship and active communication with man; who lives and rules not merely *above*, but also *in*, the world; from whose throne the current of life flows down to all creation, and lightnings, thunders, and voices go forth in every direction (Rev. 4:5, 11:19).

It must now be evident that we were thoroughly justified in applying the term non-Biblical to those other conceptions of God; and likewise the false elements which we recognized in, particularly, pantheism and deism, — viz., in the one the blending together of God and the world; and in the other, their entire separation, — are excluded by the Biblical conception. But here let us observe how the *scattered sparks of truth which scintillate amid the darkness of the other ideas of the Supreme Being, shine forth as one clear light in the view taken of him in the Bible.*

Atheism, which certainly is falsehood itself, and therefore does not contain one single spark of truth, rests upon the argument that nothing is to be seen of God. According to the Scriptures, God is really the invisible One (1 Tim. 1:17; John 1:18). So far, however, from this attribute's diminishing the reality of his being, it is precisely that which certifies to his true, eternal existence; "for the things which are seen are temporal, but the things which are not seen are eternal" (1 Cor. 4:18). The invisibility of God is not a defect, but a prerogative. For, in respect of his essence, God is absolutely exalted above everything that is created and visible, and he *cannot manifest himself directly* to the creature, but only in some shape which has a certain affinity to it.

Materialism identifies God with nature and with matter. It lays stress on the element in the being and working of the Spirit which is allied to, and interwoven with, nature. This aspect of the truth also receives its full due in the Scriptural view of God. According to it, although God is Spirit, he has nevertheless a nature, which we may term *substantial*, but not *material*. It is designated as light and fire: "We declare unto you that God is light;" "Who coverest thyself with light as with a garment," &c. (1 John 1:5; Rev. 21:23; Ps. 104:2; 1 Tim. 6:16). "Our God is a consuming fire;" "a fire goeth before him," &c. (Deut. 4:24, 9:3; Heb. 12:29; Isa. 10:17; Ps. 97:3; cf. also the visions of the prophets). However, this element of light in God's nature does not exclude its spirituality, but plainly indicates it.

The truth in *pantheism* is the assertion that God is *omnipresent* and *universally active* in the world. We have already seen that these attributes are assigned to God by the Holy Scriptures everywhere, and with full emphasis. They entirely separate God from the world as regards his nature, but most closely connect him with it as regards his will and his action. The Scriptures cannot at all imagine the life of the world without the animating presence of God in it. As an infinite Being, far exalted above all limits either of time or space, God is near to every being in every place, and that not as a mere idle looker-on, but quickening and maintaining, helping and directing it with his full power and activity (1 Kings 8:27; Amos 9:6; Isa. 66:1; Jer. 23:24; Ps. 139:7, 10, 105:7; Matt. 28:20; Eph. 1:23). But although *pervading* everything, and *in* everything, yet at the same time he is *above* everything (Eph. 4:6). Biblical Monotheism does not, therefore, at all require the aid of pantheism in order to maintain a constant, living relation between God and the world. The Bible teaches that God is the fullness of all life, and therefore recognizes a veritable presence of God in all forms of the world's life; so that as regards the fullness, multifariousness, and intimacy of the divine presence, it falls short neither of pantheism nor of polytheism. Further, pantheism fears lest the idea of personality should involve a restriction in the being of God; and there is truth in this idea to the extent that God *cannot* be conceived as a *single Person*. He would thus be degraded to the level of other personalities. But Holy Scripture also considers him not as a single person, but as *absolute Personality*, which is neither limited nor restricted by anything else; which is not a numerical One beside other single beings, but is both Unity and Plurality at once, i. e., a *triune* Being. Thus, as we shall hereafter see, room is left for the infinite fullness of life in God: and yet the great prerogative of personality is firmly maintained. Thus, moreover, full justice is done to the truth involved in *polytheism*, viz., that plurality is an elementary form of being, and therefore must be derivable from God. Pantheism likewise demands, not without reason, that a self-conscious God must from all eternity have an object which might reflect his consciousness into itself; but according to the Biblico-Christian view, God has an object of this kind, existing from all eternity, in the distinction between the Persons of the Trinity in his own being, an object which renders it superfluous to suppose that the world existed from everlasting. Because he is absolute personality, he does not exist, or come into existence, in or through anything else, nor does he only receive self-consciousness through something which encounters him, and causes him to revert upon himself; but he derives it from himself, and it flows to him out of his own essence. For he is not merely *I*, but also constitutes himself as *He;* hence he can say of himself, I am *He* (Deut. 32:39; Isa. 41:4, 43:10, 13, 25, 48:12). He is himself both subject and object.

The elements of truth contained in *deism* and *rationalism* are these, that God is a personal Being, and that, as the Creator of the world, he must be conceived as separate from it; further, that his interposition in the world is not of an arbitrary character calculated to disturb its order, but avails itself of the forces and laws implanted therein; also, that God, in his holy patience, even imposes upon himself a certain self-limitation in respect of human freedom. These truths, likewise, have due importance accorded to them in the Holy Scriptures. For the all-guiding and all-watching God of the Bible, and none other, is a God of order (1 Cor. 14:33). The entire history of his holy rule over the world, as related to us in Scripture, is a proof of this. But this order not only does not render the Providence of God in individual cases superfluous, but directly requires it. Again, even when deism goes too far in exalting God above the world, in order not to degrade him by mixing him up with the finite and with the changes and chances of the world, this idea contains a twofold element of truth: first, the separation of God from all that is impure, his *holiness* and *incomparableness ;* and next, his eternal *immutability* and *constant conformity with himself.* But what can set forth these attributes of God more prominently than do the Scriptures? According to them, God is in his inmost nature *the only holy One,* who, being strictly severed from all that is impure, and unaffected by any of the infirmities of finite beings, is supernaturally exalted above all their limitations. He is purity itself, and keeps far from him everything that is opposed to his nature (Lev. 11:44, 45, 19:2; Ps. 22:4; Isa. 6:3, 54:5; John 17:11; Rev. 15:4), because he is the incomparable One (Isa. 40:25, 46:5). And so, too, he is the immutable One. For whereas all the gods of polytheistic religions have a history full of personal events, changes, metamorphoses, and adventures, and the sacred writings of the heathen are mere collections of divine biographies, the God of the Bible has no biography and no personal adventures whatever; he is ever and unchangeably the same, because he is the only veritable *self-existent Being*, and not a being *brought into existence*. His peculiar nature also defines his relation to the world, — "I am that I am;" "Thou art the same" (Ps. 102:27); "I am the Lord; I change not" (Mal. 3:6); "With whom is no variableness" (James 1:17; cf. Heb. 13:8).

Thus, in the Biblico-Christian conception of God, all the separate sparks of truth are concentrated, as it were, in a focus. It combines God's personality and independence, his connection with nature and capability of being known, his omnipresence and omnipotence, his invisibility, incomparableness, and immutability, his supramundane, and yet intramundane existence; and, we may also add, everything which reason and conscience can, by means of natural knowledge, unveil of God's omnipotence, goodness, wisdom, and holiness — indeed, even all the *true* elements which are contained in the heathen conceptions of God, of his miracles and manifestations, his inspirations and incarnations. If one-sidedly maintained, these several elements of truth lead to a distorted and mistaken view of God; but if united, *each one checks any undue prominence of the other*, and so all contribute towards the perfect *truth, rationality, and beauty* of the Biblical idea of God.

Allow me to set this before you more in detail.

(*a*) The *intrinsic truth* of the Biblical conception of God is shown by the fact that it alone affords the possibility of conceiving God as the *entirely perfect, the truly absolute* Being. No conception of God can be the true one which does not include every perfection. But in all the other ideas of God there is something essential wanting; at one time his spirituality (materialism), or even his existence (atheism), so again his consciousness (pantheism), or his constant living activity (deism). From the Biblical point of view, however, God is made to possess all these attributes, and to possess them in the very highest degree — being and life, spirituality and omnipotence, consciousness and thought, will and freedom, and, in addition, a constant living and holy activity in the entire universe. Here alone he possesses both himself and the world, and is *absolutely the Lord*, who rules everything according to his holy aims, and guides free spirits according to free moral laws; here alone does he possess every physical and moral perfection, and become " *God*," that is, entirely and thoroughly *good*, as our Teutonic speech strikingly points out. *Therefore in this view only is the conception of the Absolute completely realized.* For God must needs determine and condition everything. But for this end it is necessary that he should be absolutely *good* and absolutely *free*. The two attributes are combined only in the God of Scriptures, — the *holy*, and therefore also the free, God, who does what pleases him, whose will no one can gainsay (Rom. 9:19); whereas the God of pantheism is neither good nor free, and the God of deism is, at all events, not free, and in reality not *perfectly* good.

Moreover, the true principle of all being can evidently be only that *from which everything that is may be derived.*

Apart from the moral sphere, God must be the unity of all antitheses. This he is only according to the Christian conception, because this alone makes him truly absolute. We can trace back to the almighty One all that is created, to the living One all that lives, to the self-conscious Spirit all the spiritually rational and personal life in the world. Here we see God as one, and yet containing in himself the principle of multiplicity; pervading everything, and yet above all; capable of being known, and yet unsearchable; condescending to the lowest depths, and yet enthroned in unattainable sublimity; eternally near, and yet eternally far off.

Again, must not that be the truest idea of God which affords the deepest satisfaction to the *religious need* of man? Such need tends to a complete union of the God-seeking soul with the Creator, and to its being pervaded, filled, and blessed by him. This, according to Scripture, is the aim and conclusion of the whole revelation and world-government of God and Christ, "that God may be all in all" (1 Cor. 15 : 28). Once more, we must aver that this consummation of the world's development is unattainable except under the presupposition of the Biblical idea of God. Neither the impersonal mundane soul of pantheism, which destroys the higher self-conscious life as soon as it takes it back again into itself, nor yet the deistical God who abides outside the life of the world, and therefore does not communicate himself to individual souls, can ever be "all in all," and thus fully satisfy the religious need of man. Only the God of Scripture can do this. And why? Because he is the perfect *Spirit* and perfect *love*, or, combining both attributes in one, *the Father*.

Here we have before us the most profound definitions of Scripture as to the nature of God, *per se* definitions to the sublimity of which the presentiments and longings of no heathen people ever rose, although the truth of them directly forces itself on the reason and conscience. God is *spirit* (Jno. 4 : 24, not "a spirit"). Man *has* spirit, God *is* spirit. In him the spirit does not form merely a portion of his being, but the whole substance of his nature, his peculiar self, is spirit. Here we have the idea of God in his *inner perfection*, just as the names Elohim and Jehovah tell us mainly his external position. As spirit, God is the eternal, self-dependent brightness and truth, absolute knowledge, the intelligent principle of all forces, whose glance penetrates into everything, and produces light and truth in all directions. Spirit! how much food for thought does this one word give! Do we not feel as though it would cut asunder the hard knot which philosophy has placed before us with its conceptions of God, so laboriously wrought out, so artificially combined, and therefore often so difficult to understand? "God is spirit." Placing these simple words side by side with all the definitions of ancient and modern philosophers, — e. g., that God is the universal relative measure of the world's becoming (Heraclitus), or the indifference of the real and ideal (Schelling), &c., — have we not even in the profound *simplicity* of the Biblical doctrine a proof of its truth? The greatest truths are always those very ones which are the most surprisingly simple in their nature, whilst that which is artificial, contorted, and complicated, is in most cases only half true or entirely false.

How clear and intelligible, too, do all the other attributes ascribed to God in Scripture become, when considered in the light of this fundamental definition of spirituality! When once I know that God is spirit, I can much more readily conceive that he is the eternally living and personal

One, and I can even forecast that this spiritual nature of fire and light may be the basis of his omnipresence, omniscience, and omnisapience, as well as of his omnipotence and glory. Nay, I can more readily comprehend those attributes, for it is only as spirit that they can appertain to him. And conversely, where once the point is settled that he, as the most perfect Being, must possess all these, it follows that he must be spirit. This definition, therefore, is *not merely a truth, but a necessity*, which spontaneously results from the conception of the Absolute.

The same is made clear to us in the fundamental tenet of Scripture as to the *moral* nature of God, viz., that he is *holy love*. As spirituality is the vital foundation of his physical and intellectual perfections, so holy love is the internal basis of his moral perfections, and a necessary deduction from the true idea of the Absolute. Benign, gracious, merciful, long-suffering, patient, faithful, true, just, and whatever other moral beauty may be ascribed to God in the Scriptures, all this he can be only because he is *holy* (cf. the passages above quoted), and because he is love (1 John 4 : 8, 16). For the same reason he is also *light*, in which there is no darkness at all (1 John 1 : 5). Light is only the necessary effulgence of his intrinsically holy nature; for the moral and the natural are in God individually one. Truly has one said, "Holiness is the hidden glory, and glory the manifested holiness of God." As holy love, God has two attributes: He is distinctly *separated*, as we have seen, from all that is either internally or externally impure and base (the fundamental conception of holiness), and is therefore higher, more glorious, and more majestic than any creature; at the same time, he is full of the most tender *condescension* and — if I may so say — self-sacrifice; in infinite compassion imparting himself to the world in order to eradicate from it sin and all impurity, and to render it a partaker in his perfect life and glory. "I am the Lord thy God," he exclaims to his people, "the *holy* One of Israel, thy *Saviour*" (Isa. 43 : 3, 45 : 15, 54 : 5 ; John 3 : 16 ; 1 Tim. 4 : 10), &c.

What teaching about God can be more sublime or more adapted to the yearnings of our heart than this ? Where do we find an idea of God which satisfies our religious need so abundantly as the truth that God is love ? Does not every heart led by an involuntary bias say "yea and amen" to this ? Does not this idea force itself directly as the truth upon all, even unbelievers ? Any man who, even in the smallest degree, acknowledges his deepest need, will lay hold on this truth with both hands, and cry out, "Yea, this is God ; and he must be this, not merely on his own behalf, on behalf of his moral perfection and beauty, but *for my sake* also, if there is to be any hope for me ; the God of *love* is the only God who can satisfy my needs."

No less comforting is the name of *Father*, as applied to God ; and following from the twofold conception of spirit and love, God is thus called, sometimes in his character of universal originator (e. g., 1 Cor. 8 : 6), sometimes in the special sense of begetting, as in the case of Christ (e. g., Ps. 2 : 7), and the regenerate (e. g., Jas. 1 : 18), but specially because he exercises loving care, education, and providence. The former universal relationship is the groundwork of the latter more special one. This, however, we do not find only in the New Testament, but also in the Old (Deut. 32 : 6 ; Ps. 103 : 13 ; Isa. 63 : 16, 64 : 8 ; Jer. 3 : 4, 19, 31 : 9 ; Mal. 1 : 6, 2 : 10) ; although, it is true, the true depths of the divine Fatherhood are first revealed to us in the former, because the relation of God to men as Father was perfectly realized in Christ alone, and through him was brought about for the whole world. This name points out his dignity no less than his accessibility and condescension, his holy prefiguration of us no less than his love and care, our own needy condition no less than our honor and dignity, as children created in our Father's image. What an encouragement and stimulus for a human heart, — how much that excites confidence, imposes awe, stimulates the conscience, and inspires love and hope, — what a sea of joy and bliss there is in that one name *Father!* "All our other knowledge of God contains nothing more than the isolated letters and syllables of this one Name" (Tholuck). We Christians possess it and enjoy it in its fullest extent. In the whole range of heathen piety we find nothing but distant and obscure presentiments of the heart's-joy which overwhelms each one who, in the fullness of his soul, can cry, "Doubtless thou art our Father and Redeemer; from everlasting this is thy name" (Isa. 63:16); who can call upon his God by all the glorious names which the Scriptures apply to him, — Physician, Stronghold, Rock of Salvation, Refuge and Confidence, Shield and Buckler, Light and Consolation, Shepherd and Helper, Redeemer and Saviour.

Again, I ask, is there any idea of God which can more thoroughly satisfy the religious need of a human heart? Indeed, in view of this name of God, I will venture to ask every one who rejects the Biblical idea of him, Hast thou ever earnestly considered its depths, in devout contemplation and active appropriation, without finding full satisfaction in it? Only we must never forget that the truth of the Biblical idea of God must be recognized principally by *personal experience.* The true God must be found by a moral search. "The desire to attain to God, without God," says a philosopher, "is just such another feat as the tempter promised to teach our first parents: how, in opposition to God, and without him, they might make themselves equal to him" (Baader).

Or must not that be the true idea of God by which I, as a sinful being, am at once *bowed down and raised up;* by which I am made to feel the whole weight of my guilt, and yet not to despair, but to hope; by which I am shown the wide gulf which separates me from God, and also the way to a restoration of unity with him? And what else in this respect can compare with the God of the Holy Scriptures, who in one breath says of himself, "I dwell in the high and holy place, and with him who is of a contrite and humble spirit" (Isa. 57:15; comp. Ps. 117:5-7), so as to make us feel at once his holy distance and his comforting nearness? or again, who, whilst asking sin-burdened Israel whether he ought not justly to make them like unto Sodom, immediately adds, "Mine heart is turned within me; my repentings are kindled together" (Hos. 11:8)? And where shall we find the way to a restoration of union with God brought so lovingly before the fallen world as by him who proclaims, "God so *loved* the world that he gave his only-begotten Son, that whosoever believeth in him should *not perish*, but have *everlasting life*"?

And finally, must not that be the true idea of God which does the most to elevate man morally, to ennoble, to spiritualize him, and to render him like God? And from an *historical point of view* we ask, Where has there been any conception of God and religion which has so much elevated, educated, and enlightened both individuals and nations as the Biblico-Christian conception? Whence may we expect a more powerful moral influence than from the worship of the God who, as spirit, desires to be worshipped only in spirit and in truth? Where is there a more forcible stimulus to purity, both of heart and life, than is found in the worship of him of whom it is written, "Holy, holy, holy, Lord God of Sabaoth;" and, "Be ye holy, for I am holy"? And place side by side the fact, that other nations, who were acquainted with none but *unholy* gods, have, through their worship, sunk into an ever-deepening moral degradation, which could not be averted even through the influence of philosophy. "By their fruits ye shall know them." And indeed the truth of this conception of God is witnessed not merely by the Holy Scriptures, but also by our own heart and conscience, and the testimony of innumerable Christians, who have recognized it in their personal experience, and have given incontestable evidence of its moral fruits in their hearts and lives; and the whole history of the world and its civilization confirms it.

(*b*) Nor does *reason* itself bear a less decided witness in favor of this view. Some one, perhaps, will say, "It is all very well to heap together the greatest possible number of beautiful attributes; but the question is, whether it is rational to predict all these *together* of God? Yes, I reply, the Biblical conception of God is also the *most rational*, and the one that recommends itself most strongly to our understanding. It is true that his sublimities far transcend all the perceptions of reason. But they are not *unreasonable* because they are beyond the scope of reason. No reasonable man can expect that he as a finite being should entirely and perfectly comprehend the infinite God; to do this, he must himself be God. And it is therefore perfectly comprehensible to any discreet, temperate mind, which remains conscious of its limitations, that the Scriptures should reserve the perfect knowledge of God for the intuition of another life (1 Cor. 13:12; 2 Cor. 5:7; 1 John 3:2). The only question therefore is, whether this preliminary knowledge of God with which the Holy Scriptures furnish us, on the express understanding of its fragmentary nature, really recommends itself to our reason, and not merely to our hearts. And this it does infinitely more than any other conception.

Is it not, I ask in the first place, the most reasonable thing we can do to adopt that idea of God which renders the necessary divine perfections, and also the mystery of the world and our own being, more intelligible than does any other? Our conception of God fulfils all these requirements. We have already seen that the attributes of eternal vitality and personality, of omnipresence, omniscience, omnipotence, &c., which we are bound to attribute to the Absolute as such, are unintelligible, unless with the Bible we presuppose God to be spirit. Moreover, it is no longer a mystery to me that God should create worlds, notwithstanding the perfect self-sufficiency of his being, if I know that he is Love, whose nature it is to desire that other beings outside itself should rejoice in their existence. It is no longer a matter of wonder to me that, in every grain of dust and in every drop of water, traces of infinite wisdom obtrude themselves on my notice, when I think of God as the highest self-conscious Intelligence. I am no longer at a loss to account for the requirements of a law in my conscience which is altogether different from that which rules in nature, when I know that the holy God is thereby teaching me his holy will. Again, it appears to me in the highest degree reasonable that God should reveal himself in the Scriptures step by step, gradually disclosing to man the depths of his own nature: first his power, goodness, and wisdom; then his holiness and justice; and last of all, in Christ, his world-subduing love. So soon as I form the idea that he is a Father who is educating man, I see why he communicates himself to him in a special manner during childhood, and then places the earlier periods of man's existence under a law somewhat different from that which rules the later ones. Yes, in view of the moral freedom of man, it no longer seems inexplicable that God should have allowed him to sin, and thereby to bring such unutterable woes upon our race, if I can believe that the purpose and counsel of God from all eternity was to redeem man through Christ, and to bring him back into blessed fellowship with himself. It no longer seems a strange chance that, in the course of the world's history, I should perceive so many traces of righteous justice and holy laws never to be infringed with impunity, when I know that a righteous God is in the seat of government, guiding everything according to his holy purposes. Nay, do not the mysteries of my own life's experience become closer and clearer when I illumine them with the utterance, "I have loved thee with an everlasting love; therefore with loving-kindness have I drawn thee" (Jer. 31:3); that is, with the belief in God as a Father, who in everything, be it love or be it severity, seeks to draw me to himself? The inmost yearning of my soul after God becomes intelligible to me, and is satisfied in its profoundest depths, only when I know that God in his compassion meets me half way and imparts himself to me, because he is love.

Once more I ask, Is it not consonant with reason to accept an idea of God which furnishes me with *a key to the most important questions connected with the world and with my life?* If the other conceptions of God lead me to only an inexplicable *something*, at which my thoughts are at rest; and if, on the other hand, the Biblical conception of God affords me, in respect to the ultimate cause of things, at least a notion, the substance of which I can in some measure comprehend, and which — even in practical life — solves many enigmas which must else remain unsolved; then surely the rationality of this conception of God must be greater than that of all others, and the words hold good, "The fear of the Lord," that is, the theoretical and practical observance of this idea, "is the beginning of wisdom."

(c) Finally, the Biblical conception of God recommends itself by its *beauty* no less than in other ways; for in this respect, too, it far surpasses all other cognate ideas. For the most part it would be hard to discover an aspect of beauty in the non-Biblical conceptions of God. Philosophical definitions of the divine nature may tickle our intellectual palate; but abstract ideas of this kind will not touch our sense of beauty. And yet the God who formed the world, as a beautiful expression of his own mind (Gen. 1:31), and then made it over to man as his beautiful image, to impress upon it the divine brightness of his Spirit, and glorify it into his own likeness, — surely this God who is the most perfect Being must also be the most beautiful, and must, therefore, most forcibly arouse and attract to himself the sense of beauty felt by his image — man. Both in his physical, his intellectual, and moral attributes, the God of the Holy Scriptures is a God of surpassing beauty. Not, indeed, his formless and invisible essence, but his overt action and self-manifestation, especially in Christ, have for this reason at all times been an inexhaustible mine of wealth for representative art, and have inspired it to its sublimest and most ideal productions.

Let us just for a moment compare the other conceptions of God with that of the Bible in point of beauty. In the one case we have an unconscious mundane soul, whose rule, in a moral point of view, is no better than that of animal instinct; in the other, a self-conscious, holy, all-wise intelligence: in the one case, a universal substance under the iron law of necessity, first begetting a world, and then again swallowing it up; in the other, a free, creative will which, in love to men, places itself in relation to them as free beings according to the moral laws: or again, in the one case, a Being who was once a Creator, but now rests in slothful inactivity, not troubling himself about his creatures individually; in the other, a Father who "openeth his hand and filleth all things living with plenteousness," who also "clothes the lilies and the grass of the field," and "feeds the fowls of the air:" in the one case, a mere indifferent looker-on, who leaves the world entirely to itself, or at best observes it from some astronomical distance; in the other, "One who keepeth Israel, and neither slumbereth nor sleepeth," and guideth his people like a faithful shepherd. Listen, on the one hand, to a Lalande, who presumptuously exclaims, "For sixty years I have surveyed the heavens, and never as yet have I seen *Him!*" or to a La Place, who says, "In my heaven I can find no God;" and hear, on the other, the king of Israel, who, in holy awe, ejaculates, "Whither shall I flee from thy presence?" "Behold, the heaven of heavens cannot contain thee:" listen, on the one hand, to a Hegel, who looks upon the starry world as nothing better than " a luminous eruption, no more worthy of wonder than an eruption in man, or a swarm of flies;" and, on the other, to the pious psalmist, to whom "the heavens declare the glory of God." Compare, I pray you, these antagonistic views of God and the world, and then tell me candidly which is the more beautiful, the sublimer, the more worthy of God and man!

On this point, however, the objection is very frequently raised, that, side by side with many exalted ideas of God, there are in the Bible, at least in the Old Testament, *many views unworthy of him.* This widely spread notion is in innumerable cases not merely a main item, but also the source of modern doubts as to the Christian faith. The objections most commonly urged are to the nature and mode of God's intercourse with man, as represented in the Old Testament Scriptures, — to his too human-like appearances and feelings, his wrath, vengeance, repentance, and the like. In the consideration of these stumbling-blocks, I would simply recommend you to keep in view two things: *first,* the gradual progress of revelation, in which God must *educate* mankind (Deut. 8:5), *dealing therefore with them at first as children,* and condescending to them in a way different from his bearing towards men; and, *second,* the circumstance that God himself and the instruments of his manifestation, such as the angels in the case of Abraham and of Jacob, are *not to be considered as absolutely identical.* In this way, very many of the situations which are supposed to be unworthy of God lose their seemingly offensive character. Furthermore it must be borne in mind that a certain distinction exists between the avenging Judge of the Old Covenant and the God of mercy and love of the New Covenant. Not that God alters in his nature; he ever was and is unalterably holy in all his actions. But times and men certainly do alter. Hence in God's educatory dealings with men, everything has its wisely prescribed season. The truth, that God is love, could not be revealed in its full depth, until the law, by its penalties, had brought about the consciousness of sin and a longing for entire release from it.

Having thus endeavored to vindicate briefly before the forum of modern consciousness the eternal truth of the general conception of God — that is, of his personality and special providence — as laid down in the Bible, we still

D

feel that we have accomplished only the easier portion of our task. For the number of those who reject the general system of Biblical theism is, on the whole, far less than that of those who entertain doubts as to the specific Christian, that is, the Trinitarian conception of God. We must therefore yet give at least some consideration to this.

II. THE TRINITARIAN CONCEPTION OF THE DIVINE NATURE.

In the so-called Apostles' Creed (as also in the Nicene), the doctrine of the Trinity is simply a confession of personal faith in God the Father, in Jesus Christ his only-begotten Son, and in the Holy Spirit. In the creed of Athanasius (likewise so called), which, in addition to the Apostles' and Nicene, is generally received in all divisions, Protestant as well as Roman Catholic, of the Western church, we have this doctrine as formulated in the school of Augustine in a much more developed shape. "*The Catholic faith,*" according to that formula, "*is, that we worship one God in Trinity, and Trinity in Unity, neither confounding the Persons nor dividing the substance.*" The persons, it proceeds to teach, are different; the substance one. Each of these divine persons is uncreate, each is eternal, each almighty, &c. And yet there are not three Almighties or three Eternals, but one Almighty and one Eternal, &c.; and not three Gods or three Lords, but one Lord and one God. The Father is uncreate and unbegotten; the Son uncreate, but begotten of the Father; the Holy Ghost uncreate, but proceeding from the Father and the Son. And in this trinity of divine persons there is none before and none after, none higher and none less, but all three coequal.

This doctrine of the church is to-day regarded by many, and by some who wish to believe in God, as a superstition. We confess, respecting it, that modern scientific theology, and, indeed, that branch of this theology which adheres most closely to the teaching of Holy Scripture, professes to find in the same (and I think, not without some reason) sundry defects. The symbol is evidently too stiffly arithmetical in its definitions and antitheses, without attempt to reconcile its obvious contradictions. It does not satisfy the questions and requirements of speculative theology, neither does it fully accord with the Scripture teachings. We will, therefore, endeavor to give what we find to be the Bible presentation of this matter.

You are all aware that no such sentence as God is a triune God is to be found in our Bible. The well-known text (1 John 5 : 7), "There are three that bear record in heaven, the Father, the Word, and the Holy Ghost, and these three are one," is now universally recognized as an interpolation. The terms *trinity, triunity, threefold personality,* and even the word *person* itself, are not derived immediately from Scripture. It fares with these as with all attempts to express human conceptions respecting the Divine and Infinite — they are but imperfect, inadequate expressions which we accept and use for want of better. The very term *persons* has something objectionable in it, suggesting at first the notion of distinct and separate individualities, which is perfectly inapplicable to the consubstantial, and therefore inseparable, *hypostases* of which the Bible speaks as Father, Son, and Holy Spirit. Our church formularies are undoubtedly right in laying stress on the unity of substance in these divine Persons; but it may be questioned whether they are also right in seeming to speak of the divine substance as if it were, in the first instance, something indefinite and universal, which was then resolved into three distinct hypostases. When we speak of "three persons in one divine substance," we use an expression which seemingly implies that the substance is regarded as something abstract and impersonal, which assumes a threefold personality in the concrete forms of God the Father, God the Son, and God the Holy Ghost. But Holy Scripture, and also primitive theology, regards the Divine Essence as in itself personal, naming it at once *God* and *Father*. These two sources agree in speaking of the heavenly Father as (not the first member of a series of divine evolutions, but) himself God, holding the fullness of the Godhead in himself, *Fons totius Deitatis*, the spring and fountain-head of the whole Deity from which Son and Holy Ghost are evermore derived. This point is one of decisive significance in determining the relations between the divine Persons.

The Trinitarian doctrine of Scripture, then, is briefly this: The Father is simply God, the God, the divine subject, the source and well-spring of the Godhead of both Son and Holy Spirit; the Son is God, true God, in hypostatic distinction, though derived from the Father; and the Spirit is also truly God in a form which is predicated of the whole divine nature (for God is a Spirit, John 4:24, and the Lord is the Spirit, 2 Cor. 3:17), but also in hypostatic distinction from the Father and the Son, by whom he is sent, and from whom he proceeds. There is therefore at once the most essential unity, and a threefold hypostatic distinction. The divine nature remains undivided; the whole Godhead ($Θεότης$) is in the Son and in the Holy Spirit — in the Son (Logos) as God's own self-utterance, in the Spirit as the divine self-consciousness. And as the Son is the uttered thought of the Father concerning himself, so it is again his office to speak out into the world the

Father's thoughts of creation and redemption, and thus to stand to the creatures generally, and especially to mankind, in an original archetypal relation (John 1:4). And finally, as the Son is thus the archetypal and ideal principle of mediation between God and the world, of creation and redemption, so the Holy Spirit is the real or efficient principle, effecting and individualizing all the creative and redeeming energies of the Father and the Son, applying, for instance, to each individual believer the justification *ideally* (i. e., in the idea or thought of God) accomplished by the Son, and so effecting a *real* sanctification and regeneration (Eph. 2:18; 1 Cor. 12:3): in which process he takes, indeed, everything from the Son, the real and actual having always the ideal and transcendent for its ultimate ground and condition.

If now we look back on the various dogmatic statements in the Athanasian Creed, we shall find them confirmed in essentials by what we have given as the teachings of Scripture: the Son and the Holy Spirit are with their immanence in the Father yet distinct persons, and with their distinct personality they continue immanent. Therefore, neither may we confound the three persons nor divide the one substance. And if the definitions of that formulary go somewhat beyond the teaching of Scripture and of the earlier church, in the *absolute* equalization of the divine persons (none before or after, none greater or less), to the partial obscuration of the truth of the derivation and subordination of the Son and Holy Spirit in the coequal Godhead, it must nevertheless be acknowledged that the church possesses and guards in the Athanasian Creed an invaluable restraint and bulwark against speculative errors, whether of a tritheistic, or deistic, or pantheistic tendency.

At the same time, it must be further acknowledged that

these definitions and distinctions are not sufficient to bridge over the chasm which still yawns between Faith and Reason. The old question is evermore recurring: How can the unity of one being or substance admit of a threefold self-consciousness? How can there be one substance in three distinct persons, and with three distinct personal activities? Eighteen centuries of toilsome thought have not succeeded in solving this enigma. The most recent efforts of speculative theology only make us feel more acutely that here we stand in presence of the mystery of all mysteries, and see only darkly as through a mirror of obscure reflection. "It is a truth" (to use the noble words of Hilary of Poitiers) "which lies beyond the domain of human language, beyond the scope of sense, beyond the comprehension of reason. The archangels know it not, the angels understand it not, the ages do not comprehend it, no prophet has discovered it, no apostle explored it, the Son himself has not made it fully known." Divine mysteries cannot, and were never intended to be made perfectly plausible to human reason; they are, and must be, in the first instance, matters of faith.

On the other hand, it is no less certain that they must also present points of contact for our apprehension; to the believing inquirer it is given not only to accept, but also to *know*, the mysteries of the kingdom of heaven (Matt. 13:11). And this is the case with the fundamental doctrine of the holy Trinity. The revelations of Scripture on this subject, however inadequate may be the forms given to them in the systems of earlier and later theology, are not only of the last importance for our knowledge of God, of man, and of the universe, but also present so many aids to fruitful meditation, and are themselves in so many ways confirmed by the witness of history and the soundest results of rational speculation, that only the most indolent superficiality would pretend to reject them unexamined. So much has been effected in our own day for the illustration of this doctrine, in the departments of Scriptural exegesis and philosophical speculation, as well as in that of dogmatic and historical theology, that we have already sufficient grounds of reason for our adherence to this the apostolic faith; which, not having its source in mere reason, is above but not against it. Only, he who would enter into this as into any other truth, must have his *standing in it* before he can *understand*. But whosoever, not in the carping, one-sided spirit of mere intellectual exercise, but in the practical way of both moral and intellectual self-surrender to the quickening and illuminating influences of the triune Godhead, seeks to apprehend this truth of the divine nature, to him an ever-widening field of rational inquiry will be revealed, and he will learn more and more to find in this mystery a key to the understanding of the deepest enigmas of his own nature and that of the world around him.

(*a*) Even the history of the principal religions of the world furnishes so many collateral supports to our Trinitarian conception that rise has been given to the assertion that primeval humanity must have possessed, in some shape or other, the knowledge of the triune God, which thence was transmitted in a distorted form to the heathen religions. For we find traces of it, not only here and there, but in the mythologies of all nations. In any case, it is certain that in a very early age men learned to look upon three as the perfect number, expressing absolute harmony, and uniting in itself beginning, middle, and end. Hence *a trinity of deities is common to all nations.* Time will not permit the giving of instances, but we will refer, by way of confirmation to our remark, to what has been said by Schelling: "The philosophy of mythology proves that a Trinity of Divine Potentialities is the root from which have grown the religious ideas of all nations of any importance that are known to us." As we confronted atheism with the fact noticed even by the heathen themselves, that all nations are agreed in worshipping some higher Being, and as we can see that this fact is a proof of our not being deceived by our consciousness of God, so we now point those who deny the doctrine of the Trinity to this general agreement of all nations, as a proof for the truth of our Christian conception of God; while, by the *pre*-Christian origin of these mythologies, we are guarded against the objection that these Trinitarian ideas might have proceeded from the influence of Christian ideas upon the heathen legends.

But in addition to this positive argument in favor of Trinitarianism, the history of religions provides us with a no less important negative support in the example of those nations whose creed has remained an *abstract monotheism* — the Jews and the Mohammedans. Here we see that the mere abstract unity of the Godhead, which does not include a multiplicity, soon leads to a cold and lifeless deism; and as soon as it has reached this point, is forced to seek refreshment from the pantheistic religions of nature. After the Jews and Mohammedans had rejected the idea of a Son who is of the same divine essence with his Father as idolatry, they were fated to find their absolutely monotheistic conception of God utterly empty and lifeless, so that they yearned after the warm vitality of pantheism. This is a phenomenon which is clearly evident from the history of the Jewish philosophers (especially Spinoza), as well as of the Indian and Persian pantheists. And so, too, it could not but happen that philosophical pantheism should tread on the heels of German deism and rationalism. If the question be put, How, then, is Monotheism to be preserved from sinking back into the deification of nature? the answer must be, Only through belief in the Trinity.

(b) This brings us to the great *advantages* derived from the Trinitarian conception, in respect to the knowledge of God in general, and his relation to the world and to man. We have already remarked, that the fullness of God's being cannot be contained in an abstract Unity, and yet that his absolute personality must have unity for its fundamental attribute. Here we find both of these in vital interpenetration. God is One, it is true, but at the same time he is the Living One, the organic fullness of power and love, and thus alone is the conception of a truly living God actually realized. Furthermore, the conception of the triune God furnishes us with the sole bridge that can fill up the breach between God and the world. None but this can fill up the void which separates the transcendent unity of God from the rich and manifold organization of natural life. Here we see the possibility of the world's creation by the premundane Word of God and his Spirit, whose work it is to realize the divine thoughts. Here, first of all, we have a connecting link between God and man in the person of the Incarnate Logos, who is the eternal Archetype of the whole creation, and especially of man, and who, for all future æons, will be the head of the whole body. Here, too, the spiritual chasm which yawns between sinful man and the absolutely sinless God-man, is filled up by the regenerating and sanctifying influences of the Holy Spirit. Hence the doctrine of the Trinity affords the most important aids in determining our *practical* relation to God. To elaborate no further, this doctrine *is the consummation and the only perfect protection of theism.* There can be no true theism without the Trinity. The one absolute Personality as such can be only the Triune God. Trinitarianism is not less true and necessary than theism; and what we adduced as proofs for the latter are mediate arguments for the former also.

(*c*) Still further, speculative theology provides us with many collateral arguments in favor of the truth and the intrinsic necessity of the Trinitarian doctrine. Nitzsch, for instance, remarks that the Divine Ego, in order to have a really living personality, must not only view its second *other* self as an object, but also revert to itself by a further act as a *third* subject, as that it comprehends its *alter ego* as the real image of itself. "If God be conceived as the primal Ego, and from this basis begets an objective *alter Ego*, this thesis and antithesis still remain several or incomplete until a third Ego proceeds from the Divine essence through the medium of the second, and thus the personality is fully consummated." So also Sartorius: "God is love — personal, primal love. What can he more delight to say than 'My Beloved'? God is the Father, the eternal Father. What is the Father's eternal and dearest Word other than Son, beloved Son (Matt. 3:17)? Through the eternal Son, God is the eternal Father, the eternally loving and eternally loved One; the eternal I and the eternal Thou, as Christ addresses his Father in loving converse (John 17:24). And this love is as ready to impart itself, as perfect and as great as God whose essence it is; and therefore the Son is not less than the Father, nor does he differ from him either in essence or in origin. How small would be the Fatherhood, were the Son but half God! We must distinguish between the love which *begets* the Son and that which *blesses* him, — the love of the well-pleased Father, and again, the *answer-*

ing love on the Son's part. The breath of that blessing and answering love is the *Spirit*. But were he only breath, and not a person, the glorification of the Father and Son through the Spirit would be egoistical. This egoistical element is removed only if the Spirit who glorifies the Father and the Son is himself a person." Similarly has Delitzsch recently attempted to reconcile the Trinitarian passages of Scripture with the idea of God as contained in our reason. But in all such attempts, care must be taken not to make that which is naturally difficult unintelligible, and at most they are only attempts at explanation, not full and perfect explanations.

(*d*) Another and more obvious series of collateral supports for the doctrine we are discussing may be found in a consideration of God's image as reflected in our own *human nature*, and in creation generally. For if God be indeed Trinity in Unity, then there is every reason to suppose that the works of his hands should, in some degree at least, reflect his nature, and especially that man, who is created in the image of God, should evince in his nature certain *analogies* which indicate a triune Creator. And what an abundance of such indications meets our eye! Christian thinkers, even in olden times, discovered traces of the Trinity in the life of the human spirit; and hence Augustine and others speak of a *human trinity*, consisting in the threefold function of feeling, thought, and will. And, indeed, these principal faculties of the spirit — presenting us, as it were, with a threefold cord, the threads of which are distinct, and yet one — do give us some idea of the united and harmonious co-operation of the three Divine Persons. As the three functions of the soul may be distinguished, but not separated, so with the three Persons who form the one Divine Being. In like manner, the *process of our thought* will explain in some degree the pre-existence of the Son as the Logos or Word of the Father. In our human consciousness a certain thought always simultaneously produces the corresponding word; we can only think in conceptions and words, for our thought is inward speech. So, too, God's thought of himself necessitates the utterance of the Word which represents the primal Thought; but the divine utterance is at the same time a real act, and hence this inner Word in God is a Being equal to Him. A similar argument for the personality of the Spirit may be drawn from our *religious* consciousness. Faith tells us that the Spirit is giving us *true* personality in the sight of God, and that without the Spirit we cannot in any way attain to full, firm, Godlike personality. But that which tends to promote true personality cannot in itself be impersonal. As in the human spirit, so also in the *outward world of nature*, there are certain indications and reflections of the Trinity. We constantly see one *life* in various *members*. In the one sun we see *light* and *warmth* as different, and yet intermingling and co-operating forces. We have the one space divided into three dimensions of length, breadth, and height; time, similarly, into past, present, and future; all bodies into solid, liquid, and gaseous. What remarkable analogies are shown, e. g., by the laws of color and of light! The three fundamental colors, red, yellow, and blue, dissolve into the unity of white light, so that an English naturalist (C. Woodward) might well call this white light a trinity in unity. But they coalesce in such a manner, "that each of the three rays preserves its distinctive attribute. Red is the caloric, yellow the luminous, blue the chemical (active) ray." God is Light; and, verily, natural light, the first of his creatures, bears the immediate impress of his triune being. No less does the number three govern the arrangement of nature's forces; and indeed so abundant everywhere in the world are the illustrations of the idea of the Trinity, that this idea may rightfully be said to be omnipresent.

(*e*) And no wonder that philosophy also — and this not only the old mystic theosophical speculation, but also modern idealism, with all the acuteness of its dialectics — has taken up the idea of a triune God, and endeavored to comprehend and to prove it. True, such attempt has often ended in proving the truth of an utterance once made by a profound divine with respect to the doctrine of the Trinity, and which I would beg my readers to lay to heart: "If we go too deeply, and yet not deeply enough, into this matter, we shall be blinded by this sun." Modern philosophy (from Jacob Böhme onwards) has shown that it feels the idea of the Trinity to be the solution of the world's enigma. Hegel called this idea "the pivot of the world." Schelling, in his Philosophy of Revelation,[1] approaches on this subject very closely to the Christian view. Still more closely come Baader and J. H. Fichte. These instances will suffice to make us comprehend what a philosopher (Braniss) some years ago most truly remarked: "*The conceptions of speculative philosophy, where they are most profound, come nearest to the Christian doctrine;* nor need we be anxious lest speculative philosophy should ever reach a height from which it may look down and say that the Christian element is left behind. No thought can transcend the Christian idea, for it is truth in itself."

Thus we are from all quarters referred to the conception of the Trinity; and should we ever be tempted to sacrifice the Trinity to the Unity, it will be well to remember that

---

[1] Philosophie der Offenbarung.

the Scriptural and Christian idea of God is justified and proved, as far as a mystery can be, by history and science, by nature and philosophy. We may apply to the doctrine of the Trinity the beautiful words uttered by Vinet, when speaking of love: "It is a mystery, the greatest of all mysteries, and the key of all mysteries, but itself has no key." The collateral arguments which we have adduced, while by no means keys that can fully open this mystery, yet show that the idea of the Trinity is really *the key to the comprehension of the ultimate world-enigmas;* of the world's eternal pre-condition in God; of its creation, redemption, and consummation. Without this doctrine, Scripture is to us a sealed book; without it, we ourselves and the world's history are a dark riddle. True, this is a problem, the rational solution of which in this life is, and must remain, mere patchwork; but even this patchwork is far deeper and more valuable for our knowledge as a whole (to say nothing of our practical religion) than all that the cheap wisdom of the street can bring forward in objection. And so, too, the very struggle to solve this problem, even though it should be without results, is of infinitely greater value than the ready rejection which we so often hear from the intellectual slothfulness of unbelief. If it is true that the darker the revelation the greater is the reward, both for faith and knowledge, which awaits those who gradually penetrate into it, then just because the doctrine of the Trinity is the most obscure and enigmatic revelation of God, the profoundest depths of knowledge will be opened to him who with earnest searchings penetrates into this revelation, and to him what is seemingly self-contradictory will appear more and more in grand harmony and intrinsic necessity. At first it appears to be quite contrary to reason, afterwards reason is more and more in favor of it, and finally it cannot give it up—it becomes indispensable for her entire knowledge of God and the world.

Just the contrary is the case with the false, non-Biblical conceptions of God. At first they please our reason, and look as if they could give a simple solution of all enigmas. But the more deeply reason goes to work with them, the less satisfactory do they become; the more do enigmas, obscurities, ay, contradictions appear, till at length it is evident that the whole fabric rests on unproven and untenable assumptions, and that those conceptions really give none of the explanations which they at first promised. Our mind, then, is expressed in the words of Joshua, the son of Nun: "Choose you this day whom ye will serve; . . but as for me, and my house, we will serve the Lord."

LECTURE II

THE DOCTRINE OF CREATION AND NATURAL SCIENCE

By OTTO ZÖCKLER, D. D.

PROFESSOR AT GREIFSWALD

OTTO ZÖCKLER, D. D.

BIOGRAPHICAL

OTTO ZÖCKLER, PH. D., D. D., was born at Grünberg, in Hesse, May 27, 1833. He studied at Giessen, Erlangen, and Berlin. In 1857 he became *privat-docent* at Giessen, and professor extraordinary at the same place in 1863. In 1866 he was made ordinary professor at Greifswald, and in January, 1885, he became consistorialrath. Besides being editor of the *Allgemeine literarische Anzeiger für das Ev. Deutschland* (1867-74), he also edited (since 1882) the journal founded by Hengstenberg, the *Ev. Kirchenzeitung*. Besides, he has been since 1866 principal editor of *Der Beweis des Glaubens*. In Dr. Lange's great *Bibelwerk*, Dr. Zöckler wrote the commentaries on Chronicles, Job, Proverbs, Ecclesiastes, Canticles, and Daniel. He has been a voluminous author. Among his more important works are his *Urgeschichte der Erde und des Menschen*, and his *Das Kreuz Christi;* the latter of which has been translated into English. His studies all along the line of the natural sciences fitted him peculiarly well for treating successfully the subject discussed by him in this volume.

SUMMARY OF LECTURE II

The biblical conception of God is in these times assailed at no point more frequently than with respect to the doctrine of creation—Particularly is there opposition to this doctrine as found in the Old Testament—Exceptions are taken to the alleged narrowness of the O. T. monotheism, to the six successive days of creation, and to the instantaneousness of the creative processes—True relation between faith and knowledge—Unbelieving science and superstition—Unbelieving science and skepticism—Illustrations of mistaken doubt as connected with geographical observations and discoveries—The same as connected with facts of modern astronomy—Also with facts of meteorology, physics, and technology—Other illustrations as connected with the science of organic nature, botany, zoölogy, and human physiology, also with animal magnetism or psycho-physics—A lesson to be drawn from these mistakes of an obdurate unbelief, is that skepticism is only the reverse side of scientific superstition—Another lesson is that many departments of physics are as yet too immature to furnish reliable conclusions—Recent origin and a running history of Geology—The Lyellian quietism is the only antagonist with which the biblical account has now to do—This question is disproved (1) by the difference in principle between creation and preservation—Disproved also (2) by incidental circumstances affecting present geological changes—Likewise (3) by the existence in times past of forces not now recognizable, that contributed to hastening the processes of the earth's formation—Also (4) by the probability that during the time of the earth's formation a higher temperature obtained than at present—Finally (5) the recent date of the oldest historic traditions is against this Lyellian doctrine—Harmony existing between natural science and the Mosaic record—Doctrine of the last things as in the Bible and as taught by unbelieving science.

II

THE DOCTRINE OF CREATION, AND NATURAL SCIENCE.

BY OTTO ZÖCKLER, D.D.,
PROFESSOR AT GREIFSWALD

THERE is no point at which the Biblical conception of God is assailed more frequently, in these times, than it is respecting the doctrine of creation; or, that God, in the exercise of his own free will, his goodness and power, created the world. True, much of what the Sacred Scriptures teach relative to God's personal existence, his working and ruling, is, even by the skeptical schools of science, admitted to be sufficiently correct; but that the entire sum of material and of spiritual being constituting what may be regarded as the world, was actually created by him,— to this the strongest exceptions are taken. In particular there has been of late need of vindicating the form in which the doctrine is found in the Old Testament writings.

The fault of this is not so much any defect in the Old Testament representation of creation, as it is rather the inability of its opponents correctly to judge of and to understand it. Exception is taken to what is termed the narrowness of the Old Testament monotheism; consisting, as is asserted, in the particular that God's all-powerful word, his repeated fiat, " Let there be!" is represented as having called all the individual creations into being. But those who make this objection forget that the New Testament also, from which they would like, if possible, to obtain a more modernized conception of creation, partakes of this same rigidly monotheistic idea, nay, it intensifies and develops this very feature. For the New Testament teaches, most unequivocally, not only that God is the author of all things (see Rom. 11:36, 1 Cor. 8:6), but also that he created the world out of nothing, existence out of nonexistence (Heb. 11:3, comp. Rom. 4:17), and, as the sole intermediate agency in the work of creation, it names no order of mere creature, neither a material energy nor a supernatural potency, but exclusively the Eternal Son of God, the personal Word, of one substance with the Father, and so really, in a concrete personal form, that creative " Let there be" of the first of Genesis (comp. John 1:3, 1 Cor. 8:6, Col. 1:15-18, Heb. 1:2, etc.)—Again, exception is taken to the alleged childishness of the Old Testament account, that it divides the creation into six successive days of labor, and then makes to follow these, as the prototype of our legal human Sabbath, a day of rest for the Creator. To this objection, as well as to the other, it may be replied, that it rests, in part at least, upon misapprehension. For the New Testament adheres just as firmly to this weekly division of the creation, as it does to the doctrine that all things were made by the Word of God (comp. John 5:17, Heb. 4:4 seq.). Besides, it is just this specialty of the days which reveals to an attentive examination an astonishing harmony between the revelations of Scripture and the affirmations of modern physics, relative to a gradual progress in the formation of the world, from the lowest order of being up to man.—Lastly, exception is taken to the immediateness and instantaneousness of the world's production, to the scantiness of time allotted by the Biblical history to the processes of creation. The opinion is entertained that we are indebted to the more recent science for a conception of the formation of matter, an idea of the development of organic existence from the lowest up to the highest species, in comparison with which all the old theories of a creation must inevitably be put to confusion, as the products of unscientific thinking or of a dreamy, misty mythology. The advocates of this view intrench themselves behind such commonplaces as: "the hypothesis of a creation, in the exact sense of the word, is the source of many scientific errors;" or, "for the conception of a creation, let there be substituted the scientifically more correct one of a development;" or, "the power required of the pan-spirit, i. e., nature, to create the world is not different from that required to uphold and govern it," and the like. But here, again, it is not remembered that the end at which such a view of the world, a view which in fact eliminates the idea of a creation, must unavoidably arrive, can be nothing short of a gloomy materialism, deifying matter, and a theory of sensuousness directly opposed to every principle of correct moral teaching and living; that, moreover, the scientific result of such a one-sided, sensuous-empirical philosophy, defying all logic, can never be more than a very ambiguous one; and that, in general, all knowledge disjoined from faith, and adhering exclusively to the phenomenal and temporal, must be considered incorrect and unreliable in principle, and, though qualified, perhaps, to solve the simple problems appertaining to man's earthly interests and his ordinary daily life, can never be deemed competent to decide those great questions which go to the first causes of things and to our ultimate destiny.

But, "In all the conflicts heretofore between faith and knowledge, faith has been invariably worsted," — thus are we saluted, in the words of a celebrated jurist and coryphæus of natural science. As finely, however, as the phrase may sound in the ears of many, we are able to discern in it not a particle of truth; it starts from an altogether erroneous idea, not only of faith, but equally so of knowledge. For that faith which has, at any time or in any place, been overcome by science, with which it was in conflict, did not deserve to be called faith, but only a superstition or a delusion. And, on the other hand, that science which should assault a true and genuine faith maliciously, and apparently, for a time, triumph over it, would not deserve to be called science, but only a perversion of science, or an impertinent short-lived sciolism. Faith and science are only two roads, differing in direction, not in aim, to one and the same objective truth. True faith and actual knowledge, so far from being contradictory, always demand and supplement each other. For faith, as the immediate apprehension of the truth by the divinely illuminated reason, is related to knowledge, regarded as the acquired apprehension of the same truth by the reason struggling towards such knowledge, as the necessary condition, the starting-point and support of all its operations. All faith is undeveloped knowledge, and all knowledge is faith unfolded and applied to the different realms of reason and experience. Had it not been for the faith of Columbus, he would never have discovered the New World; and as little, without faith, would Copernicus, Kepler, and Newton have made their discoveries in the material heavens. Zoölogists, such as Linnæus and Cuvier; physiologists, like Blumenbach,

John Müller, and R. Wagner; and chemists of the rank of Lavoisier and Liebig, would never have made the epochs which were made by them in their respective departments, had they not been guided by the star of faith. The true pioneers and promoters of natural science, and of all the other departments of knowledge, have almost invariably been men of faith.[1] Even Darwin would have been unable to achieve whatever of real significancy there is in his development theory, had it not been for that remnant of belief in a living, personal Deity, which he evinces where he speaks of the origin of the different organic species. It is only the thoroughly materialistic disciples of the great inquirer, on this and on the other side of the Channel, who have criticised him for this belief in a personal God, as the creator of the first few forms of vegetable and animal being, styling it a "lamentable inconsistency," a peculiar "narrowness in matters of faith;" and, by setting aside this remnant of a theistic method of conception, they have given to Darwinism its present decidedly pantheistic form.[2]

A science which thus, out of pure hostility, assails belief in the Divine Being and in Divine Revelation, in order to leave nothing standing as fact but the results of a wholly sensuous empiricism, does not deserve the name of science. It is at best but a half-way knowledge, inasmuch as it leaves out of view the entire realm of spiritual existence, all that belongs to the unseen world. Its innermost essence is unbelief, a denying on principle of everything not sensuous; although it can never be total unbelief, but will always

---

[1] Compare Mallet's remark: "It is delightful to see how such heroes of science as Copernicus and Kepler, as Baco de Verulam, Newton, Haller, Buckland, etc. bow in the lowest reverence before Revelation, whilst the light troops file by without so much as removing their hats."

[2] Comp. Grau, "Charles Darwin und August Schleicher," in vindication of faith (1866), p. 163 ff.

contain, be it in the form of the superstitious or of the skeptical, many remnants of faith in the supernatural. For these two intellectual processes, skepticism and superstition, form, as it were, the intercommunicating conduits by means of which the ruins of a dead and unserviceable faith are slowly carried off to the bog of a completed infidelity. Skepticism and superstition are the inseparably joined forerunners or preliminary stages of positive theoretical and practical atheism. Of both these must that science whose ultimate object is the casting off of the hated yoke of faith, the proclaiming of unconditional liberty of thought and teaching, and the establishing of absolutely irreligious States, schools, and families, have inevitably some admixture. From neither skepticism nor superstition can an unbelieving science wholly deliver itself.

Certainly not from superstition? The science which concerns itself to root out as well a genuine faith as a superstition, often enough confounding the one with the other, will it not be incapable of being complete master of at least the latter enemy? Will it not be afflicted always with the peculiar curse of falling from one extreme into another, and of becoming addicted to the very thing it desires most anxiously to avoid? As paradoxical as it may sound, we are compelled to reply in the affirmative, and, to show the correctness of this answer, it will be necessary to examine a little more closely the respective natures and the mutual relations of skepticism and superstition. This will take us so little out of our course, that it will rather open the direct way to the best treatment of our theme. For precisely the theories of modern physics regarding the Biblical account of creation offer a stronger admixture of both these preliminary stages of a completed infidelity, than can be found in almost any other department of unbelieving inquiry.

These two spiritual tendencies, the skeptical and the superstitious, have, to begin with, this in common: that they each represent a deviation from true faith, from the normal surrendering of the spirit to divine truth. Superstition, or, as from the signification of the prefix, *super*, it might be called, *over*-believing, is that tendency of spirit, or method of thinking, which believes the superfluous.[1] It attempts to bring within the domain of faith and knowledge matters which are inaccesible to the human intelligence; and so commingles, in an abnormal manner, the supersensuous with the sensuous.[1] It is the stand-point of belief and knowledge in harmony with the heathen mythologies; as also with idolatries in the church, — with the Romish worship of saints, Mary, pictures and relics; the point of view which deifies the host of heaven, and hence, according to its differences of species or of cultivation, prays to the sun and moon as divinities; interprets every solar eclipse as the endeavor of a giant dragon to gorge the sun; is afraid of every comet which appears, as ominous of some public calamity; and attempts to read in the constellations the destinies of men, as they are born under this or that one. It is the method of thought which, in times past, peopled the dens of mountaineers with all conceivable goblins and malicious gnomes; filled the chemists' laboratories with mysterious tinctures, elixirs of life, *homunculi* and philosopher's stones; caused to appear on the seas of navigators ghost-ships, huge kraken, and the like; and familiarized the offices and courts of jurists with

---

[1] Comp. Grimm, Deutches Wörterbuch, under "Aberglaube." Also Hase in Hutt. rediv. § 6, as well as the definitions of superstitio and aberglaube there given. As well. Schleiden's ingenious remarks on the nature of superstition, in his "Studi u." p. 200 ff., though these are to be received with caution.

witches, sorcerers, leagues with the devil, journeys to the Brocken, etc. For its gradual suppression of these different forms of superstition, together with their evil practical consequences, humanity is under a lasting debt of gratitude to modern science, — and especially to Protestant science, resting upon evangelical grounds, — without, however, on that account, being required, or having the right, to deify it, or uncritically to accept all its so-called conclusions. For only too frequently has it happened that science in combating superstition has gone to the opposite extreme and fallen into universal unbelief, or, to the justifiable doubts with which it commenced its assault upon a superstitious view of the world, it has afterwards added an itching for denial, a morbid propensity to criticise and object to everything apparently not in accord with its newly acquired views. Thus, from being a servant of superstition it has become the slave of skepticism; and in this process has but adopted certain forms of superstition. For if superstition believes too much, skepticism does not believe enough, and in adhering to this incompleteness it shows no less obstinacy and narrow-mindedness than is exhibited by superstition proper. In its more moderate form, that is, of occasional doubt and critical scrutiny applied to the truths accepted by faith, skepticism may in a certain sense be justified; at all events, there are uses which it may subserve. But, *as skepticism*, that is, when it is doubt developed into a system, when it is essentially only a repetition, in all instances, of the well-known question of Pilate, " What is truth?" this method of thought becomes really a mental disease, the last result of which will always be the death of the internal man, or blank infidelity; and, in its train, will necessarily appear and reappear different forms of superstition, that abnormal commingling of sensuous and supersensuous truths.[1] A few examples taken from the history of some of the more recent studies of nature, will serve to show the solidarity existing between doubt and superstition, by virtue of which, as will appear, the former is often only the reverse side of the latter.

We will commence with the department of knowledge respecting lands and peoples, with the geographical observations and discoveries, — a department which is the basis and condition of all advance in the physical sciences. In all this field, from antiquity down, what is there that has not been doubted, and perhaps pronounced to be impossible, until it has been attested by other investigations than those of the pioneers in geographical science? The list of skeptics, here, is headed by Herodotus, the father of history, himself, on account of his many incredible-looking stories, disparaged as credulous, and, much more unjustly, suspected of not being altogether veracious. He rejected the report of a circumnavigation of Africa by Phœnician sailors, in the employ of Necho, one of the kings of Egypt, for the very circumstance which to us is strongest in its confirmation, namely, that the mariners saw the sun rise and set, for a long while, " on their right," that is, in the northern half of the heavens.[2] He is followed by the master of Ancient Geography, Strabo, who affirmed that Megasthenes and Daimachus, precisely his most reliable authorities on India, that land of wonders opened to the West by the expedition of Alexander the Great, were falsifiers, because their reports differed

---

[1] A. Siedler, De Skepticismo commentatio (Halle, 1827). Stäudlin, Geschichte und Geist des Skepticismus, 2 vols. 1794. T. R. Young, Modern Skepticism, viewed in relation to Mod. Science (Lond. 1865).

[2] Herodot. iv., 42. Comp. on the other hand, the familiar sentence found so often in text-books for beginners: "Apud Herodotum, patrem historiae, sunt innumerae fabulae."

materially from some older sources which Strabo preferred. And what assaults were not the great travellers and discoverers of the last portion of the middle ages, and even of most recent periods, compelled to experience from an indurated skepticism! "Messer Milione" ("Mr. Million") was the nickname which the polished Venetians, of the 14th century, gave as a carnival joke to their renowned countryman, Marco Polo, because he had stated, that, during his journey into China, he visited several cities having a population of millions.[1] And how fully have the latest researches in China and in the islands off the eastern coast of Asia vindicated the reputation of this traveller, and confirmed, in part, even to the smallest particulars, his reports! How far off, too, is as yet many another worthy explorer of unknown seas or lands, since the days of Columbus, from receiving like amends, after having, by his own generation and others following, been traduced as either a lying reporter or a most egregiously deceived observer! I will only call attention, further, to Americus Vespucius and Fernan Mendez Piato, of the 16th century; to Baffin, the discoverer of Baffin's Bay and nearly all the seas, coasts, and islands belonging to North-eastern America, against whom Sir John Barrow, the same year in which, by the first polar expedition of John Ross, the statements made by Baffin two hundred years before were in all points sustained, opened a most sweeping and unworthy attack; to the Anglo-Indian Himalaya explorers, of the beginning of the present century, e. g., Colebrook, Hamilton, Hodgson, Webb, etc., whose accounts of the snow limits and of many other peculiarities and wonders of that grand mountain chain, the Himalayas, were so long questioned or coolly pronounced to be impossible, until,

---

[1] Strabo, Geog. xv., 1 seq. Ausland, 1862. p. 335; 1863. p. 719; 1868. p. 934 f.

by the reports of numerous other travellers of most recent times, they were put beyond the reach of dispute;[1] lastly, to nearly all the latest great explorers of Africa, especially the very worthy investigators of the countries at the sources of the Nile and in the south interior portion of the continent, — such as Krapf, Rebmann, Livingstone, Burton, Speke, etc. All these did not fare much better under the criticisms of certain overwise skeptics and theorists in geography than did the eminent Scotchman Bruce, in the last century, whose reports, resting wholly upon his own observation, concerning the natural characteristics and the people of Abyssinia, were so long doubted or declared to be falsehoods, until the most recent researches, particularly those instituted in connection with the English campaign of the past year, confirmed them throughout. What Livingstone discovered as to the identity of the Lecambye and Zambesi rivers, what Krapf and Rebmann ascertained relative to the existence of a vast lake in Equatorial East Africa (the so-called Lake Victoria Nianza, or Lake Ukerwi), — both were questioned a long while, until, by repeated investigations of later travellers, they, too, have been proven to be facts. Even that the peak of Kilimanjaro, a mountain from eleven to twelve thousand feet high,[2] is covered with perpetual snow, the learned London geographer Cooley attempted to dispute away from the missionaries Krapf and Rebmann, the first discoverers of the fact, on the important consideration that in the locality of that mountain there could be no perpetual snow, that hence the missionaries must have mistaken dazzlingly white quartz or chalk rocks for snow, — an opinion which

---

[1] Ausland, 1866, pp. 870 ff. 934 ff. Petermann's Geogr. Mittheilungen, 1867, No. V., p. 178. Rob. v. Schlagintweit, in Andreä's "Globus," Vol. xii., No. 1, p. 2.

[2] German measure. The height given generally by American authorities is from 18,000 to 20,000 feet. — *Tr.*

he abandoned only when Van Der Decken's expedition had ascended Kilimanjaro itself, and in the region of its summit found snow enough.[1]

Again, what difficulties and oppositions, caused by an intractable skepticism, or rather dogmatism, was not modern astronomy necessitated to encounter, in attaining its present elevated and secure position! What disparagements did not the Copernican system experience from not only the astrologico-superstitious Tycho De Brahe, but also from so rational and critical an inquirer as Baco De Verulam! How zealously nearly all the great physicists and philosophers of the last of the 17th and the commencement of the 18th century, — as a Huyghens, a Bernoulli, Cassini, Leibnitz, nearly all the disciples of Des Cartes, etc., — opposed the recognition of the Newtonian system of gravitation! With how much difficulty even in our century did it obtain, until, taught by Lord Rosse's gigantic telescope in Ireland, men of science have learned to believe in the resolvableness of most of the so-called nebulæ into innumerable, clearly distinguished, separate stars![2]

Numerous similar instances of a long-lived skeptical resistance on the part of scholastic learning to extensive enlargements of human acquaintance with nature, are furnished us by the departments of meteorology, physics, and technology. That it is possible for stones, in larger or smaller masses, to fall from the heavens, the wise Academy of Paris, all the last century, deemed to be a matter of doubt. To it the reports of showers or the raining of

---

[1] Ausland, 1862, p. 333 ff.; 1863, pp. 667, 719 ff. Meinecke, in Neumann's Zeitschr. für allgem. Erdk., 1862, p. 42 ff. Basler Missions-Magazin, 1861, p. 23.

[2] Comp. David Brewster, Sir Isaac Newton's Leben, nebst Darstellung seiner Entdeckungen, a. d., Engl. von Goldberg (1833), p. 137 ff. Also, by the same author, "More Worlds than One," etc. (1854), ch. 11.

stones, appeared as fabulous as the silly nursery tales about the raining of blood, the raining of frogs, and the like. What brought it to a different conclusion was that remarkable fall of aerolites which occurred near L'Aigle, in 1803, the evidences of which, while as yet they were entirely fresh and almost smoking, its commissioners beheld. This same academy, moreover, for a long while, held that the phosphorescence of the sea was a fable; and the *ignis fatuus* it pronounced to be the product of a disturbed imagination. The splendid microscopic discoveries of the Netherland naturalists, Swammerdam and Leeuwenhoeck, it attempted to overthrow, a century after they were made, and to substitute for them that axiom of scientific ignorance and indolence: "One can generally see with the microscope whatever he imagines." It hindered the inventors of the steam engine and the electric telegraph from introducing their great achievements into the business affairs of life. And, generally, by its skeptical narrow-mindedness, it has opposed the progress of the studies of nature, during their earlier stages, just as much as, afterwards, in other ways, it has helped to further them.[1]

With the science of organic nature, botany, zoölogy and human physiology, the experience has not been essentially different. Here, also, nearly every valuable discovery, as certainly as it revealed anything unusual, or restored any item of knowledge once accepted but in a subsequent age disparaged as a superstition, has had to contend with a more or less obstinate skepticism, before attaining general recognition. Those gold-diggers, who discovered in California, about 1850, the first mammoth trees or Welling-

---

[1] Humboldt, Kosmos I., p. 140. K. Möbius, Das Meerleuchten (Hamburg, 1861), Ausland, 1861, p. 839 ff.

tonians, and described their colossal height and thickness, were, in the scientific circles, a long time believed to be only bragging, or practising intentional humbug. The first billed-animal's skin that was brought from New Holland to Europe, near the end of the 18th century, was pronounced by the English naturalists of the time, "an old mole-skin fastened to the jaws of a duck," designed to dupe the Europeans. That coral is an animal secretion, the French savans of the last century, in spite of all the evidences to the fact furnished by Peysonnel (about 1727), disputed, and continued to dispute for years, until at last the Royal Society of London, by the adoption of Peysonnel's observations in their Philosophical Transactions, gave currency to the fact. Exactly so the fact brought to light as early perhaps as 1690, by Plumier, De La Hire, Geoffroy, and others, that the cochineal is not some sort of red seed, but an insect, was in many ways hindered from becoming recognized, until, finally, the Hollander, Ruchscher, in the year 1729, proved his assertion, that the royal dye-stuff was animal in nature, by "depositions taken before a notary in Mexico of cochineal-growers in that city," and so won a large wager.[1] A similar reception was accorded to the observations — so long doubted, but eventually confirmed on the authority of Cuvier, Lacepede, and others — of the Danes, Von Daldorff and John, relative to a species of fish (the Perca Scandens or Anabus Cuvieri), which are found at times climbing up into tall trees, into bushes, or up the sides of rocks, etc. ; also to the discovery, made in the Pacific Ocean, by our own countryman, Von Chamisso, of the hanging together in chain form of the salpæ and of their peculiar alternation of generation, — a discovery of inestimable worth to the department of lower

---

[1] Ausland, 1861. pp. 3, 415; 1862, p. 115; 1865, p. 20 f.

zoölogy, which only since has been cultivated with true success, nevertheless a discovery which at first brought its author nothing but ridicule and calumny; and equally so, to tne discovery made by the Englishman, Hodgson, in Thibet, of that overlooked species of antelope (Antelope Hodgsonii), remarkable for having but one — a long, straight — horn, in which animal probably may be recognized the unicorn of the ancients, long regarded as fabulous.[1]

Details of this description, possibly still more numerous, could be found in the physiologico-psychological and medicinal departments. We will here, however, refer to only three facts: to Harvey's discovery of the circulation of the blood, to Jenner's discovery of vaccination, and to Mesmer's application as a remedy of the agency known as animal magnetism, — three important enlargements of our knowledge and capability in their respective departments, which the immediate contemporaries of their authors tried in vain to doubt, to dispute, and to explain away, but which, in spite of all the abuses and misunderstandings experienced by them at the first, have, on the one hand, abundantly proved their own genuineness, and, on the other, may be regarded as the stepping-stones to wide, epoch-making discoveries in the future, particularly in the mysterious realm of the spiritualistic phenomena and the ecstatic conditions of human nature.[2]

Now, what have we to learn from all these illustrations of a wilful skepticism? This remarkable register of sins

---

[1] Ule and Müller, Die Natur (1860), p. 364. G. Hartwig, Gott in der Natur (Weisbaden, 1860), p. 183 f. K. Ritter. Erdkunde iv., p. 98. Neumann's Zeitschr. für allgem. Erdkunde, 1862, II., p. 227.

[2] Comp. Ulrici, Gott und die Natur, p. 613. Also Stevens' Hist. of the Methodist Episcopal Church in America (New York, 1865), I., p. 384, where, allusion being made to the opposition experienced by Harvey, Jenner, etc., the unbelieving attitude of science towards the same is characterized as ridiculous "pride and pharisaism."

committed by modern natural science,— a record which we could easily enlarge, nay, so interwoven and identified with the advances and relapses of natural science, for the last two or three hundred years, have been these offences, that a complete history of them would not differ materially from a history of modern physics itself, — what does this register of sins teach us?

In the first place, we learn from it, that skepticism is nothing but the opposite side of a scientific superstition, the reflex and the product of a narrow dogmatism, which, in the propagation and defence of what it believes with less heartiness than is characteristic of superstition, is, nevertheless, just as obstinate, nay, as intolerant as is superstition itself. We see that the narrowness of the standpoint of these scientific skeptics (or of these one-sided empirics on scientific ground, as they might be called) is exactly like that of the negro king in tropical Africa, who had a European imprisoned as a public impostor, because he had informed him that, with us, water becomes every year as hard as stone, so that a person can walk or drive over large rivers as on dry ground! We see, in a word, that the profound theosophist Oetinger, the "Magus of the South," was right, when he assailed the shallow dogmatism of the skeptics in his day with the words: "There are in the temple of philosophy spurious priests, who are like such youngsters as have never been outside of their own hamlet, and hence whatever is told them of the curiosities in foreign lands and they have never seen at home, they regard as fabricated; the disgrace of their own ignorance, however, they attempt to conceal by derision."[1] We see, as well, that the eminent physician and poet Albrecht von Haller characterized correctly this diminutive, short-sighted

[1] Oetinger, Lehrtafel der Prinzessin Antonie, p. 143.

stand-point when, referring to the unbelief of that African in the congealableness of water, he remarked, with his accustomed irony: "When the African, from the unvarying experience within his own limited circle, decides that water is by nature unchangeable, and when we, the wise Europeans, have decided it is also so with quicksilver, that this cannot be converted into a solid, we have by the unvarying experience of all men in all times (!) nevertheless been led into an error. And why did we err? Because, having seen many instances, we decided upon all, without having seen all!"[1]

What we can learn, furthermore, from these contributions to a history of the mistakes of modern science, is the fact, that many departments of physics are as yet so young, so immature, and so imperfectly insured as to their results, that no reliable conclusions of the more general order, particularly none which could be used for the overthrow of the venerable fundamental truths of faith, can in any wise be deduced from them. Even so exact a science as astronomy, whose statements and calculations have, in unnumbered instances, partly by the use of the telescope and partly by the occurrence visible to unassisted vision of celestial events at the moment, nay, at the very second predicted, proved their correctness, is to the present day so far from having attained to absolute freedom from inaccuracy, even respecting its affirmations relative to our planet and its more immediate surroundings, that, in spite of the rigid investigations of men like La Place, Bessel, Schubert, Schmidt, and Airy, the oblateness of the earth is as yet

---

[1] A. von Haller, Briefe über die wichtigsten Wahrheiten der Offenbarung, herausg. Von Auberlen, p. 41. Comp. also Auberlen, Die Göttliche Offenbarung Basel, 1861, p 246 ff.; and Schmidt, Lineamente zu einem schriftgemässen Pro- ... in Vilmar's Pastoraltheol. Blättern, vol. vii. (1865) p. 200.

only imperfectly ascertained, and hence quite a number of astronomical and of geographical problems connected therewith still await a truly exact solution.[1] Still greater uncertainty obtains in chemistry and physics as to what has been ascertained as yet in regard to many of their fundamental questions. The modern chemical atomic theory, for example, suffers under such serious difficulties and from such internal contradictions of a logical and mathematico-physical nature, that notwithstanding its well-nigh universal acceptance by the great chemical authorities, for the last decades of years, its speedy displacement by a wholly different conception of matter, and of the forces and essences lying at the basis of matter, can, with considerable distinctness, be foreseen. In physics, the formerly prevailing doctrine of the imponderables, or of substances thought to have no perceptible weight, has only recently been supplanted by the famous heat-hypothesis of the Würtemberger, J. R. Mayer, which, in its more developed form as the so-called Helmboltzian doctrine of the "conservation of force," makes heat, light, magnetism, electricity, the chemical forces, sound, and all mechanical motions, to be essentially identical or only different forms or varieties of one and the same material energy. But even this motion-theory, the favorite axiom of a large number of scientists and theorists of the present day, is so far from being everywhere recognized, that there are many distinguished physicists who strongly object to it, on the ground of its numerous unexplained difficulties.[2] And in how many obscu-

[1] Comp. Phil. Fischer, Untersuchungen über die Gestalt der Erde (Darmstadt, 1868), and the review of the same in "Ausland," 1868, p. 807 ff.

[2] Com. Ulrici, Gott in der Natur (2d. Ed.) p. 109 ff. W. Wundt, Die physikalischen Axiome und ihre Beziehung zum Causalprincip (Erlangen, 1866). J. Zöllner, Ueber die universelle Bedeutung der mechanischen Principien (Leipz., 1867). —Tyndall's paper before the British natural science gathering at Norwich, 1868 (for Ausland, 1868, p. 906).

rities is the subject of electricity as yet involved: for example, in regard to the connection between the electrical and the chemical processes; in regard to atmospheric electricity, the cause of which is yet "wholly unknown;" regarding the reciprocal working of animal and of inorganic electricity; and, particularly, in regard to the mysterious electrical currents which not only the electric eel, the electric silurus and the torpedo, but, also, in smaller quantities, the nerves and muscles of all other animal organisms have the power of imparting! How little, for certain, moreover, does physiological science — the domain of which we have touched upon by this last reference — know as yet of the chemical combination and the action of animal poisons! How much dissension reigned in it, until but recently, as to whether a spontaneous generation of organisms (generatio spontanea s. equivoca) was to be accepted or not as fact? And even now, how far from being settled are its disputes concerning the nature of the physical functions and forces, concerning the existence of a common life-principle, etc.! How incompetent is this same science, together with medical pathology, to give a thoroughly scientific and satisfactory explanation of the nature and cause of even a cold, the simplest and commonest form of disease to which the human system is subject! How significant it is, too, that the medical school which, to-day, enjoys the highest reputation in the scientific circles, and is most widely propagated, that of the Vienna professor, Rokatanski, deserves, on account of its extreme reserve towards most of the older theories and explanations in pathology and therapeutics, to be called the school of skeptics; and indeed, in many of its representatives, it does, and very appropriately, so designate itself.[1]

[1] Ulrici, in the before-mentioned work, pp. 145, 268 ff. Comp. Ausland, 1868, No. 42: "Die Wirkung der Gifte."

I refer to these proofs of the present unsettled condition of natural science, proofs to which I could add others by the quantity, not because it is my wish or intention to prophesy the speedy bankruptcy of modern physics in general, or to discredit and disparage its attainments, or to preach, in the sense in which the phrase is understood by an obscurantism which shuns light and truth, the "conversion of science." No one can entertain a higher regard for the great achievements of physical science, no one can cherish a more unwavering confidence in the benign influences which it will exert, by virtue of its farther advancement, even upon the religious side of human culture, than I do myself, — I, who have more than once borne the censure of the more strictly orthodox, for accepting only too readily all the chief results of science. What I have had in view, in these references, is only a well-meant caution against too unconditional and too credulous a belief in one particular branch of science, which, while it is one of the youngest of all the studies of nature, is yet one pre-eminently given to assailing the Biblical account of creation, for the defence of which we are here especially concerned.

Geology, or the science which treats of the processes by which the earth was formed, and the preliminary study, geognosy, which investigates the facts of the earth's structure, — both date back not much beyond the beginning of the present century. It was about the year 1790, when, as cotemporaries, and yet working independently of each other, the first two really scientific geologists, namely, the Scotchman James Hutton, and our own countryman Abraham Werner, of Freiberg in Saxony, began to be recognized, — the former as the founder of Plutonism, or the doctrine of the formation of the world in its present state by the agency of fire; and the latter as the author of the opposite or Neptunian hypothesis, which attributes the construction of our globe to the action of water. From the controversies which have raged among the adherents of these two rival theories, the entire present development of geological science has been brought about. And if, in these circles, not long since, Plutonism, or the central-fire hypothesis, reigned so exclusively that the participancy of water in the formation of the earth appeared to be either entirely banished or at least reduced to a minimum, the latest years have, on the other hand, found so many important arguments and learned supporters for the Neptunian theory, that now, to be a Vulcanist or a Plutonist, in the earlier sense of these names, is deemed equivalent to being almost unscientific; and so, again, as the oldest representative of this side of the question, the Bible is beginning to come into favor (comp. Gen. 1: 2, 2 Pet. 3: 5).[1] The complicated dispute, however, is still by no means settled; besides, there are numerous other dissensions, of a subordinate class, agitating this science, — a science which, in order to solve accurately all the problems which have presented themselves in reference to the primeval history of our planet, would, strictly speaking, require data to be derived not only from a geognostical survey of all the continents and islands, but also of the seas; whereas, in truth, it has as yet investigated, in exact mining fashion and to a sufficient depth, scarcely a tithe of the earth's surface. Skepticism, hypercriticism, and spurious dogmatism have here also abundantly figured, and, often enough even up to the present day, have occasioned hindrances to the advancement of knowledge. The description given by Spallanzani, towards the close of last century (1788), of the internal state of the volcano of Stromboli, was discredited

[1] See my "Urgeschichte der Erde und des Menschen," p. 35 ff.

until the beginning of this century, when its correctness was proved by the investigations of other travellers. Regarding the genuineness of the fossil skeletons of several strangely formed animals, belonging to the older world, such as the plesiosaurus, the pterodactyl, etc., there have been expressed in our century, and by men eminently schooled in science, doubts as earnest as were the judgments with which the guess-work and superstition of a century or so ago favored this same class of discoveries, — as was, for example, the opinion to which the Zurich physicist Scheüzer came (about 1530) in regard to the remains of a giant salamander, that they were those of a man who had perished in the flood![1] As there was, in that age, altogether too ready a disposition to resort to the Noachian deluge to explain by it all possible palæontological discoveries, so, from the thirtieth year of this century till most recently, the opposite narrowness obtained with most geologists, namely, the tenet that the fossiliferous strata of the so-called diluvial period do not contain any human remains; that there are no traces left of the human race destroyed by the Biblical flood, that the geological deluge, as a catastrophe occurring before the existence of our race, must be distinguished from the great flood attested by the traditions of the old world, — an error which has led not only to a hypercritical disparagement of this event as the product of ancient childish legend, but frequently also to incorrect conclusions respecting important geognostical discoveries. For example, it has led to a denial of the diluvial, or, more properly, perhaps, of the antediluvial (tertiary), age of numerous fossil skulls which have been found. This was the case with the one termed the Engis

[1] Vide my Urgeschichte der Erde, p. 45. Comp. A. von Humboldt, Kosmos iv., p. 296. Vilmar's Pastoraltheol. Blätter, vi., p. 203.

skull, discovered by Schmerling in 1833, the coming of which down to us from the diluvial epoch was so long disputed, until, of late, by the exhumation of a large number of other skulls of similarly great antiquity, it has been elevated, according to the judgment of most inquirers, into certainty.[1] But even yet, when some have begun to classify the annually increasing collection of fossil human remains with reference to periods, and, accordingly, we have mammoth-men (i. e., men of the very oldest, probably the tertiary epoch, the period of mammoths, mastodons, cave-bears, etc.) and reindeer-men (i. e., men of the proper diluvial or ice period, when all Western Europe seems to have been overrun by herds of reindeer), there are not wanting distinguished geological authorities, as, for instance, the well-known author of the "History of the Creation," Burmeister, or Professor Schaaffhausen of Bonn, who, in truth, do not deny the coming to light of petrified human remains as a whole, but yet consider it very questionable whether even the oldest fossil of this species dates back to the tertiary epoch.[2]

Though so young, so far from being relieved of obscurities and brought to reliable conclusions, and so marked by dissensions still in many of its most prominent representatives, it is precisely this one of the natural sciences which attacks with peculiar vehemence our Biblical doctrine of creation, and, with it, also most other points belonging to the Scriptural view of the world. This it does, supported by a method of reckoning the earth's chronology, which, together with the entire geological school by which this method is adopted, first began to come into more general

---

[1] Burmeister, Geschichte der Schöpfung, p. 612 ff.

[2] Burmeister, ibid.—Schaaffhausen, in Das Archiv für Anthropologie, II. (1867), p. 359.

recognition some thirty years or so since. It was in the year 1830, when the Englishman Charles Lyell came out, in his extended work, "The Principles of Geology,"[1] which was followed by a smaller manual entitled "The Elements of Geology,"[2] as the author of that novel theory of the formation of the earth which makes the lowest and oldest strata of the rocks to have been produced by processes exactly analogous to the physical changes taking place at present upon the surface of the globe, namely, by elevations and subsidences of the land above and below the surface of the sea, aqueous depositions, etc. The distinguishing feature of this hypothesis is not so much its Neptunian element, — for, with the place allowed for the action of water, Lyell vindicates also one for that of fire, in the construction of the earth, — but it is rather the extraordinarily slow and gradual manner with which those ancient operations, being made by this theory to conform to the way in which modern geological changes are effected, are represented to have been produced. This doctrine, of so extremely slow and quiet an unfolding of the history of our planet, with reference to which the school of Lyell has been appropriately styled that of the geological quietists, naturally brings this same school into collision with the Biblical account of creation, and, as well, with the ancient chronology of the Bible in general. For, notwithstanding that the days in the Mosaic record of creation may be understood as expressive of longer periods than simply days of twenty-four hours each, and, accordingly, we may interpret them as each an epoch, say, of one thousand years, for which interpretation the Scriptures themselves, in texts such as Ps. 90 : 4, 2 Pet. 3 : 8, furnish support, as well as that the old Etruscan and Persian cosmogonies (strikingly resembling the account

---

[1] 1st ed., 1830, seq., 4 vols.   [2] 1st ed., 1 vol., 1838.

of Moses) are in harmony with this view, as they both specify that the world was created in six thousand years,[1] nevertheless, between the millions, nay, the billions of years which Lyell and his school hypothecate for the continuance of the earth's formation processes and these few decades of centuries, there remains a most tremendous interval; and so, the quietistic chronology of this school removes even the last of those creative processes, the tertiary together with the diluvial formations, to such a cloudy distance, that, in comparison with its myriads of ages, the brief period, allowed by the Bible to have elapsed since the beginning of human history, shrivels up into insignificancy. Besides, this geological quietism serves as the preparation for a theory of the origin of the organic world which cannot be made to accord, either with the Biblical history of creation, or with our Christian view of the Divine Being in general. Lyellism is the basis and the indispensable condition of Darwinism, that doctrine of the development or transformation of all the organisms of the vegetable and animal kingdoms from an insignificant number of original types, which, logically carried out, not only excludes the idea of a personal Creator (though, as we have seen, the author himself shrank back from this), but also annihilates all distinction between the animal creation and man, and thus makes the first representative of our race to have sprung, through a development of the most highly organized animal, — the ape, — from a lower than his own natural order of being. The geological system of Lyell is most intimately and inseparably connected with positive materialism, whose hypothesis of the origination of man from the ape can, only under the supposition

---

[1] Suidas, s. v. γυρρηνία. Spiegel, Zeitschrift der deutsch morgenländischen Gesellschaft, v., p. 221 ff.

of an immensely long period for the existence of the human race, and as well for the development of earthly being in general, claim for itself even an appearance of truth.

From what has been presented, it is evident that the apologist for the Biblical doctrine of creation has properly to do with but one antagonist: the geological quietism of the Lyellians; — this fruitful seed-bed of all the modern materialistic doctrines; this extensive armory from which not only a Darwin, but also a Huxley, a Vogt, a Moleschott, a Büchner, etc., have been accustomed to draw the only really cutting weapons for the defence of their systems, the only clothing, ornamented with the appearance of truth, with which they have decked out their respective theories. If this one chief antagonist is overthrown, then the entire structure of materialistic hypotheses and systems has lost its seemingly scientific support, and must, in consequence, like an overturned aerial card-house, tumble to pieces.

But the downfall of this opponent can with difficulty be much longer stayed. At all events, it appears to us there is scarcely a much longer life in prospect for Lyellism than there was for many another scientific hypothesis which for a time enjoyed great popularity, but was discovered to be one-sided by a later generation. As Stahl's phlogiston theory ruled for several decades of years in the department of chemistry, then to give place to one better founded; as the atomic theory of Dalton and Berzelius, after a longer undisputed sway in the same province, seems to be at present tottering and in serious danger of being deposed by another hypothesis; as, in the domain of geology itself, one-sided Plutonism was compelled to retreat before the modern doctrine of chemical force, or chemical Neptunism; — so, to us, the days of the still reigning chronological method of the geologists seem to be numbered, and we do not consider the time to be far removed, when the onesidedness, the arbitrariness, and the scientific unreliableness of the time-reckonings based upon this method will be universally recognized. In a word, the Lyellian quietism, with its opposition to the Biblical doctrine of creation, appears to us to be one of those scientific, or rather theoretico-scientific temporary hypotheses, on the one side of a skeptical and on the other of a superstitio-dogmatical character, the eventual overthrow of which by the higher power of truth generally marks the principal steps in an advance of science from an older to a newer epoch.

In proof of this there are many evidences; a few of which may here be indicated.

1. The assumption that the earth was formed exactly in accordance with the same laws of development, and so in corresponding long periods of time, by which the changes at present occurring upon its surface are produced, involves a great mistake in principle. For it confounds the two facts of creation and preservation, the essential difference of which not only theology, but all analogies in nature and the entire realm of our earthly experience, teach. Or, where is the organism which does not, in the period of its origination and development, grow incomparably faster, change with altogether more readiness, than afterwards, during the term of its more mature existence? Where is the plant which does not first pass through a season of vigorous germination, of luxuriant growth, in order afterwards to enter upon a stage of steadier and slower development, the harbinger of its eventual decay? Where is there an animal which, while an embryo or a fœtus in its mother's womb, and also during a portion of its more independent existence, did not reveal a far more rapidly growing and developing energy, than after it had

attained full growth? And, in order not to leave untouched the domain of the inorganic processes, where is the metal, the stone, or the crystal, which, while it was liquid, alterable, adapted to quick sudden transformation, during the process of its formation, was not, on the other hand, as a consolidated body, of a nature more or less firm and enduring? Where is there a house built but that, in the masonry of it, an analogous experience can be witnessed, the experience that after a short period of variableness, while it is becoming dry and hard, it also passes into a state of greater constancy?[1] But what is true of the separate inorganic and organic elements of which the earth is composed, is also true of the earth itself. The macrocosm can have had no different history of origination and development from that of its constituent microcosms. The house, which is man's temporal dwelling-place, must have had, just as well as man or any of the different creatures about him, also its period of growth, or the period during which it was built and prepared for its inhabitant by the Divine Architect. (Heb. 3:4, 11:10.)

2. The ordinary geological changes of the present; for example, the secular elevations and subsidences of the islands and continents, with respect to the level of the sea; the destructions and depositions caused by the action of running water; the sinking of the surface in marsh and in peat localities, — all this is found by an impartial examination to be wholly unfitted to be used as the analogy, or measure, by which to determine the times of the ancient world's processes of formation. For, incidental circumstances, often of only an unimportant character, such as a peculiarly violent rain-storm, a spring-tide, or even a tree or a shrub, torn from its place by the force of a stream,

---

[1] Comp. my Urgeschichte, p. 146 f.

and stranded by it so as to occasion suddenly the formation of a sand-bank, can in a little time so materially interfere with the working of those agencies, that all similarity of their action, as continued through long periods, seems to be set aside. For primeval antiquity, however, not only these lesser disturbances, but mighty catastrophes, in part of a Plutonic and in part of a Neptunian order, are to be conceived as operative,—catastrophes of such extraordinary magnitude that the earthquake in South America the year past, or that of 1755, by which Lisbon was destroyed, can furnish us, at most, but a faint conception of the suddenness and extent of their workings; catastrophes which, whether in building up or in destroying, could produce more colossal effects over wide stretches of land or of sea, in a few minutes, than their feeble modern imitators could in centuries.[1]

3. Besides other agencies contributing to facilitate the processes by which the earth was formed, there must have been some of a physico-chemical nature, the existence of which cannot now, with certainty, be recognized by us; and especially must there have been operative then a considerably more elevated temperature than the mean degree of heat obtaining at present upon the surface of our planet; this is a particular which even the Lyellians, be they Neptunian or Plutonian in view, do not really refuse to concede, though they fail largely in deducing from it the necessary conclusions. For, given a considerably higher degree of heat obtaining in those earlier times than that now prevailing, then certain chemical changes, such as the conversion of the primeval forests, sunk under water, into the mineral coal beds of to-day, the crystallization of metallic or of silicate solutions into solid rocks, etc.,

[1] Cf. my Urgeschichte, p. 143 ff.

must have taken place with altogether greater rapidity than any similar changes in nature are at present being effected; — a conclusion which has been of late most irrefutably established by experiments instituted by prominent geological authorities, and particularly by the transformation of different vegetable and animal substances into stone coal, — a result attained by Göppert at Breslau in a few years, by the continued application of intense heat; and, being thus established, it sufficiently disproves the current geological assertion, that so many thousands of years were required for the ancient processes in question.[1]

4. This supposition of a higher temperature obtaining during the processes of the earth's creation is sustained by astronomical probabilities and postulates which learned investigation, in order to explain the phenomena in hand, is beginning nowadays to take more and more zealously into consideration; whether with Adhemar, James Croll, and others, it conjectures that a strong eccentricity of the earth's orbit, existing in connection with the precession of the equinoxes, is the occasion for an alternation between extreme heat and extreme cold, and so attempts to explain, on the one hand, the extraordinary productiveness of the ancient flora and fauna during certain stadia of the creation, and, on the other, the ice or cold epochs interrupting these periods of a more productive order; or whether it postulates, with Poison, the mathematician, and with the distinguished botanist and palæontologist, Oswald Heer, of Zurich, as the solution of this presumed vicissitude between the warm and cold epochs (or between peculiarly productive "spring times of the world" and more languid "periods of stability"), that there are in the heavens

---

[1] Andr. Wagner, Die Berufung auf die Naturwissenschaft als Instanz zur Bestreitung des mosaischen Schöpfungsberichts.—Evang. Kirchenztg. 1862. No. 10.

differently warmed spaces, through which our solar system passes in circling about its central sun. These are, of course, only hypotheses, though they are supported by important astronomical facts, and, what is more, they are not at variance with what is said in the Scriptures of an alternation between day and night in the work of creation.[1]

5. That the end of the creation of organisms, especially that the origin of the human race, should be located so extremely far back as the geologists put it, is rendered highly improbable by the circumstance that none of the historical traditions of the oldest nations, as far as they bear any traces of credibility, and have not been distorted by priestly fable into the monstrous, ever go farther back than from 2500 to 2700 years B. C., thus not beyond the Biblical deluge, — a fact which has been established recently by a thorough exploration of the earliest civil and religious histories of Egypt and of the Chinese Empire, fields of inquiry which, as long as they were investigated in a superficial, credulous manner, were, in different quarters, imagined to contain weapons especially effective for combating the ancient history and chronology of the Bible.[2]

From these considerations, the force of which is recognized by such superior naturalists as the botanist Göppert, already mentioned, the geologists Murchison, Dana, A. Wagner, W. Leonhardt, the anthropologists R. Wagner and R. E. Von Baer, etc., we cannot conclude otherwise than that the Lyellian rejection of the Biblical account of creation and of its time estimates is only an extremely

---

[1] Ausland, 1867, No. 51; 1868, Nos. 12. 28.
[2] G. T. Meadows, The Chinese, p. 34. Comp. the Duke of Argyl's "Recent Speculations on Primeval Man," in "Good Words," 1868, p. 286, sq.

one-sided skepticism, which is really only a masked superstition, reminding one, as to its figures, of the extravagant estimates given for the age of the world in some of the old cosmogonies and theogonies of the nations we have named, and so only the more clearly revealing its own want of scientific soundness. With the certain prospect, therefore, that this will ere long be the general verdict, we are unprepared to surrender our belief in the Biblical account of either the creation in general, or of the commencement of human history. We still hold fast to the fundamental truths of the inspired view of the world, as they are found, beautifully harmonizing with the results of a more thorough natural science, in the Mosaic record. Of none of the sublime truths of the Scriptural doctrine of creation are we willing to be deprived; neither of that fundamental tenet of monotheism, that God, in the beginning, i. e., the beginning of time, in the exercise of his own free will, his goodness and power, called the heaven and earth, and all things therein living and moving, into existence, nor of the more closely defined conception of this creative act, intimated in the Old Testament but brought out clearly and distinctively in the New, that it is the Triune God to which the universe is indebted for its being, or that God the Father through the Son in the Holy Spirit created the world.[1] And as little as we are willing to relinquish this specifically Christian definiteness of the creative act, as little are we ready to part with any essential feature of the facts forming according to the Biblical tradition the outward vesture of the work of creation; neither with the creation of light at the very commencement of all world-being, — for according even to the latest physics the light-force is the basis of all material existence

---

[1] Comp. my Urgeschichte, p. 28.

(see above); nor with the creation of the stars posteriorly to that of the light, — for even La Place's theory of the formation of worlds explains and supports this circumstance; nor with the fact — attested not only by the giant coal formations, but more strongly by the discoveries, recently made in Bohemia, Sweden, and other localities, of immense masses of petrified sea-plants imbedded in the transition rocks, the oldest fossiliferous strata — that the vegetable kingdom preceded the animal in the order of their genesis;[1] nor, again, with the particular, that the plants and animals were originated in different families and species, or according to the divine principle, each "after his kind" (Gen. 1: 11, 12, 21, etc.), for never will the Darwinian theory be able scientifically to establish its absurd notion of the development of all organisms from one primitive type; nor, lastly, with what the Scriptures teach of that grand final act of creation, — the bringing into existence of man; his appearance immediately after or about the same time with that of the higher classes of land mammals; his being made in the image of God, and destined to be the ruler over all the other and lower orders of creation; the commencement of his history in a world of purity and happiness, which was changed from that, its original state, into one — needing a redemption — of misery and ruin, only by his own act of disobedience, and over which the reign of death, the sad necessity of dying, was brought, certainly for himself if not for the other forms of life, in consequence only of his own fall. Particulars belonging to this, the oldest and grandest of all the paintings of the creation, may, with less facility, be adjusted into a harmony of nature and revelation. Indi-

---

[1] Ulrich Stutz, Die Schöpfungsgeschichte nach Geologie und Bibel (Zurich, 1867), p. 19. Comp. Ausland, 1868, p. 907.

vidual obscurities and difficulties, the most skilful apologete, the profoundest student of the two original sources of knowledge, the Bible and nature, may be utterly unable to explain. The question, for example, concerning the origin of death in the vegetable and animal kingdoms, or that of a somewhat similar order relative to the fall of Satan and the demons, — of these and other similar mysteries respecting which no clear and decisive knowledge is given in either the Old or the New Testament Scriptures, — a truly thorough and satisfactory understanding may be denied to men as long as the world in its present state endures. Still, we are not, on account of these difficulties, to barter away our Biblical doctrine of creation to the pantheistico-materialistic unbelief obtaining in these times. An adoption of the arid, comfortless, and monstrously irrational view of the Darwinists, of a development of the world, or of the still more gloomy doctrine taught by positive materialism, that the world is in its order eternal, in the place of our belief in the creation of all things by the Almighty Triune God of the Bible, would be one of the worst doctrinal mistakes of which we could be guilty, — an error which would work, in all the departments of our Christian theology, irreparable injury.

I remarked at the opening of this discussion, there is no point at which the Biblical conception of God is assailed more frequently, in these times, than it is respecting the doctrine of creation.

I must here so far amend that assertion as to have it include one other equally disputed point, namely, the doctrine of the last things. Of death, as the transition to a state of rewards and punishments; of a visible return of Christ to judge the world; of a passing away of the present order of things in preparation for the creation of a new heavens and a new earth, — of all this the materialist of our day is willing to know as little as he is of the calling of the entire visible universe into being by the imperative "Let there be" of a personal Creator. The modern unbelieving view of the world has as little of eschatology in its dogmatics as it has of a chapter on the creation. Regarding the future, it knows but a single prospect, — the continuation of the present order of things on endlessly; as also it has but one method of considering the past, which is to look as far back as possible for the commencement of the earth's history. Its consummation is reached in the absolute materialism of H. Czolbe, who affirms not only that the world is without beginning, but also that it will continue on without end.[1]

There is a school of theologians, of seemingly earnest and honest contenders for a true Christianity and a true church, which partakes largely of this pantheistico-materialistic denial of both the beginning and the end of the present course of the world. A zealous worshipper of the spirit of the times (des Zeitgeistes), it seeks to avoid the thought of the past birth of time out of God's eternal being, and also that of its future resumption into God's eternity. With these two points of weakness, most intimately related to each other, it thinks it can nevertheless exercise a strong faith in the central fact of revealed truth; it thinks it can, without the traditional doctrine of creation and the traditional eschatology, still have the correct doctrine of Jesus Christ. Its actual fruits in this department prove the contrary. The way it handles the historical Christ, at one time disfiguring, at another diminishing, the picture, to make it conform to certain modern deceptive

[1] Comp. Fabri, Briefen gegen den Materialismus (2d Ed.), p. 87 ff.

ideals, — the way it denies the divinity of the Saviour and disparages those Scriptures by which this essential is attested, — shows incontrovertibly that, deprived of root and top, the stock itself does not remain uninjured, or that, when the foundation is undermined and the roof is removed, the entire edifice must be precipitated into ruins. The doctrine of creation is of most indispensable need to the whole of our Christian faith, and especially to belief in the person and work of Christ. One cannot be a Darwinist, or a materialist, regarding the Biblical account of creation, and at the same time be consistently — a Christian!

LECTURE III

REASON, CONSCIENCE, AND REVELATION

By HERMANN CREMER, D. D.

PROFESSOR OF THEOLOGY AT GREIFSWALD

HERMANN CREMER, D. D.

BIOGRAPHICAL

DR. AUGUST HERMANN CREMER studied at Halle and at Tübingen. He was born October 18, 1834, at Unna, in Westphalia, Germany. In 1859 he became pastor at Ostönnen, near Soest, in Westphalia. He was made ordinary professor of systematic theology at Greifswald, and also pastor of St. Mary's Church there, in 1870. In 1879 he was a delegate to the General Conference of the Evangelical Alliance at Basel, and read a paper on the state of religion in Germany. Dr. Cremer is a profound thinker and a great scholar. He has published a large number of works. Among the best known of these to English-speaking people, because translated into our tongue, are his *Biblisch-theologisches Wörterbuch der neutestamentischen Gräcität* ("Biblico-theological Lexicon of New Testament Greek"), and his *Ueber den Zustand nach dem Tode* ("Beyond the Grave"), the last being translated by Dr. S. T. Lowrie, and published in New York, 1885.

SUMMARY OF LECTURE III

BETWEEN reason, conscience, and revelation there exists, according to some, an invincible dissonance; but we discern here a celestial harmony—Oppositions put forward between reason and revelation—What is reasonable and according to conscience?—Both reason and conscience have to do with the truth—Man's need of the truth, for which he has capability, although not naturally possessing it—Pilate's question and Plato's conclusion—Man can know the truth; affinity is its sign or proof—Truth the necessary complement of man's being; it is the standard of man, as man is also the standard of the truth—Truth is both loved and feared; it slays and makes alive—Nature of the truth to reveal itself; must be personal; must be God.—II. HISTORIC RELATION OF MAN TO THE TRUTH. Life-renunciation and life-enjoyment are the two poles at which humanity, unassisted by revelation, has often arrived—Both Stoicism and Epicureanism are philosophies of despair—When Christianity came the world had not yet found the truth, and had even lost the beginnings of this knowledge—Even to-day science (so-called) has no answer to the question, What is truth?—III. DIVINE REVELATION MEETS THE REQUIREMENTS OF REASON AND CONSCIENCE, AND THEREFORE HAS A RIGHT TO DEMAND FOR ITSELF UNCONDITIONAL RECOGNITION. Conscience was first discovered by the religion of the Bible—A self-revelation of God must be regarded as possible; it is also necessary or requisite for man's needs—God is both grace and truth; this is the Triune God, the God of Atonement—In this God of revelation and salvation, reason, conscience, the human life, all are satisfied—The entire system of revelation rests upon two propositions: God, sin—In the contest against the truth three positions may be taken: I like not, I can not, I will not. Only when the third position has been taken, does the real spiritual struggle begin.

III

REASON, CONSCIENCE, AND REVELATION

BY HERMANN CREMER, D. D.,
PROFESSOR OF THEOLOGY AT GREIFSWALD

REASON, Conscience, Revelation, — these words are regarded by some as an invincible dissonance, the key-note of which is wrong; by others as a dissonance which, though it may be and ought to be overcome, requires for this end a diminution of the intervals; while we unhesitatingly affirm that we discern here a harmony such as no earthly music can offer, such as the masters of sacred art have believed they heard, when attempting to imitate in their creations celestial choruses, in whose manifold complications there is still a prevailing harmony, comprehending and uniting the world of sounds.

With distinct consciousness, the bearers and the adherents of divine revelation perceive and affirm the sharp contradiction which this revelation offers to the methods and results of merely natural thinking, and with which it shoves aside, and passes by, not, it is true, as superfluous, but yet as vain and useless, the achievements, great as they seem to us, of the human intelligence. At the same time, however, they claim that divine revelation, and this regarded as an unveiling of hidden truth, is not merely to be received on trust, but apprehended and recognized with conscious clearness; and thus they seem to require a self-denial on the part of the human intelligence, on which many, from fear of losing what is noblest and best in them, find it difficult to decide.[1]

It is not to be wondered at, therefore, that, by the representatives and adherents of this human reason and wisdom so severely rebuked, the claim of divine revelation, that is, of the Sacred Scriptures, to be the truth, is decidedly opposed, and that the disparagements received are richly repaid. E. g., the reasonableness of that which calls itself a revelation is disputed, and belief in or recognition of the same is referred to a certain spiritual indolence, or, in the most pardonable case, to a defective schooling in the use of the reason. In no case is such a belief allowed to be compatible with sound reason, while the practice of insisting upon a recognition of revelation is characterized as obscurantism and an enslavement of the spiritual life.

---

[1] The Scripture expressions alluding thereto are familiar. When Peter says, "We believe and are sure;" and John, "We have known and believed," (John 6:69; 1 John 4:16); when Paul writes, "By manifestation of the truth, commending ourselves to every man's conscience in the sight of God" (2 Cor. 4:2), — we see the question is not concerning a faith accepted on insufficient grounds, but concerning a faith based upon and requiring knowledge, as Paul says in another place, "That the communication of thy faith may become effectual by the acknowledging of every good thing which is in you in Christ Jesus" (Phile. 6). Assent of the rationally observing and reflecting man, recognition, full, unconditionally free, and yet inwardly necessitated assent of the conscience, this the revelation whose register we have in the Sacred Scriptures — this the Bible requires. For reason and conscience are not otherwise free than that they are bound by the truth; and to furnish truth, the sole, complete truth, is the object of revelation. As to these claims understanding is possible, but more difficult is it when Paul describes the opposing "wisdom of this world" as foolishness, when he admonishes the Colossians not to allow themselves to be spoiled through the philosophy and vain deceit of human teaching, when he has so poor an opinion of the wisdom held so high in the world that in one place he says, "Professing themselves to be wise, they became fools;" and in another sets up the requirement, "If any man seemeth to be wise, let him become a fool that he may be wise." The worst, however, appears to be when he makes it a reproach of the reason that it causes men to be at enmity with God by wicked works. (Comp. 1 Cor. 1:20 ff.; Col. 2:8; Rom. 1:22; Eph. 2:3, and 4:18; Col. 1:21.)

As we are fully aware of these reproaches, nay, as we profess to understand them, and would only the more decidedly defend the claims of divine revelation, we are in duty bound to consider the former, and both to become clear ourselves as to the just grounds of these claims, and to show our opponents that divine revelation really has no need to fear a thorough examination before the tribunal of reason and conscience. We recognize ourselves as bound to investigate the claims of divine revelation to reasonableness and complete truth, to inquire into the possibility of a rational recognition on the part of man of these claims, and of a conscientious subjection of himself to them, and to judge by the requirements which reason and conscience everywhere make, whether we are to understand that the revelation of God meets, and perhaps more than meets, all these requirements, or whether humanity would have ground, in the name of reason and — as it has only recently been perfected — of conscience, to protest against this obtrusive intermingling of a revelation in the restless labor and development of the human spirit.

We shall have, then, first, to consider what it is that reason and conscience require of that which they should recognize as according to reason and conscience, — thus what agrees with reason and conscience. Secondly, we must ask, how much of that which agrees with reason and conscience has been found, without the intervention of divine revelation, by our race, in the progress of its spiritual development; and, lastly, our theme will lead us to notice, whether divine revelation, as attested for us in the Sacred Scriptures, is entitled to demand, as it does, unconditional recognition, or whether its requirement is so much the more immoderate, the more decidedly and definitely it professes by itself alone to furnish the truth.

I.

It is not accidental, or merely required in some way by the constellations of the present, that we do not now, as was formerly the custom, inquire into the relation of reason and revelation simply; but the assent of conscience also is in these times considered requisite. We should be tempted — did the matter not have a very dark reverse side — to characterize it as a decided advance, that the old one-sided opposition, in the name of reason, has changed into a stronger one in the name of both reason and conscience. For since it is the aim of revelation to furnish not merely truth, — something that is true, — but the truth, — that which alone is true, — it addresses itself not merely to our reason, but to reason and conscience, the organs and capabilities of our being which we have for the truth. As to the nature of the reason, we can and must, as will undoubtedly on all sides be admitted, describe it as not merely in general the ability to know, but more particularly the ability to know the truth, to distinguish between seeming and being, to penetrate into the nature of things. The truth, however, is that which was, and is, and is to be, according to the original signification of the word [1] in our golden German vernacular; that which has continuance and value, when all else perishes and is of worth no longer,[2] the eternal and unchangeable above all that is temporal and transitory; thus also the law that rules over all, and commits to destruction whatever does not adjust itself to it. Accordingly, the truth preserves for us a moral interest, and in the conscience now we feel, and by the conscience become aware of, the relation between our-

[1] Wahrheit.

[2] It is deeply grounded, that humanity sets nothing more readily than gold mammon, with its value, in the place of God and his truth (Matt. 6:24).

selves and the truth, of the unconditional demand of the truth upon us for its practical recognition and the subjecting of our entire selves to it, on the one hand, and of the distance at which we find ourselves from full compliance with that demand on the other. The conscience adds to the idea of the truth, as its necessary counterpart, the idea of righteousness, of the truth translated into life. (Comp. 1 John 1: 6, 8). Where truth is, there righteousness must be, and only where truth is can righteousness be.

With the truth, therefore, it is that reason and conscience have to do. This is their unifying centre and aim. Where reason is, there is conscience; where conscience is, there is reason. They must not be separated from each other, and cannot be separated. We are necessitated to think morally and act rationally; by which, however, it is by no means said that all thinking is moral, or all acting rational. That is determined by the relation into which we enter, of our own free choice, regarding the truth, as also by the extent to which reason and conscience accept the truth.

Now, since reason and conscience capacitate us for the truth, for its apprehension and its transference into life, they require the truth, both for us and of us. With the capacity for it is closely connected its need, and only when man has abandoned the morally earnest use of his reason, and foolishly and wilfully separated himself from the impulses and requirements of his conscience, can he become insensible of this need, and, as a beggar, who insanely imagines himself to be a king, be proud in the rags of his poverty, or he can substitute, in fanaticism, falsehood and unwisdom for the truth.

Hence, whatever comports with reason and conscience must spring from the truth, and only the whole truth can satisfy reason and conscience. Reasonableness and necessary assent of conscience form the standard of truth, and by this standard must be measured the thoughts of men, as well as that which calls itself a divine revelation.

It is something grand, this outfit of man for the truth, this endowment which in reality makes him the lord and centre-point of the world, — this idea of the truth, which is implanted in his spirit both as possession and as need, and which on its passage through the conscience immediately announces itself as the life-determining power. An ineradicable longing after truth and righteousness pervades the spiritual history of humanity; and how deeply the importance of the knowledge of the truth has been felt to be, we may learn from the teaching of the old philosophers, that philosophy is the guide to a virtuous and happy life, a doctrine with which even later philosophers essentially agree, only they are less enthusiastic and have their own special idea of the matter. As an electric spark, the expression or the discovery of this need arouses all the depths of the soul, and kindles in man, for the first time, a correct consciousness of his destiny, or again the deep and piercing conviction, that, estranged from his origin and his aim, he has lost himself, — his best part. All reflection of men, all spiritual labor, all seeking for knowledge has in this its point of departure and its end, and it can be readily understood how excited must be the conflict when a divine revelation, claiming to be the whole and only truth, makes its appearance and yet finds only a limited recognition. That the history of philosophy shows us less a development and constant progress in the knowledge of the truth than the remarkable phenomenon, that every new system demonstrates the untenableness of the preceding one and rejects it, and thus incessantly and unweariedly commences the work from the first, — that, so to speak, there is always heard the noise of the feet of those who come to carry out the new system, even as the former one was borne to the grave, — this more than all else attests the depth of the need of the truth, and indicates how thoroughly necessary it is that humanity should set itself right respecting everything which claims from it recognition as the truth, and so respecting divine revelation.

Now, man cannot once live, cannot understand himself, without the truth, even though he is compelled to substitute for it a thought of his own. Only by the truth does man come to his majority. Not until he has found the truth does he attain to peace with himself. It alone can give him knowledge of himself, of the ground and end of his being. It gives him the direction, the line, in which not only he must proceed, but in which alone he can freely and without hindrance order his life. *The truth for man, and man for the truth*, — this is the mutual relation in which all yearning and seeking of the spirit come to rest. Just the need of truth, which is not to be separated from the capacity for it, attests to us, that we have only then comprehended ourselves and obtained freedom and independence, when we have found the truth and submitted to it, and are reproducing the same as righteousness in our lives. The truth, and only the truth, corresponds to our life; the truth, and only the truth, is in accordance with reason, is reasonable.

After all this, we must now confess that, with our outfit for the truth, the truth itself we do not possess. We have, indeed, a conception of it, but not the truth itself, the content. Reason and conscience cannot say, I am the truth; as little can they say, of themselves alone, I have the truth; but this they can and ought to do, to seek the truth, and, wherever it is found, accept it. The truth is above us; it must come into us, since reason and conscience are adapted to unite with it, wherever it meets us, otherwise it remains external to us. This is an important result of the knowledge yet farther to be realized, that with the capability for the truth, and because of this capability, we bear within us also its need. If, however, we possess these two things, capability and need, if we have even but a conception of the truth, then we have in this an exceedingly important benefit; namely, the assurance of knowing the truth when it meets us, even as Adam, on awaking, saw the helpmeet which God had made for him, and said, "This is now bone of my bones, and flesh of my flesh." We shall be now, in some measure, prepared to say what must be the nature of the truth, provided it is the truth. We are fortunately not under the necessity, therefore, of stopping short with the question suggested by vanity, indolence, despair, levity, or frivolity,— what is truth?— as though it were in appearance wise to withhold a farther use of the reason, a continuation of that which was, perhaps, never earnestly undertaken, a thorough conscientious investigation, from such questions; as though no one could know the truth and distinguish it from imposture and delusion. And even though up till now the truth had escaped the inquiring human intelligence, still it would be an incalculable advantage to be able in every case to say, this is not the truth, this cannot be it; or, from the fruitlessness of all endeavor to have come to the conclusion of Plato, illogical yet sustained by experience, that the truth, or at least the whole truth, cannot be obtained except by revelation.

Let us hold this fast: man can know the truth. And now we ask, how can he know it? what is its sign? by what does it prove itself to our reason? by what does it bind the conscience to its moral realization in righteousness? It must be a clear, distinct sign, one visible and plain, without the eyes being armed by art and science, a sign to all, to the educated and the uneducated, to the laborers in spiritual matters, and also the laborers of the field. Because the truth is for all, it must, if it is not apprehended by all, yet be to all apprehensible. Only wilful blindness can be allowed to be incapable of discerning it, and it must be qualified to lay a well-founded claim to universal recognition, even when this is refused it.

Plato says somewhere, — and in this saying resembles that man in other respects so much his inferior of whom we read, he prophesied because he was high-priest that year, — Plato says, man is the measure of all things; and this expression finds its richest and deepest application in the question touching the sign of the truth. Affinity is the proof of the truth. This is its sign: that in it we find, and in a much higher sense than man does in woman, that which is wanting to us, the necessary complement of our being. Only with the truth and in it does man find himself; for it is this he seeks, and this wanting, the whole content and meaning of his life is wanting also. Therefore, this will be the sign of the truth: that it opens man's eyes respecting himself (as also in this "opening of the eyes" is the great, seductive power of falsehood and sin, which substitute themselves for truth). It will help him to an understanding of himself, and of all the mysterious ruling in the depths of his personality. In the light of the truth, an understanding of his needs, a knowledge of his worth, and clearness as to his capabilities and ends, will be gained by him. The truth gives me the knowledge of that which I have in myself. It accordingly offers itself directly as the ideal, to behold and become wedded to which was the unstilled longing of my soul. Now, first, do I know who I am, what I am, for what I am? not merely, I have found it, but, I have found myself! is the knowledge and confession of him who has apprehended the truth. The original affinity between ourselves and the truth, its being so completely human, and yet so sublime that it can be characterized only as divine, — thus, its divine-human quality, as it is to be called, — this is the self-evidence which the truth furnishes to him who desires it. Its signature is, all human and yet all divine. As long as we are destitute of this complement of our being, we are not, and do not feel ourselves to be, free and well; we know of nothing truly satisfying with ourselves to take hold of, and as little with all that we have gained or met of spiritual and material possessions. From this seemingly free but in reality enslaving lawlessness and insecurity, from this degrading independency, we would be absolved. The truth is freedom, light, atmosphere, and life for man; and, in this particular, He whom his church calls the God-man is at least right when he says: ye shall know the truth, and the truth shall make you free. Man is the measure of all things; truth is the standard of man, — man also is the standard of truth.

This explains why it is that there dwells in man an irresistible longing after the truth, — and yet a deep-rooted shyness of it. We love and desire it, for it is our life; we fear and flee it, for it is our death as well. This explains what is meant by the tradition about the veiled image at Saïs, that the man who raises the veil must die. He who would lift it for mortals must have the hardihood and power to swallow up death in life. Perhaps, in the conflict concerning the truth, both this seeking and fleeing are mirrored. It must appear. We are no longer children in the sense in which a child carries in unconscious and involuntary helplessness the prophecy of future freedom and independency. Our seeking for truth is conditioned, in great part, by the fact, that we find ourselves, by our own fault, afar off from the light, are wandering in the most complicated ways of error, and our thinking and living do not correspond with the truth. It is not merely mistakes and errors that truth must correct in us. Besides reason and conscience, we have a will, which goes its own way, and readily subjects itself to neither reason nor conscience nor the truth, and since the case so stands in experience, that we and our entire race are governed less by reason and conscience than by the will, the arbitrary will, we do, indeed, for the sake of reason and conscience desire the truth, for we feel that it alone is life and freedom; but we fear it, for it brings us death. We can, certainly, think of the truth as blessed life; but we always experience it first as living law, — spirit and power, — which annihilates whatever does not adjust itself to it. Because, however, man, the measure of all things, is also the measure of truth, in this is the self-evidence of the truth, that it slays, though it is the life, — nay, just because it is the life.

One thing more. All that has been said thus far leads us to the necessity of a self-revelation, a self-attestation of the truth. We have a conception of it, its idea and the desire for it, — thus everything but just the truth itself. It must be more than idea, — it is the ideal, whose idea we bear within us; and it must, again, be more than an ideal in the customary sense of an imagined object or an idol, — it must be reality, actuality. This is the desire of our souls. The truth must prove that it is the truth, by being actual. An idea in itself can be only appearance, an error, or the product of a diseased egoism; nay, we cannot, from the fact that we have apprehended and proven something to be necessary, say that it also actually exists; as a recent philosopher has rightly objected to this favorite supposition, — the bridge from logical, rational necessity to actuality has not yet been discovered. Does the truth which we seek actually exist, then it must manifest itself as reality, as reality it must at some point enter into our life or meet us.

And indeed not as a thing, an unconscious existence, be it even a combination of natural phenomena called natural laws, or the unity of the worlds and the like, but as personality. For only a personality is of equal rank with man; to it he can wed himself; in it he can find himself and his proper thou; only it is in affinity with him; — a life-dispensing, life-emitting, and even to all the world life-imparting personality, this the truth must be. For so alone does it stand by the side of man as the bridegroom, suing for his free and yet necessary love, stand as the source of life and father to him. Everything else, the whole world and its individual existences, the entire sum of natural laws, even of those yet undiscovered, is inferior to him. All this must lie at his feet; to it — the world — he cannot give himself, otherwise he would not so long already have sought the truth outside of and above the world. In a word, the truth must be God himself, a living, personal God, and God himself must be the truth, and God must be reality, not conception or thought, and God must reveal himself; for it belongs, as we saw, to the nature of the truth, that it reveal itself, or we should have it only in thought, i. e., we should in reality be eternally far from it, since our thoughts do not possess creative power and divine prerogative. Therefore the quick, sure-sighted Greeks designated the truth by a word[1] which refers to the fundamental conception of revelation. In the domain of philosophy we shall have to inquire how much truth men have thought of, and by thinking have discovered; in that of religion, how much truth they have lived, and in living have possessed. How much truth they have reproduced as righteousness in life, of this, history would inform us, if it did not show us rather the opposite.

They are grand requirements, these which reason and conscience make, — requirements, such as, if they are complied with, put before the eyes a majesty, and promise a sea of glory to him who is able to endure the glance thereof. If, however, they are not complied with, then we are doomed to submission, and there is nothing left us but either the sorrow of the world, in which we commiserate ourselves, and that we exist, and the world, and that it exists, as an eternally incomprehensible, aimless matter of fact, — only a sort of slow suicide; or else a frivolous Epicureanism and Sadduceeism, with the device, Let us eat and drink, for to-morrow we die. Renounce life, — enjoy life; between these two poles, as caprice and taste might dictate, humanity would have to move.

Let me set before you, briefly, the historical relation of man to the truth, — how much of it he has anticipated or discovered, — that we may be able also by means of this historical standard to measure the claims of divine revelation, as we possess it in the Holy Scriptures.

---

[1] Ἀλήθεια, etymologically *that which is not concealed.* — *Tr.*

II.

At one or the other of those two poles — life-renunciation and life-enjoyment — humanity has more than once arrived. India, the land of treasures, has produced also the doctrine, that nothing is the only truth, and man must renounce all, to prepare himself for transition into this only blessed nothing. It is the philosophy of despair, which there, as with us, in the poets of melancholy, confirms the saying, What is a man profited if he shall gain the world? Still, the instinct of self-preservation is too strong in man for him not to prefer, if he can find nothing better, to recompense himself with the enjoyment of the present. Therefore we find in all nations, at all times, in all places, those who prize this as the only wisdom: enjoy the moment, enjoy life. This also is a philosophy of despair, and at times one can query, which moves humanity more powerfully, the seeking of enjoyment, or the earnest though unsatisfactory search after truth? This, however, we know: the philosophy of despair, as also that of enjoyment, just because it is the philosophy of despair, does not bear on itself the sign of the truth, adaptation to humanity; and especially do we pronounce the latter, without hesitation, to be morally objectionable. We can exclude them forthwith from the answer to the question, how much truth, reason, and conscience have found, since neither of them comes legitimately within it. By so doing, however, we have excluded also both the old and the new materialism, to which it is necessary to prove, at the outset, that man is something else than an animal, though on the scale of animals the highest representative. With him, who, like the materialists, has lost his self-consciousness, there is no disputing. It is vain and superfluous, after that, to defend himself and his human rights, and we on our part have for this class of reasoners only that old and often verified saying: These speak evil of those things which they know not; but what they know naturally, as brute beasts, in those things they corrupt themselves.

By this exclusion we have already gained much. The spiritual life remaining for us to consider, has something in it more human, and struggles up nearer to the light. We enter upon a field where discussion is easier, where the battle is only the forerunner, and, indeed, the condition of peace. Let us, however, beforehand, impress upon our own memories the words which one of the world's own prophets has written: "As long as man strives, he errs."

It would be strange if at least intimations of the truth had not, at all times, made themselves known to men. Before Christianity, the religion of revelation, summoned thinking man to join himself to revelation, or to wage war with it, the thought or rather the knowledge everywhere meets us, that the truth occupies a divine relation to man; that the Deity is one with the truth, and that the knowledge of the Deity first teaches man to understand himself and the world. For this reason, man cannot live his full life without religion; and theology has ever been that which characterizes the different systems of knowing and of knowledge, distinguishing them from each other. In the popular belief of the ancients, as in their philosophy so far as it did not lapse into the doctrines of renunciation or enjoyment, we find throughout, in confirmation of the knowledge gained by us, this striving which goes beyond the world; and in all decisions respecting God and the divine, different as they are, we find yet this in common, that the world and humanity are dependent on him, and can find only in this association the full development of life. Further, we see it confirmed, that the truth in an ideal sense must be human; in the popular belief the gods were fashioned into imitations of men, with their good and bad qualities, while in the philosophy, and by the philosophy, the knowledge of a vast distance between what is divine and what is really human was made current. This also is common to both the popular belief and the philosophy of the ancients: that the life this side of death is not the whole of life, nay, that it forms a barrier to knowledge, the present not coinciding entirely with the truth; that beyond this life we shall have a look into the reality of the truth; that there, also, the truth — the rule of the gods, or of the Deity — will reveal itself in the judgment of individuals. Such intimations and perceptions, such outlines of religion, we will not embrace under the apostle's saying, that this world's wisdom is foolishness with God. He himself, with a certain predilection that way, returns to it when, e. g., in the Acts of the Apostles, he makes use of it, saying, "certain also of your own poets have said, We are also his offspring; for in him we live and move and have our being;" or when, in the Epistle to the Romans, he appeals to it, "Who, knowing the judgment of God, that they which commit such things are worthy of death." To this belong expressions such as that of Aristophanes, "Piety preserves all;" the saying of Plutarch in his treatise on superstition, "The infidel has no belief in the gods; the superstitious man would fain have none, but he believes against his will, for he is afraid not to believe;" and the old saying, "Godless and without God is polytheism." A peculiar charm is connected with these expressions, as with all intimations and prophecies, as with all germs. There is perceived in them that freshness, that originality, that earnest striving, which have become so strange to a race growing old. We are captivated by the Platonic doctrine of ideas, that at the basis of all visibility, of all manifoldness of appearances, lies an idea in real existence, thus an actual ideal; that all ideas, which form the original ground of the phenomenal world, — so, namely, that the latter is only a copy of the original picture, — culminate in the idea of the good, of the perfect, which coincides with the Deity. This doctrine is a wonderfully bold attempt to apprehend that which lies beyond the present, and still is present. Socrates and Plato, who reached the highest point, have not concealed from themselves, that the whole truth in its divine-human form they do not have; and Socrates, who refers to something that looks like revelation, complains: he held it to be the greatest good fortune to know the will of the gods; but he does not believe it can be ascertained by the conclusions of reason, and he therefore recommends divination, the art of fathoming the will of the gods from its signs. And this wisdom has never become the world's wisdom, the common property of the world and of its sages.

When Christianity entered the world, the world had not yet found the truth, had even lost the beginnings of this knowlege. The popular belief of the old nations had broken down, — unable either to endure the corrections of reason, such as Socrates, Plato, and even Aristotle, attempted, or to overcome the influences of a skeptical, doubt-seeking philosophy. Greece and Rome were sighing under a universal religious bankruptcy, which for its preservation was only able to build a pantheon, an asylum for all the gods of all nations, although Aristotle had already accented as a requirement of reason the unity of God. Philosophy was not, as formerly, advancing in a constant correction and deepening of knowledge, but had fallen a prey to skepticism, to greedy doubt and gloomy despair. The entire sum of the spiritual life, as far as it had not possessed itself of a certain ingeniousness of the moment and for this world, had become a great maze of confusion, and it is more than an accident, it is a world-historical circumstance, that over against the One and the only One who of all men ever dared to say, "I am the Truth," Pilate, his judge, must serve as Folly, with his question, as expressive of self-sufficiency as of despair: What is truth?

Yet, all the while, humanity knew not and had not the truth. Then Christianity made its appearance with world-conquering plans and — it must on all sides be conceded — with such world-conquering power, that to this hour it is the only religion which has a prospect for the future. But as formerly not even the outlines of the truth were held fast, so it cannot be regarded now as so strange, that in view of the seemingly extravagant claims of the truth, humanity again, and only the more zealously, sought it with itself, and wished to find it without the religion of revelation. A spiritual war was kindled, which still continues, and which cannot be fought out until one or the other of the parties is annihilated. What of truth humanity can find without a self-revelation of God must now appear. For it is not here revelation against revelation, nor philosophy against philosophy, but that which calls itself a revelation, and which can so little be a product of the thinking spirit, that some have wished to consider it the offspring of a morbid imagination or of a saga inventing the fantastic, — this is set against all the religion and philosophy of men, or, since no other religion can endure in the presence of Christianity, it is at last this against all philosophy. (We purposely refrain from saying, faith is against knowledge, as that is a wholly imaginary opposition). If Judaism had not produced such works of genius as did the Greeks, because it needed them not, Christianity and its opponents now led forth forces in a human point of view equally great.

What, then, has the world at this time to offer as the truth? or does it stand perhaps all the while yet before the question, What is truth? "As long as man strives, he errs,"—this is the sum, which an authority in the world has estimated. After a serious effort of thought, reason has always been forced to correct itself, and that it could not rest without perpetual correction is an evidence of its elevation and nobility. It is also an evidence of the spiritual depth of our German nation and of its special mission for the truth, that we have always taken upon ourselves the correction of systems, as well as, for the most part, the formation of them. Yet the truth cannot be found where one system is destroying another. The philosophy which was unwilling to go forward in theism—from the recognition of one living God to the God of revelation in Christ—fell away to deism, and strove in vain to make men comprehend a God who had ceased working and grown old, and as this view did not meet all the demands of reason, philosophy gave way to pantheism and was dumb. We may also regard pantheism as now set aside, partly by materialism, and partly by the decisive advances towards theism, which we greet as the early dawn of a Christian philosophy; yet the forms have not taken exact shape, and the present yet stands before the question, What is truth? *science giving to it no answer.*

It is in point to show our race that, after such results of thousands of years' labor, it is yet well worth the trouble earnestly to inquire whether the truth can properly be found except by its self-revelation. Then alone has the erring endeavor of man an end. But as this ever erring endeavor has for nearly two thousand years derived always new impulse from opposition to revelation, and has lived by opposition, so now it persists in the same. Without any bond of union, save that of denial, without being conscious of any systematic basis, it now summons to the conflict the entire sum and product of human knowledges and investigation, as aggregated in the present stage of culture. The collective consciousness of the civilized world — if such a one could be extracted — represents, it is said, at least one stage of the truth, and must be permitted to require that Christianity put itself in unison with it, instead of the reverse. Independently of its moral perversion, this reminds us suspiciously of pantheism, abandoned now in the name of reason, which taught that God becomes conscious of himself in the world, and in the gradual manner of its development. Further, natural science, on the ever-increasing height of close inquiry, in the discovery and exploration of the always unapprehended laws of nature, is, according to the latest view, to teach us the truths to which our entire being is subject; since some have gone so far, e. g., as to make of the ethical and religious question concerning the immortality of the soul a question of physiology, of physics. Anything else than the unbending course of nature is not to be affirmed; and this reminds one suspiciously of deism, which bound the Creator so mechanically to his creation, that he remained at best but bound and regulated force, no longer spirit and freedom and life. And yet the protest against deism in the name of reason has been admitted.

We have arrived at the deciding point. In the name of reason and conscience the attempts to establish and express the truth have been set aside. In no system did man find himself and his being, for which there is rest only in God. The present stage of culture can of itself, and even for our age alone, as little be the truth, as any one member or the aggregate of our race can be the truth. Does there, then, exist any right to protest in the name of reason and conscience against divine revelation, as it has furnished for itself its self-evidence in the Sacred Scriptures? This brings us to the chief and concluding point of our discussion.

III.

When, at present, not only in the name of reason, but also in that of conscience, protest is made against the religion of the Bible, — for it is that alone with which our question has to do, — it must not be overlooked, that the conscience in man and its significancy were first, so to speak, discovered by that religion. The Romans, the people of justice, knew it as the consciousness of guilt. So also the Greeks, who, e. g. Plato, conceived of it as an exercise of the memory, while more lately it was spoken of as a consciousness preceding, following, and judging of the character of actions, and was treated as an expression of the understanding.[1] But that it furnishes a measure for the truth, this first became clear when — without special show, as something self-evident — it was expressed by the apostle: "By manifestation of the truth, we commend ourselves to every man's conscience in the sight of God." The appeal to conscience we find first in the Holy Scriptures of the New Testament. There it appears as bearer of the religious need; there, accordingly,

---

[1] Comp. my biblisch-theologisches Wörterbuch der neutestamentlichen Gräcität, p. 184 ff.

it has to confirm and attest the truth of the revelation of salvation, by which this need is met and satisfied. In the conscience man is no longer, as with the Greeks and Romans, merely his own witness, but the New Testament emphasizes this, that in it he is to himself a witness of God. And everywhere this knowledge is now accepted as a literally correct and profound view of the truth. The New Testament it is that has given humanity on this point its first understanding of itself, and since, as we saw at the beginning, it is the peculiarity of the truth to acquaint man with himself, this, to go no further, speaks strongly for the truth of a revelation which, as a revelation of the truth, addresses itself to the conscience, and so not only voluntarily subjects itself to the judgment of men, but requires the same, and even points out the unknown tribunal before which alone it can be judged.

But does divine revelation actually, as it professes, satisfy the requirements of conscientious thinking? Are the contents of the Bible of such a nature that a self-revelation of God and of his truth can be perceived in them?

We have already seen this, that it would be unreasonable to deny the possibility, nay, the necessity of a self-revelation of God. The first question then is only, whether a particular revelation of God, a different one from that in the works of his creation, is possible and requisite: a different one, not in the sense, as possibly some *will* misunderstand this, that God now represents himself in a way irreconcilable with the natural revelation, but a different one, in the sense that God gives us to know something which we find neither in nature nor in ourselves. That such a revelation is possible, he will not deny who recognizes in the being of God, and in what God is and can be to us, an unsearchable depth of riches. That God both is and can be more than his works in the world show us, who will deny? But is it also requisite? It would indeed be requisite, even though sin had never entered the world. For how else could men have lived in God, except by a continual intercourse of God with them? Only revelation would probably not have been then, as now it is, something wholly special. It would have been something naturally connected with the normal moral development of life, and would certainly also have come in a different way. Now, however, since the undeniable fact of sin has caused and is constantly causing the equally undeniable fact of estrangement from God, a particular revelation must appear truly requisite to him alone who with pain becomes conscious of this estrangement, and this consciousness is the first moral condition for a right understanding of revelation and of the Sacred Scriptures. But this is also the first thing attested by our conscience, that we do become conscious of our estrangement from God, and naturally the conscience delivers this testimony with special emphasis there where God meets us. Not this became originally strange to us, whether we have a God over us. That is clear to us from the fact of our estrangement from him. But this is the knowledge which has become a want, — what kind of a God we have. Therefore that a God, that God exists, does not need to be revealed, and besides is nowhere by the bearers of revelation in the Sacred Scriptures especially taught. This is a fact of our self-consciousness, to which it cannot be objected, that there are perhaps still heathen nations on so low a grade of humanity as not to have this consciousness of God. There are also civilized men who have, to a great degree at least, lost it, and in either case we recognize a degradation, a degeneracy. This, however, is the effect of our estrangement from God, that, inasmuch as we do not now sink the roots of our entire life in him, we are not in a condition to apprehend from our consciousness of him his being, as far as this is apprehensible to men. We know by our present capability altogether too little of God to be able to be satisfied therewith, and our deepest longing therefore, rightly understood, goes out after a revelation of God. Thus also our spiritual vision suffers under the effects of this estrangement from God, and the errors of the self-ruling spirit explain themselves from its obscuration. Just as little does the conscience tell us anything of God that goes beyond the consciousness of our estrangement from him. For just in this stadium is the consciousness of distance from God. Consequently the conscience cannot give us nearer information, and so, right here, is apparent how fundamentally erroneous is the assertion of the leader of the present opposition movement, that every tenet of the Christian faith must be referred back to a deposition of the conscience. Reason and conscience must first receive new contents before they can make new depositions, and for obtaining new contents there is left no other means than that of a self-revelation of God.

Such a revelation, it is true, can by no means be a logical or natural necessity. We can claim it neither on the grounds of the universal, of even the divine reason, nor on the grounds of justice. In view of our being by our own fault far from God, it can only be an act of the divine freedom, if, perchance, it is not to be a revelation of judgment. This latter alone could be rightly and logically proven and conceived of as a necessity. The question for man, freezing afar from God, is concerning a revelation which teaches, and by facts convinces him, that he has a God different from what he could expect. So, the revelation which is to give us God, estranged as we are from him, as the open, flowing fountain of life, can be only a determination and an act of the divine freedom, and, indeed, of God's free love, of his redeeming grace. This must be the character of a revelation, such as alone can lead the human race estranged from God back to its original condition and forward to its original aim. The question, first of all, is not respecting an advance, but respecting a saving, energetic reaction. This is surely nothing unreasonable; only it is something contrary to all the expectations and conclusions of reason. If we find the same God from whom we are far off in sin, manifesting himself to us as holy love, condemning, yet saving us, we cannot say, this is a different God from the one reason and conscience attest to us; but we must say, God is different from what we expected. He is — to resume here an earlier expression — more than truth, he is grace and truth. He is our death and yet our life; he solves the insolvable riddle. These are things unfathomable to our reason, things of which the conscience has no intimation. They are directly the opposite of all original unadulterated depositions of reason and conscience, and yet not against reason and conscience, but in the highest degree for us. A morally unclear generation, to which sin is at most an error or a result of defective culture; which excuses itself and therefore believes it is able also to redeem itself, — a generation which has lost the feeling for the significancy of sin, can indeed present that as the deposition of its conscience which it did not find in itself, but borrowed from Christianity, namely, that God is love; but mark,— it is forthwith no longer in a condition to keep the unity of God uninjured; it must weaken the condemning, slaying force of the truth of God; it can no longer say of its God of love, he is my death and yet my life. And herein precisely, as we have already seen, is the self-evidence of the truth, that it is both, only no man has a presentiment how both are at the same time possible.

Now that we have such a God, that God wills to be such a God, — grace and truth, — for the world, this is the testimony of the Sacred Scriptures upon his revelation; this is what Christianity, as a religion of revelation, offers us. The God who reveals himself to our race, estranged from him, to our race, wandering far from its source of life, to bring it back to nearness with himself, does not surrender himself, as all depositions of man persisting in being far from God surrender something or even all of the truth of God, to restore at least the indispensable appearance of a nearness to him. God surrenders himself only in a certain sense, and yet remains what he is; he remains the God of the sharpest opposition to sin, and at the same time reveals himself as saving, pardoning, and redeeming love. He is the God of atonement, and assuredly not of an atonement such as to the reason left to itself and its own thinking, and to the conscience left to itself, must appear alone reasonable, and yet impossible, namely, an atonement which sinful man by an impossible reparation for his offences re-establishes, — the fundamental conception of atonement with the heathen nations, the natural expression of the religious life and thinking, — but he is the God of atonement in the sense that he himself, in the place of men, undertakes their atonement, that he takes upon himself the fulfilment of the inviolable claims of justice upon men. He surrenders not himself, for this he cannot do, without **surrendering** the truth. Therefore he reveals himself as a consuming fire. And yet he does surrender himself, and becomes substitute for men. And since this has happened, he has entered into a new actual relation to men, has become strength and life for the humanity which accepts this new relation.

You perceive I am here attempting to indicate the outlines of the self-revelation of the Triune God, of the God of atonement. Also as to this it manifestly holds good, that something is presented which does not contradict reason, but in which we dimly discern a wonderfully deep reasonableness, since in this way only is a unison possible between the God of redeeming revelation and the requirements of reason and conscience touching the truth. But, although it is nothing unreasonable, it is yet something so far exalted above all expectations, above all conceptions, above all attempts to apprehend God by the laws of logical necessity, as the One who must be the God of atonement, not first by an act of his free love, but from himself, that it is comprehensible if, to this hour, we can better adore than fathom this self-revelation of God. A twofold mistake is committed by those who oppose this truth. First, the mistake of judging of this self-revelation of God according to the natural law of the numbers three and one, without perceiving that even the conception of God as infinite life, nay, even the weakening of this conception to that of unlimited being, escapes our idea, so that we cannot with the physics of numbers enter into the metaphysical, into that which lies beyond nature. And such being the case, no proposition of metaphysics, nor in general of, say, a mathematical, or of a physical class, should in this connection be expressed. The second mistake is this, that what should be regarded as the human expression of a miraculous fact is set up and assailed not as a fact, but as a proposition of mathematics, though according to a divine mathematics it does stand the test. All rational opposition must start from an investigation of the fact. It has to inquire, Is it a fact at present cognizable, that we have such a God? To the facts the reason must confine itself, and by these correct its mistakes, as well as enlarge the boundaries of its knowledge. And this latter is far more the object of revelation than the former is its necessary accompaniment. The opposition in the name of the Christian consciousness must deal earnestly with the Christian consciousness, and not substitute mathematics, natural science, and the like, in its place. Must the reason concede that God can reveal himself, must it even acknowledge that it is in the nature of God to reveal himself, must it farther acknowledge that a revelation of God, the effect of which is not to be our death, can be only an act of the free love of God, an act of his grace,— then we must by the most earnest and conscientious search for God make the test, whether we so find God, as he has revealed himself. For the consequence of the self-revelation of God is his presence. It is not separate items of knowledge, individual notices, after the impartation of which God withdraws himself; but by revelation God enters into our presence and becomes the life-element of the man whom he meets, as water is the element of the fish. Therein must be tested the correctness of the knowledge of God which is connected with his revelations. Therein is presented continually the actuality and truth of that which was at each time imparted to the first receivers of the revelations of God,—that this something which abides is an abiding divine energy, an abiding life; and if man has, for the apprehension of spirit and life, a capability of feeling which differs from that of the five senses, if he has an ability to perceive and know what is spiritual, then he can discern, in the presence of this divine revelation which has entered into time, God himself; as, indeed, even the common consciousness of God is not a historical notice, but a present feeling of God or of personal estrangement from him. This test must be applied, and it must be conceded, that he who in this proof does not find the amount required has reason rather, on account of the importance of the matter, to doubt his proof, than the amount, and to seek the mistake rather with himself than on the other side. Commonly, however, the doubt is turned, for no sufficient reason, in a one-sided manner against divine revelation. So also it must be admitted, that, until the time when the barriers of this world fall, when the destroyed harmony between the world and God shall be re-established, the Christian consciousness, or, to speak more correctly, the personal life in the presence of God (the "witness of the Spirit") furnishes the last but irrefragable proof for him who is required to find proof. Only this we can concede to no one, that the facts in which we live are unreasonable and against conscience; and it is our great and serious task to assert and promote a recognition of this truth, so far at least, that not the reason but at most the will shall contradict it.

One thing, however, with this we must not forget, namely, the difference with which the Christian consciousness expresses itself. The facts on which it rests and which it realizes are everywhere the same. But if the way of appropriating the effect and significancy of these facts is different with different persons, so that, e. g., one sees and finds in Christ the truth, another the redemption, a third all treasures of wisdom and knowledge, still another justification, sanctification, the life, the teacher; in other words, if the facts find with individuals altogether different points at which they enter into the innermost personal life, then will the way of conveying the facts, according to their contents, connection, order, and significancy, to the understanding, be still more different. In this relation can take place not merely a greater or less. There may be misapprehensions even, unobservable to one, plain to another, which it is the office of love to reconcile. As far as the fact and its significancy for the personal life remain untouched, so far must there be allowed, on account of the limitedness and narrowness of our knowledge, a doctrinal freedom within the Christian church and its confession regarding divine revelation. And this doctrinal freedom can be allowed to that extent, because the collective life of the church in the presence of its God and of its salvation will effect a continual correction of such errors. Let us, by way of illustration, suppose that the fact of God's becoming man in Christ, or perhaps the atonement, has been apprehended by some one in faith. Now, as soon as the question is concerning the understanding, there arise, it may be, doubts, errors; incomprehensible things are in the way. We must say, on the one hand, that such doubts are of a wholly different nature where the question is concerning the understanding of the facts, from what they are where it is concerning the facts themselves, and we must guard against a mischievous confounding of the two. On the other hand, however, we must in this case claim the same privilege which is so readily, in a far higher degree than we ask it, accorded to naturalists, the privilege of seeking in different ways to comprehend one and the same fact.

Above all, we will stand by this: where divine revelation is concerned, the question is not respecting more or less comprehensible propositions, such as mathematical or philosophical formulas. It is not the object of revelation to furnish us such propositions; it proposes neither to enrich our knowledge, nor, as is sometimes with pleasure said, to augment the enrichment of our knowledge. The question is respecting divine and human pulsating life, respecting a renewal of our life in the divine mind and divine strength.

It is true, without knowledge conscious life is impossible. Hence there is no religious life without a definite religious confession, and in this sense, certainly, it is important to draw from the records of revelation, the Bible, the propositions of the revealed faith and life, that in them the facts of revelation and the present state of affairs, i. e., the presence of salvation, may be brought to expression. Of this work the Sacred Scriptures, as the "register" of divine revelation in its relations to our inner life and experience, must be made the basis, without their being so used as that they shall in any way encroach upon the reason or trespass upon the rights of conscience.

It is entirely wrong to speak of an opposition between believing and knowing in the sense that by it the realm of the religious life in general, or even that of the life in the God of present grace,— of the revealed faith, — is separated from the opposite. All faith rests upon knowledge, and when it is not produced by deduction or logical demonstration, it must ground itself upon spiritual perception and contact. Knowledge and faith are distinguished from each other like cognition and recognition, so, faith is an exercise of obedience, of recognition, and hence of trust, of surrender. Believing and knowing are also distinguished from each other like cognizing and understanding, and in all realms of life believing has the privilege of going farther than is possible to the understanding.

Let us return once more to revelation. What we find in it — the God of atonement, — He is not merely the ideal fountain of life, one existing only in thought, but since he is present, he is actually our life's new origin, and in his grace and truth we find ourselves born anew. The reason as man's sense of truth, the conscience as his sense of right, are alike satisfied by the life and righteousness which we here find. What the reason seeks, living, personal truth, a bride for the soul; what the conscience requires, righteousness, such as is good before God; what our entire being demands, life, eternally flowing, streaming, blooming life, — all is offered us by the God of salvation, of grace, of atonement; and hence we know that we were right when at the beginning we said that reason, conscience, and salvation formed a heavenly — better a divine-human harmony. All is new that revelation offers us, and yet it is to us nothing strange.

We might conclude, were it not necessary, for the sake of completeness, that we notice yet briefly one or two incidental questions. There is one which concerns the accompanying of revelation with miracles. It is really not difficult to see that the God, whose purpose is to redeem the human race from sin and all the disturbances and abnormities brought into the world by sin, must be a God of miracles, — a God who places his almighty creative power in the service of his redeeming love. Not the miracles should make us suspicious; rather would it be strange and adapted to bring the fact of divine revelation into question, if it were not accompanied with miracles. In this, however, it is implied that the miracles are not to be regarded as separate thaumaturgic feats of a magician, with the motto *car tel est mon plaisir*, but must be apprehended in connection with divine revelation and their ends. Then, moreover, it is apparent that they cannot be expressions of a self-correcting power, i. e., of a power which annuls the laws of nature, but are, at most, corrections of a mistake where in individual cases they seem to harm a natural law, extraordinary, but not unreasonable manifestations of power, wherever they occur manifestly outside of the natural connection of cause and effect.[1] Reasonable as to order, purpose, and end; reasonable notwithstanding all their deviations from nature; reasonable, i. e., not as disturbance or destruction of the otherwise uninterrupted course of nature, in the end all the miracles, even the most decried of them, can in connection with divine revelation be explained, although not naturally. Only there is needed, assuredly, neither an acquaintance with natural science, nor a contemning of all physical investigation; but there is needed a knowledge of the God who reveals himself as the God of salvation, of redemption, and so of miracles. It sounds lofty, but is, mildly expressed, a boundless immodesty, which in a reverse of positions would never be forgiven us, when Justus von Liebig so grandiosely says that, by the explanation of the force — which, between ourselves, natural science has not to this day yet discovered — of the planetary system and of fire, the earlier conceptions of God, heaven, and hell have lost their meaning. Let us, however, have the courage to set up for our Christian believing, thinking, and teaching, just as is done by the natural sciences, the claim of exact investigation, of close observation, and to cause it to be

[1] Comp. my lecture "Ueber die Wunder im Zusammenhang der göttlichen Offenbarung" (Barmen, 1865), Dr. R. Rothe, Zur Dogmatik (Gotha, 1863), p. 108. "Where does a miracle come into conflict with the laws of nature? We answer confidently, Nowhere! However, it does sharply oppose the presumed absolutism of natural law, and the idolatry which atheism would like to practise therewith. It attests that natural law is by no means the highest power in the world, but that above it rules He who made it, the living, personal God, — that in it the Creator made not a barrier to himself, by which his absolute and absolutely sacred freedom is limited, but a serviceable means, which never refuses itself to his purposes. When God works miracles, he would say thereby, that here is One who can do what created nature, what creation entire cannot do; he works in a miracle something outside of and above the process and the laws of nature." Comp. p. 100 f.

accepted, that the spirit within us, reason and conscience, are better observers than are the microscope and retort.

And now, finally, — as to the way in which the revelations of God were received, — let us not forget that their content extends beyond the bounds of the every-day and natural thinking and knowing as far as God does himself. Hence, it cannot be considered absurd and unreasonable if, wherever a man is chosen to be a receiver and bearer of these revelations, the barriers of the every-day, of the natural knowing, fall, and the man's inner sense must be opened before he can receive the impartations of God, as was the case with the seers and prophets, until all that God has to impart — the Word — has descended entirely out of its supernatural sphere into the domain of humanity, until the Word was made flesh, and is present in the Christian assembly (Tit. 1: 3), whereby the manner of New Testament knowing differs from that of Old Testament knowing.

Thus much must here suffice. The revelation of God forms a great system, complete in itself, embracing heaven and earth, time and eternity, God and man, in which all is reasonable, if the premise is correct, — God, sin. And these the conscience attests to every one. The contest against the truth and contents of divine revelation, in the name of reason and conscience, is only the second stage of a contest we all have to engage in to a greater or less extent with ourselves, — a contest in which the enemy can take three positions: I like not; I can not; I will not. The real spiritual struggle will commence only when the enemy has taken the third position.

LECTURE IV

MIRACLES

By REV. M. FUCHS
PASTOR AT OPPIN, NEAR HALLE

BIOGRAPHICAL

REV. MARTIN FUCHS was pastor at Oppin, near Halle, when he delivered his lecture in Bremen. He is now located at Cologne. He was born at Pollham, August 27, 1843. His lecture on Miracles, as presented in this book, shows him to be a very wide-reaching, clear, and logical thinker. This lecture has been pronounced one of the very best in the volume. In Mr. Fuch's conception miracles are not events that take place in contradiction of nature, or as violations of natural law ; but they connect themselves with the ordinary course of natural events, as the incoming of a supernatural force, or of some power above nature, into the workings of nature itself. They may therefore be regarded as "the high and shining points of the course of nature." Their possibility depends altogether on the conception that is taken of God in relation to the world.

SUMMARY OF LECTURE IV

With miracles Christianity can be said, without exaggeration, to stand and fall—Revelation as associated with miracles; every revelation a miracle, and every miracle a revelation—A miracle defined as the entrance of the supernatural into the connection of the natural—Two premises upon which the conception of a miracle rests: first, the real existence of the supernatural, or of a free, personal God, and of the spiritual world; and second, a living relation existing between the unseen spiritual world and our visible world—Miracles must be, therefore, wholly natural occurrences, grounded in the organization of the world and required by it—The miracle-conception is a heart-and-center point of biblical truth, yet one that in these times is very earnestly combatted—To affirm the impossibility of miracles natural science must deny either the real existence of the supernatural or the fact of a living relation existing between the natural and supernatural worlds; the last is deism, and the first is pantheism—Pantheistic view of God and of his relation to the world—Deistic view of God and of his relation to the world—The true or Christian view is a combination of the deistic and the pantheistic—Not necessary to affirm that a miracle contradicts the order of nature; the highest or common law in which all individual laws are included, is the will of God—The world's course not merely endures miracles, it requires them—Miracles are also actual, the whole history of salvation is a history of miracle—Miracles are not the chief thing in importance, but only signs following in the train of revelation; they direct attention from the outward to the inward, and also toward the future, to the great supernatural events which will occur in connection with Christ's second appearance.

IV

MIRACLES

BY REV. M. FUCHS,
PASTOR AT OPPIN, NEAR HALLE

THE subject which is to occupy us at this hour, taken in its full compass, is of such deep-reaching and determinative import for all Christian thinking, believing, and living, that with it Christianity can be said, without exaggeration, to stand and fall. The question of miracles, which the present lecture must try to answer, is as fundamental and cardinal a question of the Christian view of the world as is that of revelation, and the two are most intimately connected; faith in revelation and faith in miracles being inseparable things, each of which requires and conditions the other. Not only is revelation historically associated with miracles, so that every manifestation of God to the world is, as it were, irradiated with miracles, as the sun is with beams, but at the basis of this historical connection, of which the entire Scripture gives us evidence, there is also an inner connection of essence. Every revelation is, in the wider sense, a miracle, a supernatural event, something which has entered into the world from without, not something produced by the world itself; and every miracle, in the narrower sense, is a revelation, an immediate self-announcement of the living God. The two conceptions resolve into each other, and their distinction is only, that one represents more the content, the other more the form of the divine facts. Every revelation of God takes place in the form of a miracle; every miracle, however, has for its content a divine revelation.

But in what form, then, must a fact occur, to be qualified to claim the name of miracle? or, in simpler expression, what do we call a miracle? To the current definition, — a miracle is an event which cannot be explained from the known laws of nature, — we shall be unable to hold. For, first, this explanation draws no firm boundary line between what is miraculous and what is natural, but the division of the two realms is made dependent on the subjective apprehension of the laws of nature, so that the possibility is not excluded of seeing, in the end, with the progress of natural philosophy, all the miraculous resolved into the natural. Then, secondly, this definition is of a purely negative sort, since it tells us only what a miracle is not; but on what is the specific nature of a miracle, it gives us no information. Hence we say, better and more correctly, a miracle is the entrance of the supernatural into the connection of the natural, the intervention of a higher order of things into the lower, the immediate interposition of a God above the world in the course of the world and nature.

Let us also, to clear up the matter fully, state just here the premises upon which the conception of a miracle rests, the foundation upon which it builds itself. If a miracle is the entrance of the supernatural into the natural, then with this is premised on the one hand the real existence of the supernatural, — the real existence of a God above the world, and of a world of higher powers, laws, and orders than are those of the visible universe. On the other hand, it is premised that that invisible and this visible reality, that superior and this inferior universe, stand to each other in a living relation; that they do not, without connection and contact, continue their existence near each other, like two parallel lines which never meet, but that they are for each other; that a living way extends from the upper world to the lower, and from the lower world to the upper, on which they come constantly into contact. Just this is the peculiar view of the world taught by Christianity and the Bible: that above what is visible is that which is invisible; above the earth a heaven; above the created mundane and human existence an uncreated divine existence; nay, that to this latter, as the original entity, belongs a much higher degree of reality than is had by the former ("for the things which are seen are temporal; but the things which are not seen are eternal"); but that, notwithstanding this distinction, there yawns between the two no impassable chasm, making transit from either to the other impossible; that rather, as surely as the visible universe has the ground of its being in the invisible, there is a living connection between the two, by virtue of which the higher powers interpose continually in the earthly course of things, now quietly, now in so raised and energetic a concentration that it becomes a personal entrance of divinity into humanity. On the basis of such a view of the world, — this is self-evident, — miracles must be altogether natural occurrences, occurrences grounded in the entire organization of the world, and required by it.

You see, already, the miracle-conception is a heart-and-centre-point of Biblical truth, which frivolously to abandon, or to regard as an incidental, non-essential matter, would be a capital error, a negation in its consequences fundamentally ruinous, a surrendering of Biblical Christianity. For with its fall, fall not merely the individual miracle-narratives of the Old and New Testament, which many will doubtless in this connection think of first, but there falls the entire history of salvation, which is a continued history of miracles; there falls the miracle of all miracles, the person of Jesus Christ, with his supernatural entrance into the world and his supernatural departure from the world; there falls his heavenly origin, his sinless birth, his resurrection and ascension; there fall, in a word, all the fundamental facts and principles of our salvation in one common ruin, and there remains for us the annihilating word, "Your faith is vain!"

But, important as is the point which the adherents of Scripture truth have to affirm and maintain in the miracle-conception, it is one to just as great a degree combated. Against no other point of faith has there risen so loud and sharp an opposition as has come into existence against this. Nay, so boisterous and confident of victory is the assault which the later science and the so-called "modern consciousness" have undertaken upon this — as it is thought — most exposed post, that already the banner of triumph, with the inscription, "Miracles are impossible," seems to be planted on the battlements of the old castle, and the castle itself appears to be forever fallen. Indeed, if it were possible to kill a truth by the most multitudinous vociferations against it, it would be all over with the matter of miracles; — if it were possible to give an assumption from which one arbitrarily starts, by the boldest possible assertions, the stamp of a proved conclusion, this matter would now be in the grave. Even Schleiermacher's heart sank within him, as he saw the onset which the newer times were making, with all the means of science, upon this tenet of the Biblical faith, and he writes to Lücke (in the Theol. Stud. und Krit.): "I anticipate that we shall have to learn to do without much of that which many are yet accustomed to think is inseparably connected with the essence of Christianity. . . . Our New Testament miracles, . . . however long it may be postponed, will fall anew, but from worthier and far better established postulates than formerly, in the times of the windy Encyclopedia. What is then to be done? . . . What do you propose doing, dear friend? Will you after all entrench yourself behind the outworks, and let yourself be blockaded by science? The bombardment of ridicule will not harm you much, but the blockade!—the severance of yourself from all science, which will then, just because you so entrench yourself, be compelled by you to hoist the flag of unbelief." But should the situation be really so gloomy, so full of peril, so desperate for faith? Ought it not to have weapons of offence and of defence, which no science can shatter? Let us see.

To affirm the impossibilty of miracles, modern science must naturally seek to destroy the foundation upon which the Christian belief in miracles rests,—the Biblical view of the world which we have indicated above. Now, such attempt, in correspondence with the two moments which this view of the world emphasizes, can be made in a twofold way, either by denying the one or by opposing the other. Either the real existence of the supernatural is denied, while on the one hand it is referred directly to the realm of dreams and reveries, and on the other—which, however, in the end amounts to the same thing—it is identified with the real essence of the visible world; or the living connection of God and the world is denied, and the two are conceived of as separated from each other. The former is the pantheistic and—in its consistent result—materialistic view of the world; the latter is the deistic view. Both are sworn enemies of miracles, and the claims of both we shall therefore have to examine briefly.

Pantheism denies the existence of a personal God above the world, — of God as the Creator and Ruler of the world. It makes God one with the world. It says, God is the "Universal" lying at the basis of all the manifoldness of the world and of its individual phenomena, the universal essence which is in all; he exists not independently for himself as self-conscious being, he is only in the world as its inner ground of life, from which everything proceeds, and to which everything returns, but not outside of and above the world as its Lord and Creator. Thus God remains but an empty, unsubstantial name, and it is only the legitimate consequence of this process of negation, when at last the name is laid aside, and the existence of God is absolutely denied. Pantheism ends in that crude and unadorned species of materialism in which modern natural science sees its glory and its crown; let us rather say, most representatives of this science, for there are still noble spirits among them, spiritual relatives of a Kepler, a Copernicus, and a Newton, who were not only heroes of science, but also heroes of faith, and of whom the sainted Dr. Mallet, with joy of heart, said, "It is delightful to see how such heroes of science bow in the lowliest reverence before revelation, while the light troops file by without so much as removing their hats." Yes, the light troops, the light spirits, — they have surfeited themselves on their natural science, they have become drunken from the overflowing measure of their knowledges and discoveries, and to the delirium with which they are affected the great realities of a personal God and of a supersensuous spirit form no difficulty. Science decrees, away with them! and before this decisive sentence they must fall, just because they are miracles, i. e., facts which cannot be comprehended in the way of mere natural philosophy. For this is passing, for once, as an incontrovertible maxim: natural science is not merely the greatest among the sciences, but the only true science, in comparison with which all metaphysics and theology are but dreams; the only possible method of apprehension is by the sense-perception, and all that cannot be apprehended by the use of the microscope, balance, and retort, does not exist. Strange conclusion! It is first assumed, "there can be only the sensuous;" then the inference is boldly drawn, "consequently there is nothing supersensuous." What is proclaimed as the result of investigation is the arbitrary assumption from which they start. It is only an hypothesis, on which the entire structure rests.

But how, then, does pantheism explain the riddle of the world, if it expunges the supernatural, if it blots out the existence of a supermundane God, the Creator? It does not explain it at all; it simply interdicts the question of the whence and the wherefore of all things, — this irrepressible question which, nevertheless, rises in every human mind and heart, and has risen ever since men began to think and feel; it interdicts it, and says, "The world is because it is, and as it is, — and that is enough. The only reality is material being, matter and the forces connected with it; the only eternal and absolute entity is the atoms, the indivisible particles of matter which combine with each other, at one time so, at another differently, according to the laws of gravity, cohesion, and chemical affinity; change in matter, this is the secret of all animation and of all development. From this alternate play of the atoms and their forces has proceeded all that is, not merely the inorganic world, but the organic also, up to man; even the thinking human spirit is only a product of materiality." Then, certainly, a full end is put to miracles. If there is nothing but the regular course of the play of atoms, which goes on in eternal repetition; if there is only nature and no spirit, only the world and no God, then, assuredly, but not till then, all miracles are eliminated and banished. On this stand-point all footing for the conception of a miracle is wanting; for, if there is only a change in matter, which takes place only according to the laws inherent in matter, how can anything take place which is outside of and above these laws? From this point of view, Büchner, one of the leaders of the light troops, remarks, "How would it be possible, that the invariable order in which things move should ever be disturbed, and an irreparable rent not be made thereby through the world? Of necessity the world would forsake its poles and go to ruin. And how would it be possible," he continues, "that the invariable order should ever be disturbed, and every science not be made to appear as childish trash?" And so a God who works miracles there may not be, otherwise human science would lose its reputation; for, if it cannot force all events within its laws and rules, it would be only childish trash. Is this the humility of genuine science, or is it the swollen vanity and the drunken arrogance of autocratic caprice which here speaks? "It is not, for it must not be!"

Now, how does this materialistic view of the world bear examination, I will not say before the Bible and Christianity, but only before the thinking reason? before the light which even from nature shines in every man? We are obliged to say, it is the contradiction of all reason, the most irrational and absurd thing imaginable. Materialism, this destroyer of the spirit, is in its logical result the destruction and the end of all thinking; for it sets itself in antagonism with the necessities of thought, with the fundamental forms and laws of all human thinking, which are implanted in the nature of our intelligence, and from which we cannot depart without becoming irrational. One such necessary thought is the conception of a "First Cause." The human thinking must search after the ground of phenomena, after the whence and the why, and indeed it cannot stand still and content itself until it has come to an ultimate ground, to an absolute causality; for all intermediate causes are, in fact, not causes, but means; only the first cause is in the proper sense of the word a cause. Were there not such a one, then we should have only means, mere effects without a cause, — and that is inconceivable, that is to the human reason a wholly impossible thought; it must press forward to the ultimate cause; it cannot do otherwise. Now, if materialism says, "Matter is eternal; the atoms, of which all consists and is composed, these are the ground of all being," then the question necessarily arises, whence comes this relation and affinity of the atoms to each other? whence comes it that they remained not in their isolation, but have entered into combinations from which a whole world of harmony has resulted? If all has proceeded from the motion of the atoms, where is the moving power which has set the atoms in motion? In short, the conception of the atom is not that of a cause with which thought could rest content, but it points one back to a higher ground. Only the conception of God, of an eternal, supermundane Creator is in truth an ultimate cause, which satisfies the requirement of thought. Büchner says, "The hinge-point of the controversy between materialism and belief in a God is the question whether reason is before nature, or is in it." But Zollmann rightly answers him ("Bibel und Naturwissenschaft"): "Reason can be in nature only on condition that it is before nature. For if the existence of reason in nature is to be adhered to, then it follows that it must be in the individual atoms whose combination forms the totality of phenomena. The atoms thus would have to be themselves rational; every one would have to be endowed with the peculiar properties by which the great manifoldness of the combinations is made possible, — a reason which far surpasses that of man; for man can only with the greatest difficulty afterwards search out and construe that which the atoms have achieved. Either, therefore, the materialistic assertion that reason is in nature, has this meaning, and then man would have in every particle of matter in his body an infinitely higher reason than he himself possesses (which is nonsense); or it has no meaning at all, and it only remains for us to say, reason is before nature, and only because nature has been constituted by it is it in nature; for that cause only can anything of a rational character occur in it." Certainly, science cannot possibly conceive of matter as eternal, as having the ground of its being in itself; it sees itself rather forced by the necessity of thought to the recognition of the Biblical truth: matter is created; there is above matter and before matter a spiritual principle, an absolute and supreme reason, an eternal God, — the Creator.

Another thought-form and thought-necessity of our intelligence is the idea of design, the question as to the wherefore; and everywhere where an event bearing the marks of design and plan meets us, where an orderly development of a higher from a lower to a definite end takes place, there our thinking is satisfied, there it recognizes itself, a thinking and willing being, that pursues ends of which it is conscious. There it cannot help thinking before and above the event to the supersensuous spirit.

Here also materialism must first destroy the rational intelligence, to deny the being of God. Events bearing the traces of design, developments of the higher from the lower, plan and order, meet man in universal nature. How does materialism explain this? By attributing all to chance, to the unconscious play of the atoms! Zollmann appositely says (ibid.): "It is the most colossal chance-hypothesis imaginable; by chance ethereal atoms come together, and light is produced; by chance ponderable atoms combine and form acids and salts; by chance they form stones, plants, animals, men, fixed stars, — all things possible. Chance is the great necromancer who stands on the platform, and, with magic skill, summons up whatever the respected public wishes! To believe such an hypothesis surpasses the credulity of all believers together." We add, to require this belief of us, is to require an abandonment of all thinking.

I will not longer weary you with these expositions of the absurdity of materialism; besides, this absurdity is very easily to be discerned. I only ask, where is the charcoal-faith, — as the materialists are fond of terming in contempt the Christianity which believes the Bible, — where is it? There, where in the great, wonderful cosmos, in this stupendous structure of harmony and order, is seen the work of an Eternal Spirit, of a living God; or there, where blindly and without sense and understanding the god "Chance" is elevated to the throne? Where is reason? There, where it is believed and said, "From God and to God are all things;" or there, where all questioning as to the ground and end of things is excluded, where empirical reality is adhered to, in a stubborn do-not-know and do-not-care-to-know disposition, and where the quintessence of all wisdom is seen in the tenet, "It is as it is"? Where is truth? There, where the spirit, following its inmost tendency to truth, mounts up to the Father of spirits and bows in worship before him; or there, where, in order to avoid rendering to the Eternal Spirit the honor due him, the existence of the human spirit is denied and its nature degraded to the image of mere dust, with the destiny of becoming putrefaction? These questions need only be asked; they answer themselves in every human heart and conscience. Theoretical materialism is a web of the brain, the magical influence of which upon the present generation has its only ground in the fact that it furnishes welcome support and gives the appearance of justification to practical materialism, to the sense entangled in the earthly. Scientifically, after a short crying of victory, it has made speedy bankruptcy.

We turn now to the other view of the world, which likewise reserves no room for miracles, likewise proclaims their impossibility, without, however, in common with materialism, flatly denying the existence of the supernatural. It is deism, so called. This view, it is true, retains the existence of a God above the world, and is willing to honor him as the world's Creator; but, while it does that, it errs as to the other moment of truth belonging to the Biblical view, namely, the living intercourse between God and the world, by virtue of which a continual interposition of God in the world's course is allowed. Deism separates God and the world; it makes a stiff, mechanical division between the two. It knows only a God outside of the world, not a God dwelling in and working everywhere through the world. It decrees, at any rate, a first miracle, the creation of the world; but with this first and only miracle it closes the series for all time. Since the creation, it says, the natural forces and laws which God established have been the efficient and determining cause of the course of the world. God himself, however, has, as it were, retired to a position of rest, and only looks on, to see how the world, called into being by him and ruled according to unalterable laws, moves on. How could he interfere and help? That would be, indeed, to presuppose that he has produced something imperfect, something which after a time needed the hand of improvement. Is this conceivable? The perfect God has created a perfect world, and every interposition would be a disturbance and destruction of the whole!

Here, also, we see the inviolability and the inflexibility of the laws of nature are, in the strongest manner, accented. Natural law is made to be even for the Creator an impassable barrier. The world is regarded as a piece of clock-work which, once wound up and set a-going, keeps running of itself and allows no disturbance, as a machine which, once constructed and provided with steam-power, can be left to itself, and it works on in the regular way. God and the world stand to each other in only an external relation; they have no living communication each with the other; there is, indeed, a Creator, but no Ruler, much less a Finisher of the world.

But what a mechanical, we might almost say, what a childish notion this is of God and the world, and of the relation between them! "What is a God," says Goethe, —

"Who on the outside forces
The all, as it about his finger courses?
He should act in the world, its interests sharing,
For it in self, for self in it thus caring;

> That all which in him lives and moves and is,
> Shall ne'er his power, ne'er his spirit miss!"[1]

And what is a God, who, having departed from the world, persists in pure passivity, and in the great drama of the world plays only the idle spectator? Surely, a God who is dead and satisfies neither the wants of our minds nor of our hearts, a God who is far off in solitary exaltation, and cares not for us, and about whom we need not care! How much worthier, grander, fuller of life; in a word, how much more God-like, is the conception of God presented us in the Bible! Here we have the living God, who not merely in eternal majesty is enthroned above the world, but also in eternal activity works everywhere through the world, as the God who dwells in the world. The truth which pantheism and deism have rent in twain and divided between them, so that one knows only the internal, world-pervading God, the other only the external, world-transcending God, Christianity comprehends in one. It calls him, in a single proposition, "the God who is above all and through all and in all." And as positively as it affirms, "He dwells in light which no man can approach unto," with equal emphasis does it declare, "He is not far from every one of us; in him we live and move and have our being." Everywhere it unites the God above nature with the God in nature. Everything to be seen or heard or felt in nature is to it not merely an effect which has proceeded distantly from God, which must be traced back

---

[1] "Was wär' ein Gott, der nur von Aussen stiesse,
Im Kreis das All am Finger laufen liesse?
Ihm ziemt's, die Welt im Innern zu bewegen,
Natur in sich, sich in Natur zu hegen,
So dass, was in ihm lebt und webt und ist,
Nie seine Kraft, nie seinen Geist vermisst!"
— GOTT UND WELT.

along the threads of the natural laws and forces to the beginning of the world, to find for it a connection with God, but is an immediate manifestation of the invisible power and Godhead. God it is who rides upon the wings of the wind, who speaks in the storm and thunder, who shines and blesses in the light. God, who is above all, is also in all; upon even the natural event rests a breath of the supernatural, of the miraculous, as far as it reminds us of the divine power immediately ruling therein. The God of the Bible is not a God who, after he had created, retired to a place of rest; but he is the all-pervading life, the all-overruling power. "Upholding all things by the word of his power," is the declaration of Scripture; and the words of the Lord to the Jews who supposed the Sabbath of God was an end of all his work are, "My Father worketh hitherto." Put these two ideas together, "God above all," and "God in all," rise to the Bible's conception of the living God, then the idea of a miracle has nothing in it objectionable or difficult to our thinking. Miracles then become matters in the higher sense altogether natural.

Should any one, however, be as yet unwilling to concede to the Biblical view of the world, compared with that of deism, the right in point of truth, but should ask for farther proof, then we answer: the entire constitution of the world, of nature, as also of the human heart, decides for the Bible and against deism. How, then, is nature constituted? Reigns there in it actually the stiff, iron legalism which absolutely excludes the free ruling and interposition of God? Assuredly not. Plan there is and order, certainly, in the whole course of nature, but no stiff sameness, no unbending necessity. Nature is by no means a mechanism, a nicely defined piece of clock-work, which winds itself up every day or every year; but it resembles a well-ordered commonwealth, in which laws reign, most surely, but such laws as leave play-room for the free will. And so nature must be constituted, if it is to be the dwelling-place of man, of man endowed with free-will. Only when so constituted can it allow in it the exercise of a will that chooses among different possibilities and controls the event in nature to the attaining of its purposes. But if the free action of the human will is recognized, and room is found for it inside the laws of nature, why should just the Creator be excluded from such free action and ruling? As man in a peculiar way combines and disposes the forces in nature to his purposes, so that a result is produced which would never have been produced from the mere working together of the natural laws, so, only in an infinitely higher sense, God disposes the event in the world to his purposes. Is this a little view of God? Must it be said, "Why did he not constitute his work better, that he must constantly amend?" This objection would be just, if nature were only a mechanism, without aim and without a free man in it; it falls to the ground, because nature is something nobler, — a theatre for free acts, the human and the divine.

The entire constitution of the world, consequently, does not exclude the free ruling of God, the divine government of the world; on the contrary, it is so devised as from the beginning to have had that in view. And further we say: the human heart, also, is so constituted, that it must believe in the world-ruling God, as long as it believes itself. The human heart, as soon as it knows of a Creator and Lord of the world, cannot help praying to this God. That would be an absurdity and a contradiction, if the course of the world occurs according to unalterable laws, which form an insurmountable barrier even for God; if everything proceeds according to blind necessity. But this the innermost voice of our own nature, of which we have the immediate assurance it cannot deceive, tells us that God's hands are not bound by natural law, but that he freely rules the world and directs all according to his counsel. Therefore we pray. Can that be delusion? Can this prayer-impulse, with which every man, even the denier of miracles, is involuntarily affected, when trouble presses hard upon the soul, — can it be deception, or as the catching of a drowning man at a straw? No! it is a remnant of the truth in the human heart, which, when the earnestness of life brushes from the eyes the cobwebs of idle theories, stands out distinct and clear before the spirit. This is the remnant of truth which, after every suppression, rises again, and bursts through all doubts, denials, and negations; the remnant of truth, without which human life would be comfortless and hopeless, a lightless wandering in darkness. Where is there a praying heart, to which its experience would not with a thousand voices attest, Prayers have their influence; they do not, as sound, die away in empty space? That could not be if the world's course were a mere mechanism.

True, one could say, God's government of the world keeps within the limits of the laws of nature, and consists in only a free-ruling combination of the results which these produce; it is a guiding and adjusting of the course of nature, but no actual interposition in it, no proper miracle. Here natural law is nowhere violated and set aside, but all takes place naturally. Well, but yet belief in the divine government of the world is a prelude to a belief in miracles in a narrower sense, and leads thereto. For the divine government is after all a miracle in the wider sense; it cannot be understood from mere natural law. It proves the free ruling of the supermundane God in the world, and comes often so strikingly before the eyes, e. g., in sudden and manifest punishments of an offender, in astonishing deliverances and preservations, that we must even then, when all has occurred within the laws of nature, involuntarily exclaim, "How miraculous!"

From this point it is only a step to a miracle in the strictest sense of the word, consequently to such occurrences as the Bible narrates in such profusion, where the natural law seems to be transgressed, as in the raising of the dead, the changing of water into wine, the multiplication of loaves, etc. Here the objection rises with increased strength: God cannot violate his own order; the natural law was established by him; how could he overturn and abolish it, without setting himself in contradiction with himself, without converting the order into wild disorder? We could, in the first place, reply, Is God not master of his own work, that he may do with it what he will? Is he not Lord in his own house, and is the regulation which he has established for his house as binding upon himself as on the house? Can he not, in special cases, and for special purposes, instead of the customary regulation, introduce a higher one which sets the former aside? And is disorder produced by the lower regulation's yielding to a higher? When, on Sunday or holiday, the work-day rule of the house is suspended, and one aiming at higher ends becomes operative in its place, is confusion caused thereby in the house? Does the lawgiver come into contradiction with himself when he excepts the particular case from the general law, and puts it under a particular law? And is the general law thereby abrogated? By no means. It remains good for its domain and loses no particle of its validity. Surely, if it is God who has established the laws of nature and subjected all events to them, it is manifest that he is excepted who did subject all to them. And even for the case where it would be necessary to say, the miracle contradicts the law of nature, and it cannot be otherwise conceived of than that the essence and the properties of matter, at the instant when the miracle occurs, are changed into their opposite,— even then belief in such a temporary setting aside and changing of the elements has nothing in it suspicious for him who really believes that God, the Creator of matter, is, in consequence, absolutely master of it.

But we do not need that. It is altogether unnecessary and incorrect to affirm that a miracle contradicts the order of nature. This hypothesis results from the erroneous idea that God and the world are absolutely separated from each other, and that the world over against the Creator has an entirely independent existence. Is it so, then, that with a miracle something foreign and hostile enters by force into the connection of nature from without, something whereby this connection is disturbed, torn, and violated, whereby, so to speak, a rent is made in the *nexus rerum?* This is not at all the Biblical conception of the matter. God through all and in all, says the Scripture; all has not merely its origin from God, but also its continuance in God. He upholds all things by the word of his power; all things are, live, and move only in him. That is to say, no natural force and no natural law has an existence independent of and separated from God, but all is pervaded and upheld, animated and energized, by him who created it. All the natural forces are inserted in the living original force, from which they continually draw their life; and they work only because the original force, which is itself the life, upholds them. All the natural laws are inserted in the living original law, in the will of God; and they hold good only so far as they are upheld by the will of God. The divine power and will, these are, on the one hand, the energy enthroned above and before all the world, the energy which created all; these are, on the other hand, the living-principle concealed in the world, and lying at the basis of all the life of the world, the principle in which all is rooted, by which all is upheld, without which it would not exist. This is the point to be urged, if the Bible miracles are not to be to us a stone of stumbling; the divine creative power we must recognize as the power of all life in the world, as the energy working in and through all. Hence it is said, in the Lord's prayer, "Thine is the power," i. e., the absolute power, embracing all powers, the original force which constantly puts forth from itself all individual forces, which makes alive and keeps alive all causes, means, and instruments. Therefore, the Lord makes it a reproach to the miracle-denying Sadducean spirit: "Ye know not the power of God." Consequently, it is not true that the natural forces work their natural products without God, by themselves, in their own power and wisdom; but all natural forces have their life-root in God's creative power, and it is his power and wisdom working in them which makes it possible and necessary for them to produce this and that, so and otherwise. All these individual forces, however, which in nature are distributed according to kind, place, and time, God has forever united in his divine power, which is the life of all forces and the rule of all products; and from the fulness of this power, which flows everywhere through the world as its inner life-energy, he can at once, without the mediation of the individual forces, set forth something new, which is a manifest miracle, as the ordinary phenomena, which he sets forth gradually by means of the natural forces and laws, are a concealed miracle.

How can an abolishing of the order of nature, a contradiction of natural law, a destruction of natural force, a rending of the connection of nature, be spoken of here? These disparagements do not apply to the Biblical view. The highest law, the common law, in which all individual laws are included, and from which each of them is only an emanation, is the will of God; anything taking place in accordance with this can contradict no law of nature, because it accords with the law of all laws. And if, instead of the individual forces, the common force operates, the original force, which upholds and includes in itself all forces, how could this make a disharmony in the working-together of the forces? Then would it needs be a disharmony, whenever, in a piece of music, through the play of the notes, the key-note sounds full and clear? And is this a rending of the connection of nature, when precisely that which upholds and moves the whole course of nature, the all-pervading and all-energizing power of God, makes its appearance? Assuredly the miracles of God are not disturbances and disorders, but precisely the high and shining points of the course of nature, where it celebrates its festivals. The miracles are not something unnatural and against nature, but the supernatural beaming forth from the innermost life-ground of nature. Not something foreign and heterogeneous is here violently introduced into it from without, but its own innermost life-spirit, which is the secret of its being, comes out into the realm of the visible, the divine creative power. As the electric current, which passes through a body, under certain circumstances, concentrates and emits sparks, so with the divine power, which, as the breath of life, pervades all. Its concentrations, its scintillations, these are the miracles in nature. These are the clear flashings of the Creative Spirit through the veil of matter, while in the ordinary course of things it only shimmers through the natural event as a soft, mild radiance. But we say still more. We heighten the affirmation: the world's course endures miracles without forsaking its poles, to the other; the world's course requires miracles — miracles are not merely possible, but also necessary; by which, it is true, we have not, first of all, thought of the individual miracles, but of the chief miracle of revelation, of the connected history of miracles, which has its central point in the person of Jesus Christ, in which, however, as we shall directly see, the individual miracles, the sensuous nature-signs, have their necessary place.

The world's course requires miracles. For, without a miracle, there could be no development from the lower to the higher, no progression towards an end, but only standing still or a moving about in a circle. Developments appear only when new germs and beginnings, new life potencies, insert themselves into the connection of things, which give to the stream of the world's course new motion and direction; were it not for these, it would become a stagnating bog, a dead sea. These new life-germs and potencies, however, do not result from that which already exists; they are no product of the already given forces and conditions of the natural life, but they enter by a free creative act of God into the world, insert themselves however instantly into the regular procession of things without interruption and break, without noise and tumult. In a word, they are miracles, no product of the natural forces, but an immediate gift of God, and just this is the leaven which brings the mass into fermentation and motion, which furnishes the possibility of a progressive development.

So it is already in the history of creation. The entire creative act divides itself into a series of development-periods, — the Biblical record calls them *days*, — each of which is ushered in by a "Let there be!" With every "Let there be" a new life-potency enters into what at the time exists, and calls forth new developments, which go on according to law. Thus it comes continually to a higher grade of being, from the inorganic to the organic, from the vegetable to the animal, until at last the highest earthly grade of life, man, is reached. But even with the conclusion of the creative work, there is in existence by no means an absolutely perfect world; for perfection is not the beginning, but the end, and from that beginning to this end leads only the way of development. All is, indeed, after creation is completed, *very good;* that, however, does not signify absolutely perfect, but suited to the end for which it is designed. So with man himself; he is not created for rest, for passive existence, but he receives a commission: he must build and preserve; he is bid and forbid, — what else does this mean than that he is called to development? He must as a free being gradually unfold himself according to the divine idea lying at the basis of his being; and with him nature, whose head and centre he is. This development-course, even if it had proceeded normally, without departure from the original idea, could have taken place only under continually new supplies of life; it must necessarily have had its nodal points, where something new entered into the old, as the immediate work of God. Possibly even the Scripture hints at this, when it speaks of the intercourse of God with man in paradise.

How much more intense miracles will the world's course require, to reach the divine end of creation, after it has gone aside from the straight line of normal development and by man's sin has become distorted! This is the crying fact which every look into the history of the world and of man, every look into our own hearts, attests to us, that the course of the human race's development is a maze of misused freedom, an abnormal, sinful course, and, therefore, one tending to ruin, — a course which not only admits of a saving interposition of God, but as a work of mercy most urgently demands this. On the basis of the natural life, if the death-process into which it has fallen is not to lead to destruction and dissolution, a new life process must take place, a new, higher history, which does not grow up from the death-kingdom of this world, but from above is woven into the web of the world's course, consequently a miracle-history in the highest sense of the word. This is the deepest need of the world and of human nature. For that help from above the whole cosmos lying under the ban of sin and death cries and calls, as a prisoner cries for deliverance. And to meet this need is something contrary to nature, is a violent, disturbing interposition? Then it is also a contrariety to nature and an act of violence, when, at the right time, the hand of the physician administers to the death-sick human body the healing forces, which not only arrest the process of death, but convert it into that of convalescence!

And, thank God, this miraculous working of God, the necessity of which is as firmly established as is its possibility, has also become actual fact. Into the world's history of sin and death the golden threads of the history of salvation have been interwoven, a continued chain of divine acts of revelation for the saving of the world, which form a living organism of miracles. The record of this continued history of miracles is the Scripture of the Old and New Testaments; its culminating point is Jesus Christ, in whom not merely individual beams of the divine light and life, but all the fulness of the Godhead bodily enters into the world, and, placed under the law, interweaves a divine-human history of life into the world's history of death. And, in turn, the culminating point of this divine-human history of life, the crown and pearl of all miracles, in which the whole miracle-structure of the divine history of revelation reaches its pinnacle, is the resurrection of Jesus Christ, this banner of our faith, with which Christianity stands and falls; this sum of the Gospel, which from Easter to Easter, from Sunday to Sunday, is preached and celebrated in the Christian church.

These facts of the history of salvation yield to none of the world's history in point of historic actuality and certainty. They are attested in the surest manner by the most trustworthy witnesses and testimonies, which no historico-critical investigation has yet been able to impeach. "This Jesus hath God raised up, whereof we are all witnesses;" "We declare that which we have heard, which we have seen with our eyes, which we have looked upon and our hands have handled," — so speak the witnesses of divine revelation, with a calmness and veracity which remain unshaken in the midst of ignominy, bonds, and death. Must it not be said, if such testimonies are worth nothing, then no testimony in the world is of any worth, then every other historical fact can with equal propriety be rejected? and bare arbitrariness is set upon the throne! But men can appreciate the force of these external testimonies, in a dozen other instances; on much less important testimony, they can account a matter true; but precisely in matters of the history of divine salvation there will be no end of doubting and disputing. Here no witnesses suffice, none of all the unnumbered host who from the times of the apostles by greatness of spirit tower above ordinary men and shine down through all the centuries; in a dream and delusion they have all been ensnared! Why this difficulty of believing, this stubborn skepticism in matters of divine revelation? Just because the history of revelation is entirely different in character from whatever else human history presents. In this appears only the transitory world-life, which is infected with sin and subjected to death; but there the superterrestrial life makes its appearance, which was lost in the history of the world, but for that very reason had to be planted in it anew. Such a life must necessarily have a peculiar character and history, in which everywhere its supraterrestrial nature gleams through. Therefore the history of divine revelation, especially the history and being of Jesus Christ, cannot be understood, believed, and laid hold of by man, so long as his sense, and with that his understanding, remains fixed on the things of earth. There are inner grounds, grounds in his entire method of thinking and perceiving, which cause that to appear to him impossible, in spite of all external evidences, which is so entirely foreign to the products of the world, in which exclusively he lives. Hence no arguing and proving from external grounds ever helps one from unbelief to faith; but, if man would understand God's truth, he must consent to a change of mind. He must allow himself to be conducted from the outer world to the inner, and, instead of investigating the history of the external world and nature, he must study the history of his heart and inner life. Here is the tribunal where the right witnesses and judges can be found; where to every one his sins and mistakes, his losses and deficiencies, make themselves apparent; where all the secret troubles, diseases, and needs of human nature come to view. But so also in the interior of every man the traces of the divine image buried within him reveal themselves, which, under all the pressure of the external world, continually awaken in the deepest grounds of our being a longing for, an anticipation of, and a struggling after the supermundane life, for which we are designed. He who thus searches in himself, not merely in nature and the world, and takes along with him in his search Him who searches through all, — he who accepts and cultivates the sense for it, — he learns to view divine revelation and Him who is its centre, Jesus Christ, the life of eternity come down from above; learns to believe in, love, and understand him, and so becomes a partaker of his superterrestrial life. Such a person believes in miracles; for he has experienced in himself one of the greatest of miracles, — regeneration from death to life.

Henceforward, as may be said in conclusion, faith and understanding open for the sensuous miracle-signs in the realm of the natural life, with which divine revelation is attended on its passage through the history of the world. What are they, and what do they signify? Certainly, we must not force them up too high. They are not primary in importance, but secondary; not the chief thing, but only the signs following in the train of revelation. We believe not on account of these miracles in Jesus Christ, but the reverse; on account of Jesus Christ we believe the miracles. And only so far as they are related to him, the living heart-centre of revelation, are they a subject of our faith. On the other hand, however, they are no superfluous ornament, no arbitrary embellishment of the history of revelation, no mere display, the object of which is to charm and gratify the senses, but they have a holy purpose to subserve in the interest of revelation; and therein consists their necessity. Jesus himself repels most decidedly the curiosity which desires to see miracles merely for the miracles' sake, wherever it meets him. His miracles always have in view a moral aim, and indeed the same which is had in view by revelation throughout, — the inner renewal of man. This gives his miracles that peculiar mark of holiness by which they are so essentially distinguished from the strange and fantastic wonders described in the Apocryphal Gospels. His miracles are no arbitrary feats of power, but acts of wisdom and love designed to subserve his work as the Saviour of the souls of men. And what does this mean? In the original language of the New Testament, the miracles are called σημεῖα, *signs*. A sign, however, exists not for itself, it is not an end; but it exists for the sake of that which is intended to be signified, represented, pictured thereby. Its object is to turn attention to that, not to fix it upon itself. A sign is the visible likeness of something invisible. So also the miracles of the Scriptures are only pictures, by which the spiritual meaning of divine revelation mirrors itself in the world of sense; they are reflections of the spirit in the realm of nature. And so the sensuous miracle speaks to man, who, in consequence of his bodily nature, is most closely connected with the entire world of sense, and is in his natural condition preponderantly set thereto; it speaks to him a grand language of signs, by which the mystery of the regeneration, of the spiritual salvation and redemption at which divine revelation aims, is designed to be symbolized to him. On the basis of these signs the dim feeling of the supersensuous is to be cleared up to complete understanding, the mysterious yearning for it is to be strengthened and quickened to positive endeavor; and so they become the pioneers which direct from the outward to the inward.

And with this directing inwardly they connect a directing to the future; as they are a symbol of the spiritual renewal which can, and should even now, be taking place, so they are also a prophecy of the bodily perfecting and glorifying which is the end of the ways of God. The Scripture speaks of a future redemption of the body which is designed for the children of God, and in connection therewith of a future glorifying of nature, when the creature also shall be delivered from the bondage of corruption, from the oppression of evil, and from the ban of death. It speaks of a regeneration of the entire world, of a new heaven and a new earth, where there shall be no more death, neither sorrow, nor pain, nor crying. And to this it must at some time come. The spirit must yet be invested with corresponding body; the kingdom of heaven, which now is internal and invisible, must yet become also external, and transform even nature into a kingdom of glory. Of this future glory the miracles of the Bible are individual prefiguring beams. These acts of healing, these resurrections of the dead, — these are designed to say to us that the same power and grace of God which now are working salvation in our souls will at some future time work the same also in our mortal bodies; — and as it is now said of the redeemed human heart, it is a temple of God, so it will also be said hereafter of our entire earth, "Behold, the tabernacle of God is with men!"

This language of the external miracles, however, man will not understand, unless the Spirit of miracles, the renewing Spirit of God, dwells in him, and he has, in the power of the same, experienced that internal spiritual miracle of which the Scripture says, "God hath quickened us together with Christ, and together with him hath raised us up and made us sit in heavenly places." This internal experimental proof it is which outweighs and makes dispensable all other proofs, and which, in spite of all the contradictions of natural science and of the modern consciousness, puts in the mouth the confident confession which once the heathen king Darius learned to repeat after the prophet Daniel, "He is the living God, who worketh signs and wonders in heaven and on earth."

LECTURE V

THE PERSON OF JESUS CHRIST

By CHR. E. LUTHARDT, D. D.

PROFESSOR OF THEOLOGY AT LEIPSIC

CHR. E. LUTHARDT, D. D.

BIOGRAPHICAL

Dr. CHRISTOPH ERNST LUTHARDT is, in this country, one of the best known of the recent great German scholars and theologians. Besides being the author of many publications on a wide range of topics, quite a number of which have been translated into English, he is in Germany especially renowned as a university lecturer and pulpit orator. His style is very lucid, logical, sometimes eloquent, and of all the writers in this book he is one of the easiest to translate. He was born at Maroldsweisach, in Bavaria, March 22, 1823. He studied at Erlangen and Berlin, and was ordained at Münden, in 1846. From that date until 1851 he was teacher in the gymnasium at Munich, and was afterward *repetent* at Erlangen and *privat-docent* in the same place. Still later he was professor extraordinary at Marburg, and in 1856 he became professor of systematic theology and New Testament exegesis at Leipsic. During his long literary career he has been the editor of several German religious journals. In 1865 he was made consistorial councilor. The following may be mentioned as among the works from Dr. Luthardt's pen which have been translated into English: "Fundamental Truths of Christianity," "Saving Truths of Christianity," "Moral Truths of Christianity," "The Johannine Origin of the Fourth Gospel," "St. John's Gospel Described and Explained According to Its Peculiar Character," "History of Christian Ethics Before the Reformation."

SUMMARY OF LECTURE V

THE person of Jesus Christ is the highest theme and the common object of sacred interest to universal Christendom—Calling upon the name of Jesus is the badge of every Christian—The question about Christ is the underlying one of all—Something mysterious in Jesus' person and whole appearance—Napoleon's skeptical utterance at Weimar put in contrast with his believing testimony on St. Helena—Jesus Christ is a historical fact, that is the first point—The next point is, Jesus was a teacher, a founder of religion—Rejected by his own people, he has become an object of attraction to all nations—What is the mystery of his person?—That he was a man, we all know—That he was no ordinary man, is admitted by all the intelligent, and the church sets him upon the throne of God—What does he say of himself?—Difference in the testimony of the four Gospels, diverse and yet substantially the same—Jesus solves the mystery of man in his lowliness and exalted destiny—He also solves the mystery of the history of Israel, being the fulfillment of its hope, or the Messiah that was to come—Moreover, Jesus solves the whole history of humanity, being its end or goal and also its great central turning point—He is thus the key to an understanding of man; and no less is he the key to a correct knowledge of God—In Christ God comes down to us and becomes our Saviour—He is thus the God-man, and in him the two lines of Israel's prophecy meet—He is the Son of God and the Son of man—The gospel has brought into the world a new knowledge of God and man, and has thus caused a new epoch in the world's history—Whoever rejects Christ will soon lose a true knowledge of both man and God.

V

THE PERSON OF JESUS CHRIST

BY CHR. E. LUTHARDT, D. D.,
PROFESSOR OF THEOLOGY AT LEIPSIC

THE task has been assigned to me of speaking to you concerning the person of Jesus Christ. This is the highest theme and likewise the common object of sacred interest to universal Christendom. For in the name of Jesus Christ all in the world who call themselves Christians bow, or at least should bow, their knees. As the Israelite distinguished himself from the Gentiles by his calling on the name of Jehovah, so Christians distinguish themselves from non-Christians by their calling on the name of Jesus Christ. However the characteristic feature of Christianity may be designated, however the Christian tenets may be questioned or denied, this is the last and the deciding thing that marks the Christian,— that he bows the knee in the name of Jesus Christ. He who discards this may still call himself a Christian; we cannot in truth recognize him as such. He may be a religious man, may perhaps be in his way a pious man, — there have been and yet are pious heathen even, — but a Christian in the proper sense of the word he is not. This was the first confession of faith regarding the Risen One, the exclamation of the vanquished skeptic: My Lord and my God! This was the last, dying utterance of the first martyr of the church, his prayer to Jesus Christ: Lord Jesus, receive my spirit! This will be at the end the last prayer of the martyr church, the petition to the Exalted One with which the Revelation of John closes: Come, Lord Jesus! Between the Acts of the Apostles and the Revelation of John, however, Christians are, in the New Testament, described as those who call on the name of the Lord Jesus; and whosoever shall call upon the name of the Lord, it is said, Rom. 10: 13, shall be saved. This is the badge of the Christian.

It is the common badge of all Christians. For however much the individual churches may differ from each other, and even though they may be at enmity with each other, in the One they are all one, in their common confession of Jesus Christ and in their common calling upon his saving name. As far on earth as the salutation goes, Praise be to Jesus Christ; as far as songs glorify him who died on the cross for us; as far as the praying pray to him, and his name trembles on the lips of the dying,—so far there is Christian brotherhood, so far extends the Christian church, one, holy, universal, Christian church; but beyond these limits it does not go, for Christianity goes no further. Calling upon the name of Jesus is the common and the decisive badge of the Christian.

Just this, however, is the question at this day in dispute; for it is the kernel of the religious questions of the day. They may be differently formulized,—at bottom the dispute is only upon this. Our opponents may style themselves the knights of freedom of faith and conscience, and us the slaves of symbolism and the letter; they may inscribe upon their banners the progress of science and reconciliation with culture, and stigmatize us as the men of retrogression, consigning us to the middle ages; it may be said the point in dispute is the question of miracles and the supernatural, or how the essence of Christianity or the problem of the church is to be conceived, or however else the religious opposition of the times may be formulized; the last and deciding question, which underlies all others, is, nevertheless, the question concerning the person of Jesus Christ; and the practical and universally intelligible expression of this question is the calling upon his name.

I have always been peculiarly impressed with that word which the aged Simeon, as the Scripture narrates, uttered over the child Jesus, as the latter was brought into the temple, calling him the sign which should be spoken against. For this word, is it not, as it were, the theme of all succeeding history down to our day, and suggested by a truly wonderful glance at the oppositions which would agitate times and minds? For about the person of Jesus Christ minds have always differed, and by this to the end of days shall the thoughts of hearts be revealed. Scarcely, however, for centuries has there been a time for which those prophetic words of Simeon express so precisely, if I may use the term, the programme, as for these times of ours. This is the mystery of his being and the secret working which Jesus exercises, that he makes a decision either for or against necessary. Every one must take a definite position towards him. He can be abused, he can be reviled, he can perhaps be even hated; but ignored he cannot be. He is the ensign which God has set up in the midst of the times, and planted in the movement of history.

There is something mysterious in his person and his

whole appearance, which attracts us, and does not let go of our thoughts respecting him. And it is not merely our thoughts, which are incited by the mystery of his being to a solution of the riddle which his appearance puts before us; it is also our hearts, which are drawn towards him. For his person exercises a mysterious influence upon all nobler spirits, who are not wholly engrossed in the interests or enjoyments of ordinary existence. Into the soul of him who has once been met on his way through life by this figure, it thrusts a thorn, which will allow him to find no rest until he has found it in Christ himself, whom he seeks. And even the striving of the opponents against a recognition of him is a sign of this thorn which they bear within them. Every mystery moves us to, and requires of us, its solution. No historical greatness of humanity attains to mysterious significancy and to power over the minds and hearts of men like that attained by the person of Jesus Christ. No one can resist the inner necessity of becoming clear as to this mystery. What shall be the word that solves this mysterious riddle of humanity? What is *the mystery of his person?* Of that I am to-day to speak to you.

You have doubtless heard of that famous conversation which Napoleon had, when in Weimar, in the year 1808, with Wieland. As the latter was speaking to him of the fulfilled prophecies of Christ and his apostles, and, provoked by the scornful looks of Napoleon, began to wax warm on the topic, Napoleon interrupted him with the words, "I do not believe there ever lived a Jesus Christ." Whereupon Wieland, with earnest frankness, replied, "Then, sire, in a year from now, and at least with equal right, I shall not believe there ever lived a Napoleon." Then Napoleon changed the theme of conversation.

In Montholon's "Memoirs," published by Beauterne in 1841, there are different expressions, reported as having been uttered by Napoleon, during his last years, at St. Helena, regarding the divinity of Jesus Christ. "I know men," — about thus he is represented as speaking, — "and I tell you that Jesus Christ is not a man. His religion is a mystery, a thing by itself, and proceeds from an intelligence which is no human intelligence. Alexander, Cæsar, Charlemagne, and myself founded empires; but on what did we rest the creations of our genius? Upon force. Jesus Christ alone founded his empire upon love; and at this hour millions of men would die for him." How far these and similar words, reported of him, from the last part of his life, are historical, it would be difficult now to determine. They have probably been embellished. Nevertheless a kernel of truth undoubtedly lies at their basis. In any case they affirm what must always, in the end, be said of Jesus. From that question of the historical existence of Jesus to this of his divinity extends a — long line. This line describes the theme we are to discuss.

Jesus Christ is an historical fact. This is the first point. That Jesus lived is not a question; that stands sure. Even the heathen writers tell us he was crucified under the Roman Emperor Tiberius. And were they silent touching him, the existence of the Christian church would suffice to attest him. He lived, he taught, he died; and the disciples, whom he gathered about him, have attested the fact that he rose from the dead. With this testimony they went out into the world, and the world has been conquered by them. For this testimony they yielded up their lives.

But what is involved in this fact? That is the question. Jesus was a teacher, was a founder of religion. This is the next point.

"The Master," "the Teacher," — so his disciples call him, so he is known in the circle of his friends, — this is the picture of him which the Gospels delineate for us. What he taught was, in substance, religious. He wished to renew religion and the religious life; this is unquestionable. And the result of his work confirms it. He has founded a new religion, and renewed the religious thought and life of humanity. He was a teacher and a founder of religion. But what kind of a teacher? What kind of a founder of religion? To this it comes.

Others have gathered disciples about them, disciples that have been greatly attached to their master. When Xenophon tells us of his teacher Socrates, we discern, from his words, how his heart beat for the dear teacher. And when he speaks to us of the yearning, which all who truly knew him bore in their hearts for the departed master, we perceive, in these words of simplicity and plainness, the voice of truth. But the disciples of Socrates have passed away; affection for the noble martyr has gradually grown colder; his image in the minds of men has become more and more indistinct; he awakens still our interest, but who has an inner heart-relation to him? Socrates is a bright star in the firmament of humanity; but only one star among others; not the sun around whom the entire choir of stars circles.

There have been, also, other founders of religion; persons who have not merely gathered disciples about them, but have founded religious communities, in which their names live and are worshipped. No one, perhaps, of all the founders of religion in the heathen world is more comparable to Christ than that remarkable prince of India, Sakya-Mouni, who is called Buddha, whose worship still unites many millions of men in one religion. But, as much as Buddha's tenets seem to remind us of Christianity, and as great as is the resemblance of the outward form of the Buddhistic religion to the Romish form of the Christian religion, every observer perceives, at once, the fundamental distinction which separates Christianity from Buddhism, and, also, no less from all other religions. No religion but the Christian has disclosed the innermost nature of God; none but this has laid bare, in its peculiar centre-point, the moral nature of man. Christianity alone has taught that God is holy love; it alone has uncovered the full guilt of sin. No other religion knows of a grace of pardon and of a history of this grace, and has taught that herein is to be found the source of moral life. None condemns man so fully and yet exalts him so high, shows so much the depth of his misery, and, at the same time, the height of his calling, and opens the way to attain it. No other religion is, therefore, in the proper sense, one of redemption and regeneration. All others go no farther than the surface. They have accomplished changes in individual parts and sides of the outward social life; but an actual renewal in the innermost foundations the gospel alone has been able to effect. Hence, all other religions have their day. And when the period of decline has dawned upon them, they are unable from their own strength to renew themselves. Buddhism undertook to breathe new life into the stiffened Brahmanical heathenism, and now spiritual desolation and moral death rest more heavily and insurmountably down upon it than upon the idolatry of the Brahmans. The gospel, on the contrary, is an inexhaustible fountain. It constantly refreshes itself from itself, and so sends forth a renewing moral energy. The Christian Church has had times of the deepest decline, times of the utmost degeneracy. But from every prostration it has risen again. In it lives an eternal youth.

When, respected hearers, we transport ourselves in spirit to one of our religious services, when the Christian assembly comes before our minds, as in common with one heart it celebrates the name of Jesus, in the house where everything about us proclaims his praise, and our thoughts wander from there back to the beginnings of the Christian community and of its religious service, and tarry at last in that distant land, upon which yet the curse is so visibly imprinted, and with a man of that people which, from the oldest times to our day, despised, hated, and trodden under foot by all other peoples, has roamed restlessly over the world, everywhere resident and yet nowhere at home; when we bring this before our minds, must it not appear strange to us, that we, the proud lords in the realm of spirit, still in that which is the highest in the spiritual life, in religion, are ruled by a people with whom we have in other respects no fellowship, and by a man who died the most ignominious death known to the ancient world, and that his word has become a power which has revolutionized our entire thinking and willing? And what is the strangest of all, his own people has rejected him, and even yet knows no name it hates so much as the name of Jesus of Nazareth! Other peoples are proud of their national heroes. The greatness of Israel, as also its mission, was religion. All the world confesses, that in the province of religion Jesus is the greatest. We bow before him, though to us he is a foreigner, and his own countrymen despise him! And as we stand to him, so do all other nations, Israel alone excepted. In no other Jew do we so easily forget the Jew. But who thinks of that with Jesus of Nazareth? He is to us not the son of Israel, he is to us only the Saviour. We see in him the perfect original of humanity, as well as do the inhabitants of Greenland, or the black negroes of Africa, or the sons of the warm lands on the Ganges. Is this not a wonderful fact, which must challenge our reflection? What is the mysterious power of this One, which binds the hearts of all men of all times and places so firmly to him that they know no higher love than that which they bear to him, and for him are ready to yield up their lives? What is the mystery of his person?

That Jesus was a man like ourselves, we all know. That he was no ordinary man all the intelligent admit. But how high the line which reaches from earth to heaven must be drawn, — this is the question. The old rationalists placed him on the grade of the highest virtue and wisdom; the later exalt him to the height of genius; one of the latest calls him a man so great as to touch the heavens; the church sets him on the throne of God. So different is it that men say of him! What does he say of himself? For this will always have to be that which, after all, makes the final decision. For so much confidence we can in any case give him, — be we never so distrustful in other respects, — that he knew who he was, and did not speak differently from what he knew. For to hold him to be an enthusiast who progressed through gloomy fanaticism to imposture, this we will leave to romance writers like Renan; and to ascribe to him arrogant self-exaltation, which would have reached the bounds of insanity, this was reserved for a David Strauss.

Do we, however, wish to know what Jesus said of himself, then we must consult the writings of the Evangelists. For these are the only source of that information. But whether they are also a reliable source? This is doubted.

It is not the place here closely to discuss the matter. This one thing can suffice for us. The Gospels are not literary productions of individuals, who have deposited therein their particular thoughts and discoveries, but the common consciousness of the Christian community has found expression in them. Concerning many questions, doubts and controversies obtained in the oldest church; never any doubt obtained respecting the reliableness of what the Gospels report of Jesus Christ. And yet there could not have failed to be doubt, had there been opportunity for any, because what Jesus said and did took place not in a corner, but had many witnesses. This consideration alone can suffice to assure us that we have here a trustworthy report of Jesus. And did we wish to reject never so much in the particulars, the principal thing would still remain, the essence of his wonderful works, the kernel of his words and of his testimonies regarding himself, and that is enough.

But do they not contradict each other?

Certainly, one can say, there is a difference between the first three and the fourth Gospel. This difference has at all times been remarked. Even the old church busied itself therewith. In what does it consist? From antiquity down it has been thus described: the first three present more prominently the human side of Jesus, the fourth renders his divine side more prominent; those draw the line from earth up to heaven, this draws the line from above down to earth; the former portray his relation to the world, the latter his relation to God; the former describe the Son of man (God), the latter, the Son of God. This difference is unquestionable.

Indeed, the first three Gospels differ among themselves. Matthew writes for Christians from the Jews, Luke for

Christians from the Gentiles. The former portrays him, therefore, as the hope of Israel, the latter as the object of the yearning of all nations. The former traces back his lineage to David and Abraham, the latter to Adam; the former portrays his birth in the house of David at the time of King Herod, the latter his birth by operation of the Spirit of God at the time of Cæsar Augustus. The former shows us how in Jesus the history of Israel, the latter how in him the history of the world, has found its end; the former how Jesus is the higher completion of the old time of the law and prophecy, the latter how he is the beginning of the new time of the Holy Spirit. Mark, however, delineates for the first stage of the instruction of Gentile Christians, in vivid colors, a picture of the victorious power of God over even the spirits of the deep, as it was manifested in the person and works of Jesus, and consumed in indefatigable service on behalf of men. But as much as these Gospels and the pictures of Christ which they respectively give us differ from each other, over against the Gospel of John they form, nevertheless, a class whose internal difference recedes before their unity, when compared to the difference by which they are separated from the Johannine Gospel. For if Matthew goes back to Abraham, Luke to Adam, John goes back to God and the eternal being with God. From the eternal bosom of the Father he represents the Son as proceeding, and to the eternal world of God he connects the threads of the history which took place on earth and in time. And everywhere with him, through the lowliness of human existence, shines the eternal Godhead, who in the flesh has made his abode with men.

Are these opposites, which exclude each other, or only different sides of the same thing, which mutally require each other? And if the two belong together, how are we to conceive of this?

There is, on the part of the first evangelists, a saying of Jesus which forms, as it were, the iron fastening which binds their representation of Jesus inseparably to that of John. It is that great saying whose Johannean cast has at all times been observed and recognized, and which, besides the wonderful depth of its content, is of so peculiarly marked and complete a form that no one can doubt its having come from the mouth of Jesus. It is that saying in Matt. 11 : 27, — " All things are delivered unto me of my Father; and no man knoweth the Son, but the Father; neither knoweth any man the Father, save the Son, and he to whomsoever the Son will reveal him."

I said, the first evangelists represent Jesus' relation to the world, John his relation to God. The two are here united. "All things are delivered unto me of my Father," — this describes him as the Lord of the world. But this his unconditioned relation to the world rests upon his absolutely unlimited relation to God. He is the Lord of the world, because he is the Son of God; he is the former in the unconditioned sense, because he is the latter in the unconditioned sense. His unconditioned divine sonship is the necessary presupposition of his all-embracing rule of the world, and, in turn, his all-embracing rule of the world is the natural consequence of his unconditioned divine sonship; that is, he is what the first evangelists portray him, only because he is also what John announces him to be. It is as with a great painting. What those portray of Christ forms the foreground of the same, the part which first catches the attention; what John announces of him forms the more removed portion, or background, — a background which stretches away into the concealed depths of heaven and into the endlessness of eternity. The two sides belong together; the one is correct as representative of Jesus, only because the other is also.

"No man knoweth the Son, but the Father; neither knoweth any man the Father, save the Son, and he to whomsoever the Son will reveal him." By this Jesus describes himself as a mystery. He includes himself in the divine mystery. As God is a mystery, so is he. For he belongs with God. It is true, he and the Father are known and open to each other. But to the world he is a mystery as undisclosed as God is himself. But he wishes to be known. For to that end he has revealed himself. And the knowledge of him discloses the mystery of man and the mystery of God. The mystery of man he discloses, so far as he is the Son of man; the mystery of God, so far as he is the Son of God.

Man is a mystery. For the contradiction which he bears in himself is a riddle. From of old this enigma busied man. Its profound expression is given in the eighth Psalm: "Out of the mouths of babes and sucklings hast thou ordained strength because of thine enemies, that thou mightest still the enemy and the avenger. When I consider thy heavens, the work of thy fingers, the moon and the stars which thou hast ordained, what is man, that thou art mindful of him? and the son of man, that thou visitest him? For thou hast made him to be but little lower than God,[1] and hast crowned him with glory and honor. Thou madest him to have dominion over the works of thy hands; thou hast put all things under his feet: all sheep and oxen, yea, and the beast of the field; the fowl of the air,

---

[1] So the lecturer, "Du hast ihn nur wenig lassen unter Gott sein." The Hebrew, וַתְּחַסְּרֵהוּ מְּעַט מֵאֱלֹהִים, Gesenius (Robinson's) translates *thou hast caused him to lack but little of a God.* — *Tr*

and the fish of the sea, and whatsoever passeth through the paths of the seas. O Lord, our Lord, how excellent is thy name in all the earth!"

It is the contradiction which in man is reconciled, between lowliness and loftiness, between the lowliness of his natural condition and the loftiness of his destiny, between the feebleness of his present and the glory of his future,— this strange riddle of the human existence, which awaits its solution, is that which this profound Psalm celebrates. But Jesus is the end of the human race and of its history; he is the Son of man absolutely. He is thus the solution of the mystery which man is.

Every lower grade of being receives its light from the higher. Nature becomes intelligible to us only when we place it in the light of human destiny. Then we perceive, that it exists not for itself, that it is a preparation for man, that it is something on the way to him, that it points beyond itself, that its existence means man, that it has been advancing towards man, that it is as it were a gradual becoming of man himself. In itself it is incomplete, forms no unity in itself, is not a whole by itself; not till man has come does it find its aim, attain its destiny. Only in connection with him, therefore, can it be understood; considered by itself alone it is full of mystery and contradiction. The knowledge of man is the solution of the riddle which nature is.

Man, himself, however, in turn, is equally a riddle and full of contradictions. For in himself, it is true, he is the harmony of the world, but through sin he has fallen into contradiction with himself and with the world; because he has fallen into contradiction with God, in whom alone he holds his unity. Thus that deep schism has come into him which has made of himself and of his life a life of the sharpest oppositions and contradictions. We cannot understand this contradictory existence of man, except we find its solution in Him in whom sinful humanity attains its end, and the history of the same its destiny; that is, in the Son of man. A similar position to that occupied by man with respect to nature is occupied by the Son of man respecting humanity become sinful. As the former is the end of nature, and hence the light by which it is understood, so the latter is the end of humanity, and hence the light by which it may be understood. As man is the son of nature, but its higher son, and, therefore, its lord, so Jesus is the Son of humanity, but its higher Son, and, therefore, its Lord. Man unites the preceding grades of being in himself, but he exalts them to a higher sphere. So Jesus sums up entire humanity in himself, and exalts it to a higher grade. He is, as a profound old church father has called him, the recapitulation of the human race and of its historical unfolding.

Therefore, Jesus loves to call himself the Son of man.

What is implied in this name?

The apostle says, "When the fulness of the time was come, God sent forth his Son." Did Christ come in the fulness of the times, then he appeared as the end of the times and of their history, — as the end of the history of Israel, as the end of the history of humanity. The former is implied in the name Christ which he bears; the latter in the name Son of man. The former, Matthew renders particularly prominent; the latter, Luke.

Jesus is the Christ, the Messiah, i. e., the fulfilment of the hope of Israel. In him the prophecy of Israel was fulfilled, in him the entire history of Israel was fulfilled. For not merely single words of the Old Testament Scriptures are prophetic, but the whole history of Israel, as it is deposited in the Sacred Scriptures of the Old Testament, is prophetic. For every stage of the same points beyond itself to a future, in which it is to find its completing truth; as well the priestly time of Israel, which began with Moses and Aaron, as the regal, which attained its typical culmination in David and Solomon, and the prophetic, whose blossoming period coincided with the fall of Israel. And as the times of Israel are prophetic, so their bearers, all the servants of God under the old covenant, from Moses, the covenant-mediator, down to the prophets, who were rewarded for their service with persecution; and as the bearers of the history, so no less the regulations of the law. They are all, as the apostle calls them, a shadow of good things to come; their reality, however, is Christ. And, lastly, as the law is prophetic, so, too, all the word of the prophets from beginning to end. This is the truth of the Old Testament, that its present includes a future, in which it is to attain its consummation, in which its infolded substance is to be unfolded to full bloom.

Jesus is the Christ, i. e., the fulfilment of the history and of the hope of Israel. Hence, he says to his disciples, "Blessed are your eyes, for they see; and your ears, for they hear. For verily I say unto you, that many prophets and righteous men have desired to see those things which ye see, and have not seen them; and to hear those things which ye hear, and have not heard them." (Matt. 13: 16, 17.) He is the object of the yearning of the old time. Therefore, he is the Lord of the church, the Bridegroom of Jehovah's bride, and the greatest of the Old Testament prophets. John the Baptist's mission it was to be bridesman. He led the bride to the bridegroom, to be united to him in marriage, to be made one with him. This is the end of the history of Israel. Jesus Christ is the end of that history. For he is the Messiah.

But if in him the infolded substance of Israel is unfolded to full bloom, this happens not for Israel alone, but for all the world. For from the beginning, even from the days of Abraham, the salvation which is deposited in Israel, and here has its history that attains its end in Jesus, is destined to become the salvation of the world. In Abraham's seed shall all the nations of the earth be blessed. This destiny fulfils itself in Jesus. His position respects not merely Israel, but the world; he is not merely the end of Israel, but that of humanity; he is not merely the Son of David, but the Son of man.

He is David's Son and David's Lord; he is more than the prophets, he is more than the temple, he is the Lord of the congregation and a Lord of the Sabbath. But he is all this, not without being also the other: the Son of man, the Lord of the world, the object of the yearning of every human soul.

When he calls the world the field on which the seed of his word is to be sown; when he says of himself, that all things are delivered unto him by his Father; when he ascribes to himself all power in heaven and on earth, even the power to forgive sins; when he characterizes himself as the future Judge of all men, before whose tribunal all nations are to appear and receive from his mouth the sentence which decides as to their eternal state, — in all this he designates himself not merely as the Lord of Israel, but as the Lord of the world. He is the Lord of the world, because in him humanity has attained the end of its history and of its destiny. For this is the position of man as the eighth Psalm marks it: all things are put under his feet. But this destiny has not been realized in man. The world has not become subject to man, but man has become subject to the world. For he has become subject to sin, and so to death. In this way he has not gained, but lost his rule over the world. Then Daniel announces a future, — after the time of the power and rule of sinful men, which he designated by the figures of the four beasts that come up successively from the troubled sea of national life in the four great kingdoms of the world, — a time of the God-given rule of the Son of man, to whom the Ancient of days commits all dominion and power and the greatness of the kingdom under the whole heaven (Dan. 7). Then the destiny of man is to be fulfilled in the Son of man. In Jesus, the Son of man, it has been fulfilled, but, as the Epistle to the Hebrews (chap. 1) teaches, after we had fallen into sin and death, in the way of humiliation and of death, on account of man's sin. Jesus is the goal for which humanity and its history were destined. He stands in the middle of the times. All the previous history of the nations tends towards him. In him centre the manifold ways of national history. In him the old time comes to an end, and a new begins. He is the great turning-point of the times. This is the loftiest view of history, one which has inspired our greatest historians, and has made out of a John Müller a believing Christian. From Jesus as the point of vision we understand the course of the world, — from him alone. From him we also understand ourselves.

For he is not merely the end of our race as a whole, he is also the end of every individual soul. For him the soul is designed; in him alone it finds what it wishes and seeks, often without knowing what it purposes; in him it reaches its destination, in him it comes to its truth. For he is the concealed law of our being. As long as it is yet on the way seeking, it is full of unrest. He is its rest, its peace. "Come unto me, all ye that labor and are heavy laden, and I will give you rest." He is our end. We understand ourselves only in him. What we wish and purpose, what we ought and seek, is to ourselves unknown; our entire being is to us full of riddles, our entire existence full of contradictions. But the riddles all and the contradictions of our being and life resolve themselves in him. In him we understand ourselves. The mystery of Jesus Christ is the key to the understanding of man.

Let us sum up what has thus far been said. The history of Israel is a riddle, until we place it in the light of the knowledge of Jesus Christ; then it becomes clear to us. Humanity and its history is a riddle, until we see the end of their ways in Jesus Christ; then they become intelligible to us. We ourselves, our being and life, are a riddle, until we find Jesus Christ; then we understand ourselves and what we ought and wish. The mystery of Jesus Christ is the key to the understanding of man. This is one part; the other is, that it is no less the key to the knowledge of God. For he is the Son of God.

In Jesus to behold the Son of man, the original of humanity, in which our race unfolds itself to its fullest and most beautiful bloom,—this is, in modern theology, the reigning view, as particularly Schleiermacher gave it form and currency. It makes an important step beyond the old rationalistic notion of the ideal of virtue, and has in itself something which can give not merely to the understanding, but also to the deeper need of the soul, a higher degree of satisfaction. But the whole truth it is not. It might, perhaps, be correct if there were no sin. For, according to this view, Christ is only the highest unfolding of that which from the beginning was designed and deposited in human nature; he has proceeded only from the deepest life-sources which we have within us. In him the world of creation has found, in the way of its self-unfolding, its end. But we need more than that. Since sin has entered into the world of creation, we have need not merely of a complete ideal of the world of creation, but, above all, of an atonement for our sin, of a mediator of redemption, of a revelation of the grace of God.

The Son of man is the exaltation of man to nearness with God. "Thou hast made him to be but little lower than God,[1] and hast crowned him with glory and honor," it is said in the eighth Psalm. This is the end of creation, — a man so great as to touch the heavens, as Jesus has been called. But it is not merely needful that we mount up to God; it is especially needful that God come down to us. It is not enough that we open ourselves towards him; the main thing is, that he open himself in grace towards us, and impart himself to us. The old heathen world knew of godlike men, men who ascend to Olympus. The moral philosophy of the ancient world is the exaltation of the human to the divine. The highest virtue of its noblest representatives is love, which soars above the earthly to the world of eternal ideals. Christ, as merely the Son of man, is the ideal of these thoughts of the heathen world. But the gospel preaches not merely a love of exaltation to God, but especially a love of the condescension of God to us. And this has saved the world. Even the noblest idealism of the Platonic school had at last to confess its impotency, and the heathen philosophy closes in one of its final representatives with the acknowledgment, that in this way the end is not to be found: "Man cannot approach unto the gods, the gods must come to men." The first

[1] See note under p. 125.

hymns of praise, however, at the threshold of the New Testament, exult, "He hath visited and redeemed his people." This was the fulfilment of the old prophecy.

Through the prophecy of Israel run two lines. One makes a bridge from man up to God, the other from God down to man. The former shows us a man full of the spirit of God, a man standing in the service of God, a man advanced near to God and furnished with his gifts and powers. The end of this line is the Messiah and the Son of man. But by the side of this runs another, which announces the future revelation of Jehovah, his gracious presence with his people, his reigning as King over the nations. Man is to approach unto God, and God wills to come to men. The two lines meet in Jesus. In the Old Testament they proceed near each other; they approximate, but as yet do not unite with each other. A man who is the appearance of God himself, a revelation of God, who is God become man,—this thought was far off from the whole ancient world, was far off even from the Old Testament. For it is a wondrous thought, one which the human mind has not the courage to think of itself. Heathendom obliterated the boundaries between God and man, Israel kept the two sharply apart. The God-man, therefore, in the proper and full sense, neither the one nor the other find. Still, in the last of the prophets, in Malachi, the two stand near each other: the Lord who comes to his temple, and his messenger of the covenant. The times before Christ do not know the idea of the God-man, because they know not the fact of the same. For the idea did not produce the fact, but the fact produced the idea. First the God-man came, then men dared to think him. Jesus Christ is the point in which the two lines come together. He is the man who is God; he is God who is man. Here is more than the ideal of humanity, here is the revelation and presence of God himself; he is not merely the Son of man, he is the Son of God; in him not merely the bosom of humanity has disclosed itself, in him is disclosed the eternal bosom of the Godhead. God was in Christ,—this is the theme of John's Gospel. Again and again this thought returns, and in a multitude of forms. He is the Word, i. e., the absolute revelation of God; he is the Life, i. e., the disclosed content of God; he is the Light, i. e., the appearance of the holiness and truth of God; he is the Way, i. e., the mediation to fellowship with God, for he is the presence of God himself: "He that hath seen him hath seen the Father." This is what the Gospel of John understands by the Son of God. Between him and the Father there is no barrier, either of sinfulness or of finiteness: He is the Holy One and the One unconditionally in unity with the Father,—Eternity in time, Divinity in actual humanity. For the divine which we believe and confess to be in Christ does not hover above him as perchance an idea, but is realized in him as a fact, and hence is to be found only in his human reality, in him, the One become flesh. It is true, he has resigned his world-position of power for the position of a servant in feeble flesh,—into this glory he first recedes with his exaltation. But the completeness of the Divine nature and life, full of grace and truth,—this glory of holy love he bore constantly with him, and this shone forth in his every word and act. In the latter the former was brought low and lifted up. For a twofold position God has to the world: he is power and he is love. But the power serves the love and determines and limits itself by the love. In Jesus Christ the Eternal Love, when it descended into the society of fallen men, enclosed its power within the limits of an earthly human existence, to pass, after having accomplished the work of redemption, up from lowliness to loftiness, and out from narrowness to the breadth of world-embracing power and efficiency. This is what the Scripture teaches us of Jesus Christ, the Son of God, and of the history of his divine Sonship.

Son of man, Son of God, — these are the two sides of the being of Jesus Christ, the exaltation of humanity to God, the condescension of God to us. That mysterious saying of Matt. 11 : " All things are delivered unto me of my Father, and no man knoweth the Son but the Father, neither knoweth any man the Father save the Son and he to whomsoever the Son will reveal him," — this saying joins the two sides together in unity.

Jesus represents himself here as a mystery, but as a mystery revealed. Confessedly[1] great is the mystery of godliness: God manifest in the flesh. This mystery discloses the understanding of man and the understanding of God. For the deepest thing in man, and his peculiar nature, is that he is destined for God. Whatever else we may say of man, it all does not concern the centre of his being, unless we understand him in his destination and in his susceptibility for God. And the deepest and innermost thing that we can say of God is, that he is holy love, which wishes man. For higher than his power and wisdom goes God's love. To understand God rightly is not to understand him as the Infinite Spirit, as the Power of all things, as the Source of all life, but as eternal self-imparting Love. This is the highest and best thing that we can say of God. And this knowledge of God is the knowledge of the gospel of Jesus Christ. The gospel has taught us to understand not merely

---

[1] Ὁμολογουμένως, 1 Tim. 3:16, is rendered in the German of the lecture (as in Luther's version) by kündlich, *known*, adv. *manifestly*. — *Tr.*

man, but it has taught us to understand also God, in the God-man Jesus Christ.

Every higher stage in the history of humanity is an advance in man's knowledge of both himself and God. All true advances of the human spirit, also all progressions of culture, are thereby conditioned. Whatever does not further us in this knowledge, while it may beautify our earthly life, enlarge our knowledge of the world, exalt our position in the world, is not for man a true gain. The gospel has brought a new epoch into the history of our race, and has caused an amazing advance in the entire spiritual life of humanity. It could not have attained to this significancy and have produced this effect, if it had not brought a new knowledge of God and of man, a knowledge unknown to the ancient world. That man is a rational being, this the Greeks and Romans knew. But that his soul was created in the image of God and longs for God, that its hunger and thirst are appeased only when God graciously unites himself in personal love-association with it, — this the world learned first through Christianity. And whatever advances in the humanities we have since made, the starting-point of all is this Christian knowledge of man, of his being and destiny. Farther, that higher powers rule in the world, that a Supreme Spirit hovers over all; of this also the heathen world had a dim apprehension. But that above the stars is enthroned a God whose heart is moved towards us men with love, and who seeks his happiness in our happiness; who forgives sin and pities the sinner, and, to save us from a lost condition, hesitates not to sink himself into our flesh, thus to impart himself fully and wholly to us, and to teach us what love signifies, — this not even the thought-flight of a Plato approached, and the science of an Aristotle would have considered it foolishness. To us, however, this knowledge of God has become a fountain of comfort and of wisdom. By this knowledge we now live; our hearts, our minds live by this.

Thus, with the truth of Christ, the God-man, is connected the whole advance which Christianity has, by means of its new knowledge of man and God, brought to the world. To deny that truth is, not merely to deny a dogma, but to call in question the whole gain of Christianity. This is the tremendous import of the contest of the present. The question of Christ is the question of Christianity itself. Those who oppose the church's doctrine of the God-man will dispute this, and I doubt not that many of them are earnestly and honestly disposed towards that gain which Christianity has, through its higher knowledge of man and God, brought to us. Not immediately at the beginning do the consequences of a principle reveal themselves. But they work out from an inner necessity, and depend not on the wish of the heart or the ambiguity of the thought. The branch which the storm has broken off the tree preserves for a time its freshness and the green color of life. But gradually its sap dries, and the leaves wither. The effects cannot be forever parted from their cause. He who discards the latter will soon lose also the former. The attitude a person holds to the question of Jesus Christ determines his answer to the question of man and to the question of God. He who rejects Jesus Christ will lose also man, and will have left, instead of the eternal soul hungering after God, a slave of natural necessity or a tyrant of selfishness, in whose heart no sun shines, because he knows not the sun of God's grace in Christ. And he who will know nothing of the Son will soon lose also the Father, who will be found only in the Son, and will have remaining, instead of him, only an idea of the universe, which sees not, hears not, and has no heart for our sorrows, or only a cold inexorable law, which, as often as anything lives, swallows it up in the night of death, the contemplation of which finally makes even the heart of a living man grow chill in the gloomy waste of resignation.

It is not merely individual tenets of belief that are at stake in the great spiritual conflict of the present, but the holiest interests of humanity, — the holiest interests of our minds, of our consciences, of our hearts. The centre-point of that conflict is the question of Christ. This is the mystery of the person of Jesus Christ, that with him what is best and highest of all that belongs to us stands and falls. But just on this account we need not fear. For that the highest blessings of humanity will not be lost, but will always find those who preserve them in their hearts, this is certain. And so we can be also certain, that to the end of days Jesus Christ will have a church of those who thankfully confess what he is to them for this world and the other, and who therefore bow their knees in his name and salute each other with the salutation: **Praise be to Jesus Christ forever!** Amen.

LECTURE VI

THE RESURRECTION OF CHRIST AS A SOTERIOLOGICO-HISTORICAL FACT

By GERHARD UHLHORN, D. D.

FIRST PREACHER TO THE (LATE) COURT OF HANOVER

GERHARD UHLHORN, D. D.

BIOGRAPHICAL

DR. JOHANN GERHARD WILHELM UHLHORN, the famous court preacher at Hanover, was born at Osnabrüch, Feb. 27, 1826. He became *repetent* and *privat-docent* at Göttingen in 1852. In 1855 he was made consistorial councilor and court preacher at Hanover. In 1866 he became a member of the consistory, and in 1878, abbot of Lokkum. He produced a large number of literary works: among the most significant and well known of which is his *Der Kampf des Christenthums mit dem Heidenthum*, translated into English by Professors E. Smith and C. J. H. Ropes. English title: "The Conflict of Christianity with Heathenism." Another very excellent publication of Dr. Uhlhorn's that has been translated into English, is his (English title) "Modern Representations of the Life of Jesus," published by Little & Brown, Boston. His style is clear, scholarly, logical, at times eloquent, and always interesting. It would be difficult to find anywhere a more thorough-going and satisfactory discussion of the resurrection of Christ than is the one furnished by him in this book.

SUMMARY OF LECTURE VI

Just now the resurrection of Christ is probably the most hotly contested point in the great battle between faith and unbelief—Not only is the fact of the resurrection in dispute, but also its significance—The matter is, first of all, a historical question, and such questions are not to be decided according to dogmatic postulates—The earliest church believed in Jesus' resurrection—This belief rested upon the testimony of eye-witnesses—Necessity of explaining how this belief originated—The old theory that Jesus was only seemingly dead, is now generally conceded a failure—The theory of visions among the early disciples is at present most widely held—Nature of a vision, how it is produced—Views of Renan and Strauss—Holsten's view, and argument by which he advocates it—This theory is disproved by mistake made as to Paul's great motive in persecuting Christians—Disproved also by the fact of Paul's not already believing in the resurrection of Jesus—Also by the consideration that at most Paul's state of mind must have been one of doubt, and doubters have no visions—Disproved further by the fact of the large number of the witnesses, also by the simultaneousness of the origination of this belief and the shortness of time allowed for it—Strauss' resort to the notion of popular delusions, in order to help out his vision theory—In the way of more positive evidence, the handling of Jesus by the disciples after the resurrection, and other matters of that kind, might be adverted to—More important is the empty tomb—The resurrection was not a subjective event, but an objective fact—In several ways the resurrection of Jesus has a bearing upon the redemption accomplished by him.

VI

THE RESURRECTION OF CHRIST AS A SOTERIO-LOGICO-HISTORICAL FACT

BY GERHARD UHLHORN, D. D.,
FIRST PREACHER TO THE (LATE) COURT OF HANOVER

AS I have been commissioned to speak to you on the resurrection of Christ, I am placed at that point of the great contest obtaining at present with regard to the fundamental articles of the Christian faith, where, probably, for the moment, the battle rages most vehemently. If this contest has centred more and more about the person and life of Jesus, so, in turn, this latter has collected with increasing force about the resurrection. Here rests, as is felt on both sides, the decision. Always as one accepts or rejects the resurrection, will he think differently also of the person and life of Jesus, and so, too, take a wholly different position towards Christianity and the church.

All, however, is so combatted here, that I am no longer expressing universal convictions, but propositions which have been made subjects of dispute. For not merely the occurrence of the resurrection, but also what significancy belongs to it, is under dispute. While some, and not merely such as recognize the resurrection to be a historical fact, but also such as deny it, see in the belief in the resurrection the shibboleth of Christianity, one of the fundamental articles with which it stands or falls, others have asserted that the question whether Christ rose from the dead is simply an historical one; be it accepted or rejected, Christianity and the Christian life are in neither case affected.

If the question then is, on the one side, concerning the resurrection as a historical fact, and on the other, concerning the significancy of this fact for our salvation, I have endeavored to put the two sides together; having so conceived of the theme, whose closer understanding was left freely to me, that my wish and purpose is to speak to you of *the resurrection of Christ as a soteriologico-historical fact.*

Whether Jesus, as the Christian church believes and teaches, on the third day after his death, actually came forth from the grave alive, rose from the dead, — this is, surely, first of all a historical question. For as an alleged fact of history the resurrection is reported to us. Whether it is that or not, whether what is here related happened as is related, or happened otherwise, or happened not at all, — to attain to certainty on these matters no different course can be adopted from that taken with other historical questions. A historical fact may be proven only by historical testimonies, and only on the ground of such can be set aside. It can on grounds of the universal reason neither be proven when these are wanting, nor be set aside when they are sufficient and at hand. The inquiry is, therefore, Who was present, saw, and heard that which is said to have occurred? are the witnesses trustworthy? does the testimony suffice? or is it to be rejected as untrustworthy and insufficient?

This being the question, I must, then, to begin with, characterize one stand-point in it as an unwarrantable one, namely, the stand-point of those who enter upon a historical examination with the dogmatic postulate, There are no miracles. With such no discussion in a historical way is possible. For if one had proved to them, by ever so ample historical testimonies, the fact of the resurrection, they would reply, It cannot after all be true; for the resurrection is a miracle, and there are no miracles. All testimonies, be they never so reliable, do not suffice to establish a miracle. It is always more probable that the best of witnesses may have erred or designedly falsified, than that a miracle has occurred.

This stand-point I denominate unwarrantable, because a person has no right to decide historical questions according to dogmatic postulates. To be sure, I well know that it is manifoldly asserted, that the only truly historical method is just this: that the recognition of miracles be absolutely excluded. For a miracle is the inexplicable something that cannot be understood from the natural connection of cause and effect, is not, therefore, properly a matter of historical inquiry. As if it were possible for history everywhere to trace up its objects to their ultimate grounds, everywhere to show an unbroken chain of natural causes and effects. That a miracle is inexplicable excludes it not from being historically considered. Justly it would be so excluded only on the ground of its being incognizable. But incognizable a miracle is not. For even though it is the working of a higher causality, it comes, nevertheless, as worked, wholly within the natural connection of cause and effect, deports itself, on the other hand, in its workings and results, like every other fact, throughout in accordance with the laws of nature. It is, therefore, as a fact cognizable, and is legitimately a subject of historical inquiry, which has to do with facts. The exclusion of miracles is not historical impartiality, but dogmatic prejudice. In this sense one commences the examination impartially when judgment is withheld, until it is seen whether there are not facts, occurring in a strictly historical way, which to us are miracles. I can recognize, as warranted from a historical point of view, only the requirement, that, when the question is regarding facts which deviate from the customary course of things, the examination and testing of the witnesses should be the more earnest and stringent. And, since the resurrection is such a fact, I do not object to your requiring here a rigid historical proof. Only this I cannot consent to, that you shall bring with you dogmatic postulates over against which all historical proof is impossible.

Now, as after these preliminary remarks we enter upon the historical examination itself, let us start from a fact which is denied by neither side, and which cannot be reasonably denied; I mean this: The oldest church believed that Jesus rose from the dead. Do not misunderstand me. Whether this belief had sufficient ground, or whether it rested upon delusion, that does not as yet concern us; that will hereafter be the subject of our inquiry. At present we affirm only the undeniable fact, the oldest church believed, and, indeed, with a confidence lifted above every doubt, in the resurrection. This is the kernel and centre-point of the apostolical preaching. Where Paul, in 1 Cor. 15, states the sum of the gospel which he preached in Corinth, he reduces it to the words, that Christ died, was buried, and rose again. Where he brings the contents of saving faith to its briefest expression (Rom. 10: 9), he says, "If thou shalt confess with thy mouth the Lord Jesus, and shalt believe in thine heart that God hath raised him from the dead, thou shalt be saved." He declares himself to be a false witness, his preaching and the faith of Christian believers vain and groundless, if Christ be not risen. And, as with the Apostle Paul, so everywhere (the Acts of the Apostles attests it) the resurrection forms a chief element of the apostolical announcement. Faith therein is also the foundation of moral life, according to the New Testament view. It is living in Christ and for him who died and has risen for us, with whom we must die and rise. Here is rooted the whole joy of faith, which becomes a joy of suffering and dying for the Risen One. From this faith the apostolic age drew its strength for its victorious contest against the heathen world. Here are, also, the starting-points of the Christian worship and of its peculiar forms. The day of the resurrection becomes the weekly festival, the day of the Lord; the yearly celebration of the resurrection is the first deposit for the formation of the ecclesiastical year. In short, on whatever side we choose to consider the life of the oldest Christian community, we always come upon living faith in the resurrection as the impelling and actuating power.

But we can go one step farther, without leaving the ground of wholly undeniable facts. The oldest church based this its belief upon the depositions of such as professed to have seen the risen Jesus. Here again we at first only state the fact, without estimating the worth of the witnesses' depositions. So much is certain, that a great number of persons were convinced that the risen Jesus had appeared to them, and upon the testimony of these, those who had not seen him for themselves based their conviction that he had truly risen. At the place already referred to, in the first and indubitably genuine Epistle to the Corinthians, Paul says expressly, that he himself had seen the risen Lord; and when he farther narrates, that also Peter, James, the twelve, five hundred brethren at once had seen him, this narration rests, it is unquestionable, upon the testimony of these men as Paul himself had received it, and is accordingly, considering Paul's unassailable veracity, as good as a self-deposition.

With the statement of these facts we have not indeed, I repeat it, by any means as yet proven that Christ actually rose from the dead, as those believed. The possibility must be conceded that the witnesses of the resurrection were self-deceived, and so that they deceived also the oldest believers. But this we have gained. We need no longer take up with the mere denial of the resurrection, or with the doctrine so commonly advanced that the witnesses were self-deceived. We can now demand an explanation of these facts; we can require that it be shown us how, without the actual occurrence of the resurrection, that belief in it could have originated; how those men, ingenuous and veracious as they were, came to the conviction of having seen the risen Jesus. If such explanation cannot be given us, then that fact of the belief in the resurrection returns directly with all its force, and demands as a necessity the simplest and the only possible explanation, namely, that to the belief the reality corresponded; they really saw him; he has actually risen from the dead.

Only at a price can this result be avoided, namely, at the price of giving up every explanation, of saying, The resurrection, as the church affirms it, certainly cannot have happened; but what did really happen, how the belief in it originated, that cannot now be known, that must be left as an insolvable riddle. Closer consideration, however, shows that this cannot be done. For let us not forget that this belief in the resurrection marks the chief turning-point in the history of humanity, the end of the old, the beginning of the new era. To give up the explanation of this belief is to leave as an insolvable riddle the fact which more than any other marks the profoundest revolution in human thought and life, is therefore to relinquish an understanding of the history of our race at precisely its most deciding point. Such a relinquishment can indeed be expressed by individuals in momentary embarrassment, but to carry it through is simply impossible. The consequence would be only a repetition of that already noted. Such a merely negative relinquishment would not hold out long before positive assertion. If it be impossible to explain satisfactorily the belief in the resurrection in any other way, then the fact that Christianity and the church rest upon this belief, that from this belief the new era has originated, will ever necessitate the conclusion that the resurrection is itself a fact.

Indeed, while Bauer yet occupied this stand-point of relinquishment, and asserted that what the resurrection is in itself lies outside of historical inquiry, and it is enough for the latter to know there was belief in the resurrection, this stand-point must be regarded as one already abandoned. Rather is the problem, positively to show how the disciples came to such belief, recognized as one demanding solution, and to this — as must be granted even though the results of the labor be not regarded as correct — much diligence and mental labor have been directed. Whether the solution has been found we shall now have to prove.

One solution is now universally considered a failure, nay, it is overwhelmed by all sides with scorn and contempt, though formerly numbering men like Schleiermacher among its representatives. It is the view that the actuality of the resurrection consists in the resuscitation of Jesus from an apparent death. Not really dead, but only in a death-like deep sleep, he was by the coolness of the tomb and the seasonable help of confidential friends — whom the old rationalism, with its naturalistic explanation of the miracles so readily summoned to its help — restored to life, and thus showed himself to his disciples. That this view is untenable, no extended argument is needed to show. It does not agree with the surely attested facts, neither with the fact of his death, which was doubted only to be able to have him the more easily raised, nor with what is reported of his appearances after the resurrection. Besides, it does not at all suffice to explain the belief in a risen Lord. "A half-dead man crawling out of the grave," says Strauss justly, "a man creeping about, sickly, in need of the physician's care, of bandages and restoratives, could never have made upon the disciples the impression of his being the victor over death and the grave, of his being the Lord of life, which impression lay at the basis of their subsequent career, could never have changed their mourning into enthusiasm." To-day, as said, this hypothesis is one of the past. I would scarcely have alluded to it, were it not of interest to see in it an example of the way it goes with such hypotheses. In their time commended as the truly scientific, as the only tenable views, they are a few years later brought forward with a pitful smile as mere antiquities.

Undoubtedly, as I am willing to grant, the step from the old rationalistic view of an apparent death to the view obtaining most widely at present, that of visions, marks an advance. The opposition has become more historical than was the thoroughly unhistorical old rationalism. It is admitted, as, indeed, in view of the evidences at hand it could not but be, that the disciples really saw Jesus after his death, alive, risen; only their seeing was not objective, not the seeing of an actually existing object external to them, but a merely subjective occurrence. an internal seeing, a vision. Because they were not in condition to distinguish this visionary seeing from the seeing of an actually existing object, they were of necessity firmly convinced, and with them the churches believing their testimony, that the Lord was actually present, that he had risen from the dead and appeared to them. The question, accordingly, shapes itself thus: Were the appearances of the risen Lord, which Paul recounts, actual, real objective appearances, or mere visions?

To come nearer to this question, I shall unavoidably have to premise somewhat on the nature and origin of visions in general.

All sensation, seeing and hearing, is an internal occurrence. Our nerves of sense, the optic and auricular nerves, are excited by the pictures and sounds of the world about us. The sensations thus occasioned are internal; we see the pictures and hear the sounds within. But we learn by experience to think of the objects which occasioned these sensations as being in the world about us. Now, the nerves of sense can be excited wholly from within as the result of peculiar physical or mental states. Then we see pictures and hear sounds in themselves distinguished by nothing from the excitements produced by external objects. These are produced by the unconsciously working imagination; and just because it does work unconsciously these excitements are independent of the person's will, because, farther, these pictures are not, like those of the consciously working imagination, lightless, colorless, and soundless, but appear in the eye's field of vision with full lustre of light and color, are heard with full sound by the ear, quite naturally the visionary, following his other experience, thinks of the pictures he sees, of the sounds he hears, as being in space outside of himself, and is convinced of having seen and heard that which was truly objectively present.

Still more important for us is a look into the origination of a vision, if we would understand fully what those have to do who undertake to explain the appearances of the risen Saviour as visions. Evidently what the vision-seer sees and hears must have lain previously in him. The vision-seer's imagination produces nothing wholly new; it only reproduces that which lived beforehand in his consciousness. While he is busying himself constantly therewith, separating himself from the actual world and burying himself meditatively in himself, an unnatural tension of the nerves arises. The excitement of the mind works upon the circulation of the blood; the activity of the central organ, the brain, increases; the circulation of the blood is accelerated; upon the excited nerves a pressure is exerted; and suddenly the picture already in the thoughts rises up with full lustre of light and color before the eye; suddenly the words engaging his meditation strike aloud upon the ear. What he sees is nothing new; it is only the embodying of that with which he had long been meditatively carrying himself about; and what he hears is only the voicing of that with which he was long inwardly agitated. The vision is, though unconsciously to him, his own act, the product of his own inner life.

It will now probably be understood what is the task devolved upon those who assert,— the appearances of the risen Lord were only visions. They must show us that such visions, as acts of the disciples themselves, as products of their inner life, were, according to the peculiarity of this life and under the circumstances historically demonstrable to have existed in connection with it, possible.

The mere assertion, they were visions, settles nothing;

for no one will fail to see that there are presented, even to first sight, at least circumstances which are anything else than favorable to the originating of such visions. How, it is involuntarily asked, could there have originated with the disciples who by the death of the Lord were so utterly disheartened, and with Paul, the rage-breathing persecutor of the Lord, from within, by the action of their own minds, the picture of this same Lord risen from the dead? So frivolously as Renan essays, with his "hallucinated woman who has given to the world a resurrected God," this difficulty is not to be overcome, and it must be mentioned to the honor of German science, that it has not so lightly dealt with it. Strauss, and especially, in later times, Holsten, have directed much labor and ingenuity to proving the possibility of visions.

To the idea of a vision the appearance of Christ, granted to Paul on the way to Damascus, is best adapted. Accordingly the custom is to start from this, in order afterwards from its visionary character to draw conclusions respecting the appearances witnessed by the other disciples, which Paul evidently ranks in the same class with the one granted to him.

A circumstance here affords much help. Paul had besides this other visions. He was, it is said, a vision-seer, constituted such in body and soul. The easier is it thus to explain, also, the appearance of Christ which formed the turning-point in his life, which converted him from a persecutor to an apostle. And yet even here great difficulties arise. Certainly, Paul had visions. He himself tells us, in 2 Cor. 12 ch., of the visions he has had. That these visions were also revelations, — the vision thus becoming the medium for divine revelation, — this we may let pass. The main thing is that Paul, as no one who impartially compares his own reports will fail to see, speaks altogether differently of the appearance of Christ near Damascus from the way he does of these visions. Of these he speaks evidently with great reserve. Hitherto he has not mentioned them. He comes to them only when compelled to do so by his enemies. These form a part of his private life, which he only reluctantly discloses. Of that appearance of Christ, on the contrary, he speaks with entire openness. He often appeals to it. Its narration unquestionably formed an element in his public discourses. Moreover, where Paul speaks of these visions, he describes very plainly his state as one of ecstasy. Whether he was in the body, or out of the body, he is even unable to tell. Nothing of all this, where he narrates the appearance of the risen Jesus. There he uses the simple expressions, " He has appeared to me ; " " I have seen the Lord." Add to this, that he portrays that occurrence near Damascus as an altogether extraordinary one, which was never repeated with him, nor afterwards happened with others, — for what is worthy of especial notice, he calls this appearance the last, though he subsequently in a vision saw and spoke with the Lord, — that upon this appearance he grounds his apostolical authority, while visions were allotted to others also who were not apostles; and you will not be able to escape the impression, that Paul very consciously makes a distinction between those visions and this appearance. However, I do not now straightway conclude that because Paul regarded that appearance of the risen Lord not as a vision, it could, consequently, have been none. For to this it might be replied, All visionseers are unconscious that what they see has no objective reality corresponding to it; rather are they, since the vision makes upon them the impression solely of objective reality, able to think of such alone. I conclude only, and this I believe to be just, that Paul received from each of the two events an altogether different impression, and also that in each case his bodily state must have been a different one, and I think this knowledge is, to say no more, not exactly favorable to the hypothesis of a vision.

But the decision cannot rest here. It rests with the question, whether it is possible to understand the vision as an internal act of Paul himself; whether the attempt to explain psychologically, according to the peculiarity of Paul and his state, the arising of such a vision in him, has succeeded. No one has undertaken the matter more fundamentally than has Holsten. Let us, then, take his representation as the basis.

Paul — so Holsten argues on this point — stood towards Jesus as the other unbelieving Jews. To him Jesus was a false Messiah. The sufficient proof thereof was his death on the cross as the manifest judgment of God upon the impostor. So he believed he was fighting for the truth, for the will of God, and became a persecutor of the disciples. Precisely his own feeling, however, in accordance with the entire nature of the man, had to become the means of his conversion. His persecuting zeal brought him into continual immediate contact with those who believed in the Crucified One as the Messiah. So this belief was made a subject of his emotional interest. According to his spiritual endowment accustomed to consistent thinking, he was necessitated to endeavor to apprehend, in the thinking spirit, the contradiction between that Messianic belief and the divine truth of Judaism. Accordingly, while still an enthusiastic zealot, he carried about continually with him the elements of that belief, though in the negative form and negatived. Nay, he penetrated deeper into the thought of the death on the cross, though always yet in the interest of denial, than did his then opponents. If this death appeared to him to be the one sufficient proof against the Messiahship of Jesus, his opponents held up on the other hand the fact of the resurrection, by which the offence of the cross was for them set aside. Impostors, as Paul could soon see, these his opponents were not. Considering the clearness of his sense and the profoundly religious tendency of his mind, he must rather have been convinced that the resurrection was, to his opponents, a subjective certainty. And having once conceded that, he had no tenable ground left for denying its objective certainty. For that a man could rise from the dead, Paul as a Pharisee did not deny; the resurrection in itself was rather an article of his own belief. What reason, then, had he for denying that this Jesus had risen? The hitherto purely negative elements began to assume a positive nature. What if these Christians were right? What if Jesus had really risen from the dead? Might not even the death on the cross be conceived of as in accordance with God's will, nay, as necessarily belonging to the Messianic work? And if this was so, was he not, then, under the delusion of his fighting for God against falsehood, rather fighting against God for unbelief? Such thoughts as these busied him more and more, and the contradiction thus arisen in him, a man like Paul could not leave unsolved. It forced him into a brooding subjectiveness of life, in which all the powers of his spirit were directed to solving this contradiction. In this agitation of his inward being, it was always the risen Lord towards whom he looked; the risen Lord was the thorn on which his soul was wounded. His picture lay, therefore, already in the soul of Paul. It needed only a profound shock of his spiritual life, which, working upon the tension of his nervous life, affected the optic nerve, and the picture of the risen Lord, transfigured in celestial glory, stood before his eyes.

However consistent this picture, drawn not without psychological art, of the change of the inner life with Paul may appear to many, I must nevertheless affirm, it is limned from the imagination, and does not agree with what we know thereof from history. The presupposition of the given portraiture of the conflict arisen in Paul is, that he persecuted the Christians on account of their Messianic belief, that the fighting between him and his opponents, which was then repeated in Paul himself and there spiritually fought out, finds its acme in the question, Is Jesus the true, or a false Messiah? This, however, is already a departure from the historical representation. Where Paul tells us, in Gal. 1, how he persecuted the church of God, he adds, "And I was more exceedingly zealous of the traditions — i. e., the law — of my fathers." Because he saw the law was threatened, he became a persecutor, not because the Christians affirmed, Jesus is the Messiah. So also the Acts of the Apostles attests that what brought the first persecution to an outbreak was the danger to the law from the Christians. This, moreover, independently of the Acts, stands sure; for undoubtedly the persecution did not commence immediately after the founding of the Christian community, but this had first a period of rest. As certainly, however, as the believers from the beginning with full definiteness confessed Jesus as the Messiah, so certainly this confession cannot have been the cause of the persecution, or it should have broken out directly. Not until the opposition of the new community to the legal establishment became evident, and indeed first in Stephen, did the persecution break out. It was this also that made of the Pharisee Paul a persecutor, viz., his zeal for the law. Not the question about the Messiahship of Jesus can, therefore, have marked the acme of his opposition to the Christians, but the question about the law and his significancy. It must, therefore, have been also this that preponderantly busied him. Not that the question, Is Jesus the Messiah? did not also engage his thoughts, but the all-controlling question filling his whole spirit, it cannot have been.

If thus the foundation of Holsten's representation falls already, it does not do, in other respects, what was required of it. To make us understand that a vision could have arisen in Paul, Holsten must show us that Paul believed already in the resurrection; for you remember, the imagination does not produce, it only reproduces,—the visionary picture rises only where it lies already in the soul. Therefore, Holsten adduces the considerations, that the joyous certainty of the believers made an impression on Paul, that he could not take these to be impostors, that he must have been convinced of at least the subjective actuality of the alleged appearances of the risen Lord, and then had no ground left for his denying their objective actuality. I ask you, how does this accord with the description which Paul himself gives of his spiritual state at the time, in Gal. 1, where we read nothing of wavering and becoming doubtful, but all indicates growing zeal in persecution and increasing blindness? "I profited in the Jews' religion above many my equals in mine own nation." How does it accord with the fact that Paul here represents the transition as one altogether sudden? Should any one, however, wish to say, that, up to the moment when the vision occurred, he was unconscious of the change which had really already taken place in him, that now first it comes clearly to his mind, — then, I ask, Did Paul never think of that afterwards? Would not his clear, inquiring intelligence, going everywhere to the ultimate ground of things, have subsequently perceived that the first impulse to the entire change was, after all, given by the testimony of the believers? And, if this cannot have remained concealed from him, how can he, then, with such definiteness disavow all human mediation in his conversion, and affirm that he was called, not of men, neither by man? How can he refer all so exclusively to immediate revelation?

But here is a still more questionable weakness of the development that Holsten gives. I will, if you please, grant that doubts could have risen in the soul of Paul, whether he was in the right, or the Christians; questions such as, Could it not, indeed, be true what those affirm of the resurrection of this Jesus? That, however, is far from sufficing to explain a vision. Such an event occurs only where one thought with full certainty fills the whole soul. Doubtful-minded persons have no visions, but believers who with their whole souls are wrapped up in what they believe. Because the Maid of Orleans already believed with the fullest certainty in her mission, she saw sights and heard voices which conveyed that mission to her. Holsten ought to have shown how Paul, without having yet had the appearance, could come to the firm, at least, for the moment, firm conviction: This Jesus has really risen from the dead! Instead thereof, he speaks always only of a contradiction, of a conflict in Paul. It avails nothing to paint for us this contradiction as an unendurable one, which had to be solved, this conflict as one which took hold of Paul's entire being, forced him wholly into subjectiveness. The question is, What was there in this contradiction that decided Paul for the faith which till then he had so energetically persecuted? What was there in the conflict that determined the victory on the side against which Paul had up to that time with all his power striven? The testimony of the believers? But they were, in his eyes, the enemies of God, against whom he defended the traditions of his fathers! The circumstance, that he could oppose nothing to their assertion, Christ has risen from the dead, because he himself believed in the resurrection of the dead? Then all the Pharisees would have had to become Christians, for this was the case with them all. His already gained conviction, as Holsten intimates, that the death on the cross might be understood as belonging to the work of the Messiah, as willed of God? This, however, he could have comprehended only on condition that he already believed in the resurrection, and so the offence of the cross was set aside! Here Holsten entirely fails us, and here is, in fact, a difficulty which one can surmount only by accepting the occurrence of some sort of an event which produced the change. Without such an event, this change remains forever inexplicable. The conversion of Paul, which transformed him from a persecutor to an apostle, cannot, as simply a necessary development from within, be understood; it requires rather, necessarily, the appearance of Christ as an objective actual fact. Even the master of the Tübingen school, Bauer, saw himself necessitated to acknowledge, that " by no analysis, psychological or dialectic, can the inner mystery of the act in which God revealed his Son in Paul be disclosed." Bauer, whom no one will call miracle-seeking, sees therein a mystery, a miracle.

But even if it had been shown successfully that a vision on the part of Paul was ever so probable, what would be gained thereby? Paul is only one witness of the resurrection. Besides him, there is a long line, — Peter, James, the twelve, the five hundred. The conclusion, If the appearance of Christ to Paul was a vision, then all the others were visions, — this conclusion is wholly unallowable; for, as long as it has not been shown that these others were really visions, the reverse conclusion is equally valid: Because the appearances of Christ to Peter, James, etc., cannot have been visions, that to Paul cannot after all have been a vision, to say nothing of the possibility of attributing to each of the two kinds of appearance, as, e. g., Keim has done, a totally different character. The problem, thus, would be far from being solved. It is essential now, also, for these other appearances to furnish the proof that they were visions.

Need I demonstrate that still greater difficulties oppose themselves to that? In the case of Paul, the already existing conviction of many believers, the fact that many were convinced of having themselves seen the Lord, could be adduced as a co-operating factor, and you recollect how largely Holsten makes use thereof. Now that help is wanting, and the task is to show how and where the thought, Christ has risen! was developed at first altogether spontaneously. In the case of Paul, moreover, there was at the disposal of the historian a considerable time for the internal conflict whose last result was the vision, but in this only three days. In not even three days, in but little more than twice twenty-four hours, from Friday afternoon to Sunday evening, must the wondrous transformation from the deepest sorrow of complete dejection to full, joyous vision-producing faith, from the "We trusted that it had been he which should have redeemed Israel!" to the "The Lord is risen indeed!" have taken place.

Strauss felt well enough that this was quite impossible. Hence he seeks to gain time for the change. The disciples, he conjectures, fled first, without having had an appearance of the risen Lord, into Galilee, and there the change gradually came to pass. This conjecture, as Holsten has openly conceded, is uncritical. "The third day he rose from the dead," looks too definitely like a constituent part of the original tradition. How could the disciples, if the earliest appearances of the risen Lord followed only after a long while, have hit upon the third day as the day of the resurrection? On this third day the appearances must have had their beginning, — that stands historically sure; to assail that is caprice.

Holsten, who has given that up, seeks to gain time in the opposite direction. Peter, he thinks, must not be regarded as going about, spiritually asleep, in the days before the death of our Lord. The death was not a fact breaking in precipitously and suddenly; its expectation had ever since the departure from Galilee busied the soul of Peter. Consequently, when it actually occurred, it did not so stupefy him that he awoke only after many weeks again to thinking. It only sharpened the pain of thoughts already pondered, the pain of emotions already experienced. It called forth only the most intense spiritual unrest, that state of the soul from which visions arise. One thing now formed the centre-point of all his internal agitations, the mystery of this death. Before him stood the picture of the living Lord, and then his death. Was he indeed not the Messiah? — after all, a false prophet? How could He whom God had so endowed, who had spoken such words, done such deeds, be a false prophet? But his dying, his dying as a criminal on the cross, — was not that a proof thereof? Why had God forsaken him? This contradiction between the once living and the now dead Messiah was the deciding occasion for the vision of Peter. It forced him into a purely inward life, and since the picture of Jesus in its ideal purity was the centre-point of all his thoughts, this picture could, with the over-excited condition of his mental and nervous life, have come, in its radiant features, apparently objectively real and still visionary before his eyes.

I will only, in passing, remind you, as to this picture, that it is psychologically incorrect to suppose the expectation of the death weakened in any degree its impression. The presentiment had been, could have been, after all, but one which alternated between anxiety and continual hope, and the consummated fact did not thereby lose in force. It must have sunk the soul of Peter the deeper into sorrow and despondency as the denial with its depressing influence was added. From the deepest dejection to the full joy of the resurrection remained, therefore, only a period of scarcely more than two days. Ask yourselves, whether, as occurring in this period, such a change is conceivable? And how far does Holsten bring us with his development of the mental state in the case of Peter? Only, again, to the feeling of the contradiction, of the enigma. The question is the same as in the instance of Paul, what brought the solution of this enigma? Over against each other stand the remembrance of the life of the Lord and the crushing fact of his dying as a criminal on the cross. What was it, then, that caused the former to triumph over the latter, and not the latter over the former? On this point the answer fails. Nay, even if, without the occurrence of any new fact, Peter really worked through to the conviction that the crucified Jesus is nevertheless the Messiah, from this conviction to the belief, He has risen, is yet a long way. Whence came, then, the thought of the resurrection? That Jesus had previously announced this, and this previous announcement was understood and so firmly believed by the disciples that the prophecy became the source of visions, this the opponents will least of all admit. On the other hand, they will have to admit, that he often and very definitely spoke of his return in glory. The firm conviction of the primitive church requires this. But then the question presents itself, why do not Peter's thoughts turn in that direction? If anything appears to be a natural result, it is the entertaining of the hope, He is still the Messiah, he will come again in glory and as such reveal himself. But the thought of the resurrection, where are the points of connection for that? We stand, here also, before a riddle, which can be solved only by our concluding to accept, in place of mere internal events, external facts, in place of a visionary appearance, one objectively actual.

There are left us yet the appearances which James, the twelve, and the five hundred had, and which we can regard as standing historically sure beyond a doubt. Was James also, then, a vision-seer? And the twelve in a body? Of James we know little; what we do know of him would scarcely betray visionary capacities. And the twelve? was there not, then, among them a single considerate spirit? mere visionaries? What kind of a picture do we get of the circle of the apostles? and do you not observe how little this agrees with the picture of the apostles given in the New Testament?

Lastly, the five hundred. Let me lay particular stress on this appearance. You remember that to the originating of a vision certain physical and psychical dispositions belong, over-excitement of the nervous life, intense activity of the central organ, etc. Is it, then, to be believed that these dispositions are found with more than five hundred men, and indeed simultaneously, for "at once," Paul says expressly, the Lord appeared to them, — thus with above five hundred men at the same instant, the same nervous over-excitement, the same excessive activity of the central organ, the same accelerated circulation of the blood, the same pressure upon the optic nerves? It is only needful, I think, for one to understand what that means, to see its impossibility. Strauss, accordingly, here abandons the visionary explanation, and speaks only of delusion of the excited imagination. He mentions that when Duke Ulrick von Würtemberg was banished from his country by the Swabian League, persons here and there pretended to have seen him, or even harbored him in disguise under their roofs. Similar delusions may have crept in also here. So far have we now descended, that the appearances of the risen Lord are only delusions. Upon delusions rest the beginnings of the Christian church. Such is the sandy foundation upon which the structure has strangely, now for more than eighteen hundred years, stood. Truly I envy not him his understanding of history who considers this possible.

More earnest and worthy of notice is it, when the attempt is to show that these visionary states have in them something infectious, by which, as by sympathy, they are propagated from one to the other, attacking even considerate souls, overcoming even doubters. That is correct. I will remind you only of the visionaries in the Jansenistic controversies and in the Cevennic war. Other not innumerous examples of the kind will readily occur to you But no observation, I believe, is better adapted to set strikingly in the light the difference between those states and the appearances of the risen Jesus in the oldest church. Where is, then, here the over-excited, fanatical temperament which accompanies those states or is their cause? On the contrary, we find a considerateness, clearness, and repose of spirit, an earnestness of moral endeavor which absolutely forbids making of the primitive disciples a company of visionaries, in which one infects the other with his fanaticism. Is natural law so much appealed to, then I shall be permitted for once also to appeal thereto. It is a natural law, that those states should continue, should immoderately increase, until they find their limit in a reaction, and then, in place of the agitation and over-excitement, come the greater lassitude and inactivity. Now, pray tell me, where is there even the least trace of this in the apostolic age? The appearances of the risen Lord do not continue, do not become an abiding, or even for a time an abiding element of the life in the churches. They have their wholly determinate boundary, and, indeed, one very narrowly drawn. Even those who are not inclined to accept Luke's account of the ascension and the forty days' limit therein given, as historically established, will, nevertheless, have to admit that the number of the appearances, at the time of Paul's conversion, had long been closed. The appearance granted yet to him was something altogether extraordinary; besides, was nowhere repeated. It is, then, definitely the last. Exactly so there is not the least sign of a reaction, of a lassitude after the excitement. Rather the certainty, Christ has risen, forms continually and increasingly the source of the victorious joy of faith in the severe struggle through which the oldest community of believers had to pass. He who considers the actual circumstances of the church, and puts no imaginary pictures before his mind, will be forced to concede, then there is presented here something else than morbid nature given to visions.

But perhaps it will be replied, The possibility that all these appearances were only visions still remains, for as yet we are proceeding solely on the ground of the subjective spiritual life. Yes; not unless it has been shown that the risen Lord interposed at some place or time in the objective world, did or worked something in and upon it, or that there is a necessary connection of those appearances with an objectively real fact, will it be proven that they cannot have been simply subjective visions, but must have been objective appearances of the actually risen Lord. Were I permitted now to appeal to all the evidences which I personally regard as trustworthy, I would point to the facts, that Thomas laid his hand in the places of the wounds, that the risen Saviour ate in the presence of his disciples; and I will not, at least when opportunity for it offers, suppress the remark, what peculiar significance these incidents, thus regarded, attain. But I will not appeal to such particulars, for I know that they are doubted or wholly rejected by opponents. On the other hand, there is presented one fact which cannot well be doubted, and which of itself suffices to prove that we are not proceeding here on the ground of subjective visions.

The tomb of Jesus must have been empty. This appears not merely from the testimonies thereto, which are only arbitrarily to be doubted; it is required also by the fact from which we started, — the belief in the resurrection. For we shall easily persuade ourselves that this belief could not have originated from visions alone. These might, it is true, cause the disciples to believe that Jesus was alive, but the additional conviction, that he had risen out of the grave! For that, unquestionably, the fact that his body was no longer in the grave was needed. Without this fact, the unbelieving Jews would have had it every moment in their power to put an end to the whole belief, and one must have a strange notion of the enemies of the young community, to find it intelligible that, nevertheless, they did not do so. They did indeed manufacture the story, that the disciples stole him away; but they never affirmed that his body might be found in the tomb. Without the fact of the empty tomb, there would have been wanting, even on the part of the disciples, so necessary a portion of the proof of the actuality of the resurrection, that belief in it could not have maintained itself even with them.

If, however, the tomb was empty, then the question is unavoidable, What became of the body of Jesus? Who removed it from the tomb? His enemies? Impossible! for then they needed only to say so to annihilate with a single blow the hated belief in Jesus as the Messiah, and that they would have said so, their hatred assures us. His friends? His disciples themselves? Again, impossible! For then they must have been impostors, and that the church is not indebted to imposture for its origin you do not need that I should prove to you. Else unknown persons? some accident? No less impossible! for as little as upon an impostor, so little can the existence of the church rest upon an accident. What if this accident had not occurred? what if those unknown parties had not taken him away, or had not been so obstinately and unaccountably silent respecting their having done so? Then there would have been no belief in the resurrection; then, consequently, there would have been no church and no Christianity; for even those who do not concede that these rest upon the resurrection itself must yet admit that they do rest upon the belief in the resurrection. Will you, then, really refer the greatest and most beneficent change which the history of our race has ever experienced to an accident? Will you really attempt to hang the world on the thread of a spider's web?

On the side of the opponents the danger lying in such reflections has been clearly seen. It is, moreover, no longer possible to evade the question, What became of the body of Jesus after it was deposited in the tomb? Therefore the assertion has of late been hit upon, that it simply remained in the tomb; but that concerned neither friend nor enemy, for no one in those days so much as thought of the reanimation of this body. The prevailing idea was rather that the soul of Jesus, having been by death divested of its earthly body, was reinvested with a new body. This was the national Jewish view of the resurrection, the view which Paul held, and which must have been participated in by the other disciples also. Not till afterwards was the thought of the reanimation of the buried body resorted to. Accordingly, the body, remaining in the tomb, could have formed no moment whatever of proof either for or against the resurrection. The disciples could not have based their faith on the fact that the body was no longer in the tomb, nor could the enemies of Jesus have come to the thought of showing, by an examination of the tomb, that the announcement of the resurrection was a falsehood. After the dead body, it is said, no one inquired.

The embarrassment must indeed be great when recourse is had to such acts of violence; for as an act of violence in the face of clear and positive testimony, I must characterize this assertion. I will not ask, how, then, the faith of these oldest Christians is properly to be conceived of, who at first are totally indifferent as to the dead body of Jesus, believing that he is invested with an entirely new body, and then very soon abandon this view and remember that the body was restored to life and raised up from the tomb. For so unquestionably in all the Gospels and in the Acts of the Apostles the resurrection is conceived of. Suffice it to prove that Paul also so understood it. To do this, I will not appeal to the Epistle to the Philippians, where in the well-known passage it is said that "Christ shall change our vile body that it may be fashioned like unto his glorious body," I will confine myself entirely to the epistles universally accepted as genuine. I think an unprejudiced exposition cannot here fail to discover, that Paul conceives of the resurrection as a reanimation of the buried body, as a restoration to life, which is indeed also a glorification, so that the body which was deposited in the tomb in truth arose, but not as it was deposited; it arose a changed, a glorified body. Else what mean the expressions everywhere used, "rise," "rose from the dead"? What does it signify that Paul in 1 Cor. 15, between the words "died" and "rose again," inserts the word "buried," if this burial has no reference whatever to the following resurrection? Read, I pray you, Rom. 8: 11, "But if the Spirit of him that raised up Jesus from the dead dwell in you, he that raised up Christ from the dead shall also quicken your mortal bodies." How can the apostle from the raising up of Jesus draw a conclusion as to the quickening of our "mortal bodies," if the raising up of Jesus himself was not a quickening of his body? Or read Rom. 6: 4, "Therefore we are buried with him by baptism into death; that like as Christ was raised up from the dead by the glory of the Father, even so we also should walk in newness of life." How can the submersion in the baptismal water and the emersion from the same be to him a picture of Christ's burial and resurrection, and our burial and resurrection the repetition of that which happened to Christ, if in Paul's view the body of Jesus remained in the grave? Indeed, Paul cannot have thought otherwise than thus, — Christ's body came forth from its place of burial; and as Paul, so thought the other disciples. But this faith could have originated and maintained itself only on condition that the grave was empty. Then, however, we have before us, in the fact of the empty tomb, an objective, actual fact, which furnishes the proof that we are not proceeding here altogether upon the ground of subjective visions, but on the ground of real objective facts.

In this connection, I must also characterize Schenkel's view as historically untenable. Schenkel has taken it very ill that he is classed with the deniers of the resurrection; and with those who recognize here nothing actual whatever, he really does not belong. Rather does he expressly declare that the recognition of mere visions will not suffice, and that he, on his part, regards the appearances of the risen Jesus as " real manfestations of his death-surviving and glorified personality." But after all, he denies by this the resurrection in the sense in which Christendom has hitherto believed and taught it. In his view, the body of Jesus is not restored to life, but the glorified personality of Jesus manifests itself " in a higher, glorified body." So there is something altogether extraordinary left, something which happens with no mere man. For never yet has any other representative of our race manifested himself in such a higher, glorified body. The laws and orders of nature, which, to our experience, hold good everywhere else, we have thus overstepped, and Schenkel's opinions cannot favor those who are willing to see in Christ nothing but what is human, and nowhere in his life a transgression of natural law. We have a miracle, only now a miracle to which every historical attestation is wanting. For the historical testimonies at hand pertain not to such manifestations of the glorified personality of Jesus, but to a resurrection from the dead. If any one believes that these testimonies cannot be regarded as sufficient, then he must reject the fact of the resurrection; but so to halve matters, on the one hand not accepting what those witnesses depose, and yet on the other not breaking entirely with what the church believes, thus suiting a resurrection to one's self, which still is no resurrection, — that is to abandon history and to substitute for it fictions. The resurrection is historically attested just as the apostles announced it, this and nothing else; and Christendom believes it on their testimony.

This, however, as I think has now been proven, is satisfactorily attested. Every attempt to explain the belief therein otherwise than by recognition of the fact, shows itself to be inadequate, becomes entangled in the greatest difficulties and creates insoluble riddles. If one weighs without prejudice the importance of the testimonies at hand, if without dogmatic postulates the result is drawn from the historical inquiry, this cannot be other than, Christ actually, the third day after his death, rose again and appeared to his disciples.

Do I think, then, to be able thus to compel you to believe in the resurrection, as it is possible to compel assent to a rightly constructed mathematical argument? Deem me not to be so foolish! It is true, I am convinced, if the question here were concerning an historical event like every other, like perchance Alexander's expeditions of conquest or the deeds of Charlemagne, no doubt would arise; every one would accept it as sufficiently attested. But the resurrection is not a merely historical, it is a soteriologico-historical fact, which, as such, works with determining influence upon our thinking and living; upon its recognition depends nothing less than one's entire view of the world and of life. Whether you believe in the expedition of Alexander to India, or hold it to be insufficiently attested, this of itself does not affect you, your thinking and living, in the least; you remain, for all the effect of that, still the same. Whether, however, you do or do not believe in the resurrection of Christ, this makes necessarily a difference, and a radical difference, in your whole thinking, living, striving, and hoping. For the resurrection of Christ from the dead is one of the fundamental facts of our salvation, of our redemption in Christ, and, as far as the Christian faith is faith in the accomplished redemption, an essential element of the Christian faith. Therefore, surely, there belongs to belief in the resurrection more than simply that one assents to a historical argument. Moreover, on this account, one's assenting to this argument will depend upon wholly different co-operating factors, of whose working he may be conscious or unconscious.

Is it really so? Does the resurrection have such significancy for the Christian faith and the Christian life? In support thereof I could appeal to testimonies from right and left. Strauss has declared that with the resurrection Christianity, at least, what has hitherto been known as Christianity, stands and falls, and Presensé once said, " If the resurrection does not continue an integral part of Christianity, it no longer pays to speak of the rest." But as this expression, even at the Ministerial Conference where it was uttered, called forth vehement opposition; so elsewhere, it is frequently asserted, that the resurrection has for Christianity no import, it can as a matter of history be accepted or rejected, — this is a historical question, this affects not

Christianity itself. For not the belief that he came forth from the tomb alive, but the belief in the living Christ, is an essential element of Christianity. In regard to that historical question every one can hold whatever view he chooses, provided he only believes that Christ lives! So doing, he has retained the kernel of the resurrection-belief, has full right to celebrate Easters and rejoice in the risen Jesus. You see the drift of all this; it is to make of the resurrection simply a historical fact; no longer is it to be soteriologico-historical in nature.

The greater, now, the delight taken in expatiating with much rhetoric on the tenet, "Christ lives," the greater the need of observing with all dispassionateness what is left to those who reject the resurrection. We must, then, start with the premise, that nothing happened with Christ which does not happen with every other human being. He died, his body remained in the tomb and corrupted. Now, if the immortality of the soul is held fast, then Jesus is immortal, and, in this sense, he lives; lives personally, and, indeed, since even here he stood in the most intimate fellowship with God, lives in celestial glory. But on this continuance of life no stress is laid, and rightly, for it has no significancy to us, since he is thus in his person removed from the sphere of our life. We have of this his life neither an understanding nor an experience. Moreover, it is not this which is meant, when the living Christ is spoken of; but that he lives here on the earth, continues to live, as all great men do, only in a wholly extraordinary, unparalleled measure. Closely scanned, however, this saying, He lives, is only a rhetorical trope. Not he, not his person is meant, but his memory, his words, his thoughts, the life excited and awakened by him; or, if you wish to personify it, not the personal Christ, but the thought-

Christ, the Christ in idea. The question, then, comes to this, does that suffice? For, if that suffices, then truly the resurrection sinks down to the rank of a historical question, which can have had, at most, the import of lifting up the dejected spirits of the disciples. For us, to whom without that it stands sure that he so lives, the question whether his body was reanimated has no significancy at all, and, as regards Christianity, it is utterly indifferent whether criticism answers that question in the affirmative or the negative.

Does this, then, suffice? suffice? for what? Manifestly to re-establish the fellowship with God which sin has interrupted, to put away sin and its consequences, to renew what has been spoiled by sin. We stand at the deciding point. Some one has of late said, the Christian faith can be proven only to those who have a bad conscience. If you have not that, or, in other words, if you recognize not the fact of sin, then the Christian faith will always be to you a strange and incomprehensible one, for it is the faith in an accomplished redemption from sin. Or, to refer still more definitely to the resurrection, If you feel yourselves to be well, perfectly well in the body of this death; if you never have sighed under the want and misery of this life; if you dream that this present world is a perfect world, as much so as when it came from the hand of the Creator,— I should not know how I could make clear to you the import of the bodily resurrection. Then, indeed, no resurrection and renewal would be needed; then, indeed, all is good, as good as it should be, and I understand perfectly only this, that to you the resurrection as an incidental historical event is nothing, that you can quite unconcernedly leave the matter of its actual occurrence or non-occurrence undecided.

Let me not be misunderstood. I make here a presupposition, and readily admit that without it I can proceed no farther. I presuppose the fact of sin and of its consequences, — that man has apostatized from God; that an opposition between the holy God and sinful man actually exists; that sin, as it is not a disturbance in thought, but a subversion of the relation between man and God, has interposed destructively also in the present world; that this body has become through sin a body of death, and this present world one in need of being renewed. If it is not so, if there is no sin, if what we call sin is only a stage of natural development, a necessary transition-point, then surely no redemption would be needed. Or if sin is merely a disturbance in thought, if between God and man an opposition exists not actually, but only in our thought, in our idea, then also only a thought-redemption would be needed; then it suffices that the opposite idea be expressed, God is our Father; then also we have enough in an ideal Christ and an ideal resurrection. If sin, however, is a fact, then this redemption in thought suffices not; the facts of sin and death, to be cancelled and put away, must be met by facts.

These facts are the death and the resurrection of Christ. The two, as Scripture always conceives of them together, belong inseparably to each other. I do not mean merely for the reason that, without the resurrection of Christ, we could not apprehend his death as the ground of the redemption, or that so the justification of his dying as a criminal on the cross, and the Amen! of the Father to the It is finished! of the Son, would be wanting. That is true. But the significancy of the resurrection goes much farther. It does not suffice that sin has been atoned for and can now be forgiven; we must also be renewed, and this our renewal is based upon the resurrection. "Christ was delivered for our offences, and was raised again for our justification (righteousness [1])," says the apostle Paul, and in the first Epistle of Peter significantly enough regeneration and resurrection are connected with each other. We are born again by the resurrection of Christ. This renewal extends as far as the corruption extends. If this comprehends the entire man, then the renewal must also comprehend the entire man, in soul and body. If death is the recompense of sin, then even death must be overcome, and it is overcome by the resurrection of Christ from the dead. Hence not even a mysterious manifestation of Christ, such as Schenkel substitutes for the resurrection, satisfies. Only the bodily resurrection is in truth the overcoming of death, and only in the so risen Christ have we the assurance of our resurrection. In a Christ so risen, however, we surely have it; nay, in his resurrection a beginning of the resurrection has already been made. He has become the first fruits of those that sleep. From his resurrection hope looks on to the final complete renovation. What the Scripture prophesies of a new heaven and a new earth has in his resurrection already commenced. Without the resurrection there is an end to our Christian hope.

Only the Risen One can dispense the salvation acquired, only the Risen One can continue the work begun, to bring it yet to a conclusion. Take away the resurrection, and it is he, indeed, who gave the first impulse to the development, but this now, disconnected from his person, continues itself. The risen Jesus, on the other hand, is the living head of his people, to which from him constantly new life streams. He stands in personal fellowship with his

---

[1] Gerechtigkeit, as in the original lecture, and as Luther's version renders δικαίωσις of the Scripture quoted. — *Tr.*

disciples, speaks to them in his word, gives them to eat and drink his body and blood. This personal fellowship you break up the moment you deny the resurrection. Then you can have, it is true, a remembrance of him, a picture of him, indeed, the words he uttered, the thoughts he expressed, but not himself; you can have certainly a thought-Christ, a Christ in idea, but the personal Lord himself you cannot have. And if Christianity is living in personal fellowship with Christ, then with this soteriologico-historical fact of the resurrection of Christ from the dead Christianity stands and falls, and that remains true which, to appeal yet to a higher witness, Paul says, If Christ be not risen, then is our preaching vain, then your faith is also vain, then ye are yet in your sins, then they also which are fallen asleep in Christ are perished. The truth of the resurrection is the truth of our redemption.

Permit me, in conclusion, to direct your attention to the entire present situation of the church as connected with this one question.

The ancient church had to undergo, in the second and third centuries, a severe struggle with a tendency which set out to volatilize the facts of redemption into ideas, and to substitute for faith in those facts knowledge of the idea, called on that account Gnosis. Sprung from a combination of Christian and heathen elements, it built up its strange huge systems, all of which aim at changing the redemption by facts into a redemption by thoughts; at displacing the historical Christ by an ideal Christ. Counter to it the church faithfully confessed and victoriously defended the fundamental facts of redemption, of the history of Jesus as the history of redemption, as they are summed up in the Apostles' Creed. We are to-day in a similar situation. To us, also, a gnosis, composed of Christian elements and of elements of culture which are, alas, in many ways estranged from Christianity, is opposed; a gnosis which, as different as it is from that of the earlier times, has this in common with it, that it resolves and volatilizes the facts of salvation into ideas. Suffer not yourselves to be deceived by the circumstance that much is said about history and an historical apprehension of Christianity. The history, the facts, are to this tendency only the shell, which is thrown away after the kernel has been pretendedly extracted therefrom. It is all-important again, as at that time, to defend the simple facts of salvation, as they are contained in the Symbolum Apostolicum. Let us faithfully fulfil this duty of the present, and not lose courage, because now, as in those first centuries, knowledge and culture are seemingly on the other side, because a great multitude stands there. The facts rest upon a sure foundation; and, as they outlasted that storm, will also, undoubtedly, survive this of to-day. Let us, however, never forget that the primitive church was enabled to carry the conflict successfully through only because it preserved the historical facts, not as past and dead, but as living and present facts; because it had life and love, which latter the apostle sets higher than all gnosis. This puffs up; love edifies. Only he in whom these facts have repeated themselves, who, from his own experience and not merely through scientific argumentation, has apprehended their truth, he alone in the end can answer for them. He who has died and risen with Christ, who, in repentance, dies with him daily as to the old man, and rises with him daily as to the new man, he can respond to the Easter salutation, "The Lord is risen!" with full joy and victorious confidence, "He is risen indeed!" To him that was dead, and, behold, he lives, and has the keys of hell and death, to him be praise and thanks forever.

LECTURE VII

THE SCRIPTURAL DOCTRINE OF ATONEMENT

By W. F. GESS, D. D.

PROFESSOR AT GÖTTINGEN

BIOGRAPHICAL

WOLFGANG FRIEDRICH GESS, D. D., was born at Kirchheim, in Würtemberg, July 27, 1819. He studied at Tübingen from 1837 to 1841. Between the latter date and 1850 he was assistant pastor, *repetent*, and pastor in Würtemberg. Between 1850 and 1864 he was theological tutor in the Missions House at Basel, and member of the Board of Directors. From 1864 to 1871 he was ordinary professor of theology at Göttingen, and from 1871 to 1880 the same at Breslau, besides being a member there of the Silesian consistory. In 1880 he was made general superintendent of the province of Posen, *emeritus* in 1885. Among other publications written by him, are the following: *Christi Person und Werk, Bibelstunden über John 13–17, Bibelstunden über Rom. 1–8, Bibelstunden über den Brief des Apostels Paulus an die Römer, Cap. 9–16.*

SUMMARY OF LECTURE VII

JESUS revealed himself gradually to his disciples—First makes known his Messiahship at Cæsarea-Philippi—Directly afterward begins to talk of his suffering and death—The necessity of his death repeatedly mentioned—Then in the neighborhood of Jericho he announces that the purpose of his suffering was "to give his life a ransom for many"—Afterward he spoke of the Jewish passover in connection with his death, and still later explained that his blood should be shed " for many for the remission of sins"—The same evening, in his parting prayer, he says, "For their sakes I sanctify myself;" as a holy offering—These four utterances are the main roots from which have grown the apostles' testimonies concerning the atoning significancy of Jesus' death—Man is everywhere free and guilty; the pre-supposition of this fact is the groundwork of the atonement—A regular law that seems to control in the commission of crime, as shown by statistics—This suggests and helps to prove the Scripture doctrine of man's being a "servant of sin," and of there being a regular "law of sin"—While man is thus estranged from God it is neither meet nor possible for him to enjoy the divine favors, and especially the Holy Spirit, without an atonement—To make an atonement for sin three things are requisite, with not one of which is man naturally able to comply—Jesus' intercourse with men soon convinced him of their moral and religious state as very different from his own—This led him to intercede for others, and finally to pray that the Father would receive him as the Atoner for his brethren—Though sinless, Jesus took the place of sinners, endured the whole curse, vindicated the righteousness of God, and confessed the condemnatory nature of sin—How Jesus' atonement becomes available for man.

VII

THE SCRIPTURAL DOCTRINE OF ATONEMENT

BY W. F. GESS, D. D.,
PROFESSOR AT GÖTTINGEN

THE instruction which the intimate circle of the Lord Jesus' disciples received from him regarding himself, was imparted to them with gradually increasing fulness and clearness. During the first year and a half of their association with him, he expressed not to them in direct words that he was the Messiah, i. e., the King of Israel and of all nations whom the prophets had foretold. By the hearing of his words of eternal life, by the seeing of his wonderful deeds, by the holy impression of his entire personality, they were to be led of themselves to this conviction. Towards the end of this year and a half, the enthusiastic applause which had for a time been accorded to him was, with the mass of the people, greatly decreased. On the other hand, the enmity of the Pharisaic party had risen so high that Jesus could no longer dwell in peace at one place, but had to change continually his sojourn. First now, and precisely now at this critical period, Jesus, on a certain occasion, suddenly addressed to his disciples the question, whom they held him to be. It was near Cæsarea Philippi, far up in the north of the land. And as now, notwithstanding all the disfavor of the outward situation, the joyful confession followed from the mouth of Peter, "Thou art the Christ, the Son of the living God," Jesus then solemnly assured his disciples, that he was what Peter had declared him to be.[1] With this closed the first stage in his instruction of his disciples. But he immediately commenced the second. The evangelists narrate particularly that at just this hour Jesus began to announce the suffering which awaited him. Moreover, he added to the words concerning his death, that he would at length return in the glory of his Father with his angels, and then reward every one according to his doing. Intimations of both Jesus had already given; now, however, these two themes, the Messiah's dying and the Messiah's return, became, in Jesus' instruction of his disciples, cardinal points. As a third subject, this also was joined to the two, namely, that even in the interval between his dying and return he would, invisibly but in efficacious reality, remain with his followers.[2] This second stage of the instruction, which continued till his death, can be reckoned at perhaps three fourths of a year.

It is Jesus' utterances concerning his death that we are at this hour more closely to consider. For the New Testament doctrine of atonement is to be now the question, and for this Jesus' utterances concerning his death form the most important source.

Since that occurrence near Cæsarea, our Lord, from time to time, and in nearly the same words, repeated the announcement then made, that the Son of man must be put to death. But at first simply repeated. He named the place at which it would happen, — Jerusalem; he named the men by whom it would happen, — the heads of the Is-

---

[1] Matt. 16: 13 ff. [2] Matt. 18: 20; John 14: 16.

raelitish people; he set forth prominently that it *must* happen, and would not, therefore, occur as a casualty, but by virtue of a necessity; yet by virtue of what necessity and to what purpose, he did not as yet explain.[1] Still on the journey to his death, he repeated in this wise his saying.[2] We may ask, why he, foreseeing that he will be put to death, nevertheless undertakes the journey? His duty to preach in this metropolis the kingdom of God was already by him abundantly fulfilled. Often had he, to use his own words, endeavored to gather Jerusalem's children about himself, but they would not.[3] Why does he not now remain far from this city? We see it is that "must" which impels him. He has perceived in his death a divine decree. The hatred of men it is that will accomplish his death; but he knows that they only do what *must* happen. Nevertheless, even during the journey, — it took place from the Sea of Galilee down, on the left side of the Jordan valley, — he does not yet explain himself on the purpose of this decree. He who reflects with due attention upon the history of our Lord will learn generally to wonder at how much Jesus understood the art of waiting. Nowhere any precipitation, everywhere calm considerateness. Not till they arrived in the neighborhood of Jericho, and so were distant from Jerusalem only one day's journey, does he avail himself of an opportunity to disclose the purpose of his dying.[4] Two of his disciples, John and James, had brought before Jesus the petition that, when he set up his royal throne, he would make them the first among his mighty men; for the disciples could not yet relinquish the notion that the establishment of the throne was nigh. Jesus answers them, that they are not called to rule over

[1] Matt. 17: 12, 22; Mark 8: 31; 9: 12.   [2] Matt. 20: 18 f.   [3] Matt. 23 37.
[4] Matt. 20: 23.

men, but to serve. And then he adds, "As the Son of man came not to be ministered unto, but to minister, and to give his life a ransom for many." Consequently, Jesus came to serve. Day after day, in this year of his public working, his whole strength was consecrated to the greatest rvice which a man can render to his brothers, the announcement of God by word and work. Yet, not his working alone, but also his dying, is to be a service for men. And indeed his dying in a different manner from his working. He would surrender his life as a ransom, — as a ransom for many; therefore, as a substitutional ransom. Those for whom he surrenders his life are, then, in imprisonment. And they could not escape from this imprisonment, unless Jesus would give his life for them. We see, this first word which Jesus uttered on the purpose of his death was sufficient of itself to open to the reflection of his disciples a fruitful look. But, a few days afterward, he added to the first word a second. It was on the Tuesday before his death that he said to his disciples, "Ye know that after two days is the feast of the passover, and the Son of man is betrayed (delivered up)[1] to be crucified."[2] Noteworthy connection! What have these facts to do with each other, — the Jewish people's paschal supper and the Son of man's being delivered up to crucifixion? It was soon to become clear. For as now, on Thursday evening, the Lord sat with his disciples, after the custom of the feast, to eat the lamb, he took bread, and then the cup with wine, and said, "Drink ye all of it; for this is my blood of the New Testament, which is shed for many for the remission of sins." The day following, his blood was shed on the cross. The passover served to commemorate the establishment of

---

[1] So παραδίδοται is rendered in the version quoted by the lecturer.—*Tr.*
[2] Matt. 26: 2.

the old covenant, when Israel was delivered from the land of bondage, exalted to be the people of God, and led out towards the land of its home. Every covenant was consecrated by the blood of lambs. Now a new covenant is to come in the place of the old. But for that purpose Jesus' blood must first be shed, — shed for the remission of sins. First the obtaining of God's pardon of sins, then God's new covenant can enter into life.[1] And it is the Son of man, that is to say, the Son of humanity, the long-promised and wished-for, its noblest scion, who now is delivered up to crucifixion. For the new covenant is not, like the old, a covenant with Israel alone, but with humanity. On the same evening Jesus spoke, in the parting prayer, the word, "For their sakes I sanctify myself."[2] As a holy offering he goes to his death.

These four utterances of our Lord are the main roots from which the testimonies of the apostles concerning the atoning significancy of the death of Jesus have grown. Peter and Paul repeat, in their Epistles, the word of the ransom.[3] Paul and John amplify the thought, that in Jesus the true Lamb of God, of which Israel's paschal lamb was only the type, was given to humanity.[4] The Epistle to the Hebrews calls the blood of Jesus the blood of the eternal covenant, by which the conscience is purged. What Jesus spoke of the sanctifying of himself to be a holy offering is amplified in this epistle to the effect that Jesus was both the priest and the victim, and that, since he through the Eternal Spirit dwelling in him sanctified himself as a holy offering to God, an eternal redemption was accomplished by him.[5] Not upon an invention of the church, but upon the apostolical word, then, does the belief of Christendom rest,

---

[1] Matt. 26: 27 f.   [2] John 17: 19.   [3] 1 Pet. 1: 18; 1 Tim. 2: 6.
[4] 1 Cor. 5: 7; John 19: 36.   [5] Heb. 13: 20; 9: 14.

to wit, that on Good Friday the atonement of human sin was accomplished; i. e., the forgiveness of our sins was effected by Jesus with his Father. This apostolical word rests upon Jesus' own word.

There are in the present times many who deny that man is free, i. e., has the ability to choose among different ways of action possible for him. They affirm that everything which man has done or will do in life, he must do as he does, by virtue of a necessity lying partly in his peculiar nature, partly in his outward situation. There are many, indeed, who protest that they have no souls, but are mere matter. The most effectual way of opposing such assertions is by referring to inner experience. Man has experience of freedom, for he has experience of his obligation to obey a moral law, and of his responsibility for obedience or disobedience to this law. With him who has the resolution to deny the fact of this experience no farther discussion is at the outset possible. But it is also unnecessary. For the unprejudiced part of mankind is so conscious of its inner experience of freedom that it quietly proceeds on its way. The state will continue to care for the education of the young and for the just punishment of criminals, that is, to presuppose the freedom of man; for education, as well as punishment according to principles of justice, is to be spoken of, only on condition that the inner experience of freedom is true. In like manner, my friends, the Christian church, when it speaks of the atonement for sin through Christ, presupposes an inner experience; and indeed the experience that God is holy and that men are guilty. For him who denies God's holiness and his own guilt, discourse on the atonement for human guilt has no meaning. For him who in fact does not deny both, but holds them to be matters of trifling moment, the whole subject of the atonement appears to be not exactly foolishness, but it leaves him cold. The Christian church will not on this account suffer itself to be confused in its annunciation of the atonement; for it knows that every man who attentively gives heed to his conscience can learn by experience, that God is holy and that man is guilty, nay, that for every one an hour comes when he must learn this. This experience, it is true, has something more of concentration and energy in attending to the inner voice than has the mere perception that we are free, but it lies in the same line, only one must go deeper down. This inner experience I also presuppose. Only those who are agreed on the same can have an interest in the discussion of the atonement and an understanding of the manner in which it happened. To this understanding let us now seek to come nearer.

Christ has expiated our sin, that is to say, he has effected with God the pardon of our sin. With this, to go no further, is connected that which is strange to many. They say, God is love; how was it necessary, then, that Christ should first work out pardon for men, and altogether by his death? Surely, the God who is love pardons every one forthwith who asks him for pardon. I will reply to this first, Bremen had, in the first third of this century, among its preachers, a man who belonged to the most spiritual theologians of the evangelical church, and, besides, was of the greatest independence of judgment. All that appeared to him to be merely human tradition, he esteemed not; on the other hand, he was totally penetrated with the divine authority of the Scriptures. I need scarcely say that I mean Godfrey Menken. No one can speak more strongly on this great theme, that God is love, than did Menken. Just this man, however, hesitated not to attest that Christ—I give Menken's own words—"paid the debt of humanity, averted from us God's displeasure, disclosed to us by his death a new right and a new way to eternal life."[1] To him, then, it was no contradiction that God is love, and that, nevertheless, Christ had to work out the pardon of our sin, had to atone for our sin. But I ascend from the disciple of the apostles to the apostles themselves. John it is who first uttered that great saying, "God is love." Directly, however, after he wrote this saying in the fourth chapter of his first epistle, he adds, "Herein is love, that God loved us, and sent his Son to be the propitiation for our sins." So John knew of no contradiction between the idea that God is love, and the proposition that our sin had to be expiated by Christ. But we will ascend still higher; from the apostles of the Lord to the Lord himself. From the Lord Jesus humanity has learned that it is permitted to call God by the name of Father; the prophets of the Old Testament never ventured to commence their prayers, Our Father. But our Lord declared that he would give his life a ransom for many; that his blood was the blood of the new testament, shed for the remission of sins. Under these circumstances, a clear-seeing man will deliberate well, before he joins in the assertion that, because God is love, no atonement was needed; for he will say to himself that he by whom the Father-name of God was made known to humanity must certainly have been better acquainted with the ways of the divine love than is the present generation. At present men talk of the divine love; Jesus lived in this love. Moreover, it is not difficult for a somewhat more deeply thinking man to perceive why God's love and God's requirement of an atonement do not exclude each other,

---

[1] Comp. the Versöhnungslehre by Dr. G. Menken.. In verbal extracts from his writings. 1837, pp. 13, 20, 21.

rather are in harmony. This can be made intelligible even from our human relations. When a man of character is compelled to know that his son, by a grievous offence, violates the moral order, his love to the son does not, on that account, cease, but rather evinces itself in the earnestness with which the father seeks the son's conversion. Yet in the converse of the father with the son a change takes place; intimacy ceases; perhaps the son is even wholly excluded from intercourse with the father, and this until a suitable expiation of the offence has been made. The simple word of the son, that he is sorry for the offence, does not satisfy a father of character; he asks the proof of earnestness by an expiatory act. And this is not want of love, but true love; for true love knows that the son's welfare can only then be secure when he has bowed in the fullest earnestness in submission to the moral order.

Perhaps what has just been said gives occasion to a second objection. That human father, one will say, requires then the expiation of the offence from him who committed the offence; God, however, is represented as having required the atonement from the only person who was without sin. I enter upon this question the more readily, as it makes it necessary for us to penetrate more deeply into the kernel of the matter, namely, into the way in which Christ accomplished the atonement for our sin. And this is the principal thing. As long as a truth is not rightly understood, many an objection presents itself with force, which, for him who has gained an insight into the matter, immediately becomes forceless. I commence this discussion with a remark which, at first sight, may appear extraneous. No one of us will wonder, that the relation of deaths to the number of inhabitants remains every year about the same. We think, death ensues according to a natural law, and this law works every year with like strength. Now, however, our statisticians, in the last decades of years, have found the same regularity in the case of crimes. "As long as the course of justice in regard to the prosecution and punishment of crimes in a state does not change,"—these are the words of the reliable statistician, Dr. Wappäus, in his General Statistics of Population,[1]—"the crimes repeat themselves according to their number and kind, as well as according to their distribution as to sex and age, with the greatest regularity."

Many may query whether this is not a proof against all freedom. But the criminals themselves have the definite consciousness, that they could have refrained from the crimes, if they had only earnestly willed. Besides, the statistics furnish other facts, which show that freedom is not a dream, but a reality. (I can also for this refer to the work mentioned.) Thus much, however, is incontrovertibly clear from this regularity with which crimes return, that it does not stand as it might and should with the development and use of the freedom innate in man. It is, according to the testimony of every conscience, a wicked contrariety to nature for a man to murder his brother; but so much have the mass of men surrendered themselves to the power of the passions that every year about the same number of men yield to temptation working with constant strength, and commit the unnatural crime. A hundred times offence has been taken in the name of enlightenment at the Scripture, because it declares man to be a servant of sin and speaks of a law of sin;[2] now come the figures of the statisticians and prove it is nevertheless so.

Does not the fact here present itself with frightful force

[1] Allgemeinen Bevölkerungsstatistik.   [2] John 8: 34; Rom. 8: 2.

before our eyes, that the way humanity goes is a wholly different one from that which the holy Creator from the beginning has indicated to it? And if this is so, is it not then intelligible, that the majesty of God demands of humanity an atonement for its sin? that the fellowship between God and man cannot be again restored, the Spirit of God cannot be communicated to man, before the atonement has been made? God bestows even upon those men who are far from him many favors. The heathen nations to this day enjoy God's sunshine and rain and the filling of the heart with many joys. The same blessings are allotted, among Christians, even to the despisers of God. But these external benefits are not the highest benefit. Only he who has God himself, in that God's Spirit dwells in him, has the highest good. And these earthly benefits give strength and gladness for only this earthly life. Imperishable life can only come from fellowship with the living God.

He who will think somewhat more deeply can easily perceive, that, especially after death, the impossibility of remaining vigorous and joyful without the Spirit of God will become apparent. For by death man will be deprived of the earthly sources of nourishment. During the earthly life the self-delusion, that the earthly can satisfy man, is possible; but from what source in the future world is the nourishing, strengthening, beatifying to come, if not from God himself? What the Scriptures call *being lost*, is, where the Spirit of God is wanting, indeed the natural, self-intelligible, necessary result. To receive the Spirit of God is, therefore, for man in the fullest sense of the word a life-question. And yet it is, as before remarked, contradictory to the majesty of God to give his Spirit, and so himself, to men, before an atonement for sin has been made. And how, now, is this to be effected? Men have tried in different ways to bring about an atonement. They have offered animals as sacrifice. But a human offence could not possibly be expiated by that means. They have imposed upon themselves grievous performances, as wearisome pilgrimages, or painful tortures, e. g., by scourgings. But also these do not change the heart, and therefore before God can have no worth. The atonement for a misdeed could obviously consist only in the man's earnestly bearing, in humble acknowledgment of God's righteousness, the evils which fall from that righteousness upon the misdoer as the reward of the misdeed; secondly, in his utterly breaking with the evil disposition from which his evil deeds proceed; thirdly, in his leading from this time forth a righteous life. Where, now, are the men who are able to do this? — and indeed do it before they have the Holy Spirit? For this can be given to man only after the expiation has occurred. There may, it is true, be many who imagine they are fully able to comply with that threefold requirement, and thus to become their own expiators. But this is a self-delusion. These men know not that there is a law of sin; that sin is like a revolving wheel which turns round with itself every one who becomes entangled in it. Our great poets know well of this revolving wheel. How powerfully Shakespeare speaks of it! But let us not in this connection think of merely such monstrous offenders as Macbeth and his consort. To be selfish is to be sinful. Whether the evil dwelling in man makes its appearance in great or small dimensions, in ugly and rough, or in seemly and polished forms, is a secondary matter. Ugly animals, when through the diminutiveness of their figure their ugliness hides itself from the human eye, are on that account not less ugly; he who arms his eye with a microscope is shocked at their ugliness. Before

God's eye, however, everything stands as it really is. Even this is a secondary consideration, whether the evil comes to be action, or remains locked up in the heart. God looks at the heart. Before his eye, a very real murder can be committed by mere thought. Even the selfishness remaining concealed in the depths of the heart is a governess over man; he can at the best hinder it from manifesting itself by word and work; but he cannot expel it from his heart.

I am speaking here of such men as have not yet the Holy Spirit. To me it seems that it must now be clear that no man can himself atone for his sin. And yet an atonement for our sin is necessary. Accordingly we have now come to the point from which we can begin to understand the appearance of Jesus on our behalf. The eternal Word of God is in Jesus become flesh, a complete real man. Now as Jesus, sinless but truly human, truly human but sinless, grew up in Nazareth, he must soon have learned, by contact with those who met him, that none of them stood to God as he stood to him. To Jesus intercourse with God was as necessary for his soul-life as was the breathing of the air or the seeing of the light for his physical life. Moreover, he nowhere found a separation between God and himself. To pray and do the will of God was his delight. His inmost consciousness told him that he was God's child and God was his Father. With men in the society about him he also found, indeed, a need for God, but neither this constancy of seeking for God, nor this child-intercourse with him. As the boy became a youth, and his look extended to his people, and as through the reading of the Old Testament the history of his people and a part of general history became known to him, the universality of human sin, and how entirely destitute of the

Spirit from God humanity was, came more and more forcibly before him. Farther; we can regard it as certain, that in the same measure in which Jesus began to come to this knowledge, his prayer-intercourse with his Father became an intercession for his Nazareth, for his Israel, for humanity; for living intercourse with God becomes necessarily prayer, and true prayer becomes necessarily intercession. No less certain, however, is it, that Jesus must soon have perceived how mere intercession could not suffice to save his people and humanity. Even the Old Testament law, then also the Old Testament prophecy, pointed to the necessity of the atonement. Humanity is restored to life only by the Spirit from God; the Spirit from God it receives only when an atonement for its sin has previously been made. The intercession of Jesus became, then, the prayer that the Father would accept him as the Atoner for his brothers. For where was there a holy one, save him? And only one who is holy can become an atoner. But how did he wish to bring about the atonement? "To atone for" is actually to take back the misdeed committed, actually to plead for the pardon of it, actually to break the staff over it. This Jesus wished to do in the name of his brothers. But in what manner could he do it? If he set his entire strength on attesting God to his brothers and leading them back to him; if he was willing to endure all sacrifices on account of this attestation of God; if, in the midst of this labor with sinners, he experienced also all the misery which the righteousness of God attached to their sin, but bowed his soul willingly under it, because where sin reigned for the sake of God's righteousness misery also must reign,— if he did all this, and did it till the last breath of his life, is not this so to interpose in the process of the holy God towards sinful humanity that he, in the name of his brothers, laid before the throne of God an actual acknowledgment of the perfect wrong of man and of the perfect right of God, and an actual plea for the pardon of our misdeed?

To become in such a way our advocate was the resolution with which the holy Jesus came from Nazareth to the Jordan. Many readers of the Gospels have wondered that our Lord began his public ministry by suffering himself to be baptized by John; for this baptism was usually connected with the confession of sin. The immersion was in itself a symbol of the desire to wash away the defilement of the soul. Jesus, however, was, as he not merely once, but one would be authorized in saying a hundred times attested, without the least impurity. Wherefore, then, with him the water baptism? The matter explains itself by what he subsequently said of the baptism of suffering which was to be accomplished in him. It was the willingness to this that he symbolically expressed in his participation in the Jordan baptism. He who alone of all men had no part in human sin desired, nevertheless, to take part in human sufferings, which are the wages of sin, in order thus to become helpful to sinners. This willingness he confessed by his baptism, and his Father accepted this confession.

Three times in the life of our Lord a voice came from heaven attesting that his Father was well pleased with him, and each time it was occasioned by an attestation of Jesus of his willingness to suffer. The first instance is this at his baptism. The evangelists relate that as Jesus went up from the water a voice came from heaven, saying, "This is my beloved Son, in whom I am well pleased." The second voice from heaven occurred in connection with the transfiguration of Jesus on the mountain. This took place six days after Jesus had given to his disciples, when near Cæsarea, that solemn announcement of his impending death, which we mentioned at the beginning. Again the voice sounded, "This is my beloved Son, in whom I am well pleased." This voice, as well as the whole transfiguration on that mountain, stood in intimate relation to the announcement made by Jesus of his suffering. Jesus humbles himself before his disciples to the confession that he, the Messiah, will be abased even to an ignominious death; the Father glorifies him by the breaking forth of the inwardly concealed glory of Jesus in his outward appearance, then by the coming of Moses and Elias, and, lastly, by that voice from heaven. Jesus is by this transfiguration recognized as one belonging to the heavenly world, who, when on earth he dies, dies not as a man naturally subject to death, but as the shepherd who, out of love to the flock, voluntarily suffers death. The third instance took place after Jesus' formal entry into Jerusalem, a few days before his death. The thought of the approaching death had, as John narrates in the twelfth chapter, at that time suddenly filled Jesus with deep horror. He cries out, "Now is my soul troubled." He asks himself whether he shall pray the Father to save him from this hour of anguish. But as he is willing to bear death itself, so is he willing to endure also this anguish and the humiliation, before those about him, connected therewith, if only the name of his Father will be glorified by him. Then, once more, comes the voice from heaven. It attests that, as Jesus' life up to that time had been, so will also his impending death be, simply the glorification of God.[1] These were assurances of the Father how well pleasing to him was Jesus' willingness to suffer. But we can likewise understand by these voices from heaven, with which the Father answered Jesus' willingness to suffer,

[1] Luke 12: 50; Matt. 3: 17; 17: 5; John 12: 27 f.

how severe was the suffering of Jesus. These encouragements which he received from above give us a look into the depths of his conflict.

It must not, moreover, be supposed that Jesus' suffering first commenced in the last week; it extended through his whole life, especially through its last year. If the question is asked wherein, then, it consisted, three ingredients come particularly under consideration. First, what befell him from the hatred of men. How disdainfully he was often treated! A servant of the devil he must suffer himself to be called in reproach. But not merely the enmity of men did Jesus have to endure. His heavenly Father put him to a severe trial also by often concealing from him his presence and love. Jesus' whole life was a walking by faith. Ever anew it was necessary to break through obscurities. This concealment of the Father reached its height precisely when the enmity of men became the greatest. Whoever of us leads his life far from God ought justly to confess his unfitness to judge in any degree of the mystery of the life of Jesus. Even the life of a pious man, as, e. g., of a Luther, and especially its deepest kernel, remains necessarily an enigma to him who is remote from God, for, naturally, only like can understand like; how much more, then, must the life of the only begotten Son of God remain a mystery to him! On the contrary, those to whom an intimate intercourse with God is a felt necessity will find it intelligible, that, with Jesus, the higher the enmity of men rose, the greater became the desire of the soul for the internal experience of fellowship with the Father. Instead of that, precisely in his outwardly most trying hours, namely, in Gethsemane, when he knew the arrest was nigh, and, above all, on the cross, when the derision of his enemies and his physical distress had become greatest, the internal fellowship with the Father was concealed, the inner voice, assuring him of his being the beloved Son, was silent, so that Jesus, who was always the perfectly true, could not do otherwise than break out before his revilers in the cry of humiliation, "My God, my God, why hast thou forsaken me!" And now came death itself, death which, according to the universal testimony of the Scripture of the Old and New Testaments, is the wages of sin, and, consequently, for the holy Jesus was an experience that militated against his nature.

So fiery were the trials in which Jesus had to prove the earnestness of his zeal for the honor of God, and of his commiseration with sinners, of his intercession on their behalf. The sinless Jesus had to share wholly the lot of sinners. Men treated him as though he was the most odious of criminals, and God preserved him not from this mistreatment; he delivered him up to their hatred; he was silent; he delivered him up to death. So fully had Jesus to experience the consequences of having to do with sinners, of wishing and purposing to save them; he, the Holy One, had to taste the entire curse which through sin has come upon humanity, as though he himself was a sinner. He, however, remained a willing sufferer. He despised not the condition under which alone he could interest himself in sinners, namely, becoming involved in the curse resting upon our race. He knew that this curse lay upon our race justly; that it was the retributive justice of God that imposed it on us; and since he willingly suffered the whole lot of those whom he wished to help as his brothers, he has actually acknowledged the righteousness of God and the execrableness of human sin. By just this has he become our expiator. The expiation of sin must take place by the actual acknowledgment that it is purely and perfectly wrong, and that God, in the decreeing of all the misery in soul and body wherewith he requites our sin, is in the right. By such an acknowledgment the majesty of God, ignored by sinners, is satisfied. Jesus has in the name of humanity pronounced the verdict upon human sin, therefore God can forbear to judge us.

My friends, as I have endeavored to open a look into the way in which the atonement for human sin was effected by the Lord Jesus, I am far from supposing that by what has been said this great theme has been exhaustively discussed. One thing, however, I affirm with confidence, that even this discussion is sufficient to show how superficial are the objections with which opponents are accustomed to load the doctrine of the atonement. Where, I ask, remains, e. g., the disparagement of God's doing injustice to Jesus, if it was the inmost desire of Jesus himself to be permitted to appear for his brothers as their priest? Or how can it be said, that, according to the doctrine of atonement preached in our churches, God punishes sin first in Jesus and afterwards in us also? Of external punishment, with which human magistrates, in their proceedings against the transgressors of civil law, must content themselves, we are here not speaking. That sinners are in the way to ruin breaks forth from the nature of the case itself with inner necessity; for he who separates himself from the living God by this very act chooses death. What, however, Jesus suffered, he suffered because the free constraint of his love impelled him to suffer with and for his brethren. As little ought a thinking man to say, that, according to this doctrine, God asked a double expiation of our sins, the first of us sinners, the second of the holy Jesus. For in the misery which we ourselves through sin inflict upon ourselves can be no expiation; because only holy suffering is an expiatory suffering. Our suffering, however, is an unholy suffering; the holy and therefore propitiatory suffering was to be found with Jesus only.

In conclusion, permit me yet a few words on the question, how after all it can come to pass that Jesus' atonement is available for others, for humanity, for every one of us. He who would understand this must make clear to himself two things. First, the being of the expiator, Christ. Self-intelligible is it that Jesus, if he was himself a sinner, could not have become our expiator; for then he would have needed rather himself an expiator. But not even sinlessness was sufficient to qualify him to make atonement. Humanity may be compared to a tree. Ordinary men are, then, the leaves. Prominent men, who form the support for others, are like the twigs. The greatest among men, those whose spirit influences whole nations and generations, as, e. g., a Luther, can be called the boughs of the tree. But the tree of humanity must have also trunk and root. And if the question is concerning the representation of entire humanity before God, this can be done only by a man who could be designated as both the trunk and the root of humanity. This man, according to the Scriptures, was Jesus Christ. For he is the Word of God become flesh, by whom and for whom the whole world, and so also humanity, was created.[1] This Word, become flesh, could alone be the representative of humanity. He only had an insight into the entire depth of human sin, therefore he alone could treat in a priestly way with God respecting it. Jesus only could be sensible of the whole, full anguish of soul, on account of human sin, corresponding to the greatness of the misdeed. When the frivolous son of a noble father does a grievous crime, with whom is

[1] Col. 1: 15 f.; John 1: 3.

the inner anguish afterward the greater, with the son or the father? According to experience, with the father. This will help us to understand the agony of Jesus on account of the sin of men, for Jesus is the eternal Son of God become man, by whom and for whom we were created; from the creation we have been his possession. Yet of the inner being of Jesus I will at present speak no farther; it formed the subject of an earlier lecture.

The other thing which one must make clear to himself, to comprehend the availableness of the atonement of Christ for us, is the nature of faith. Only for the believer does the atonement of Christ avail. That to a great many men the Christian doctrine of the reposing of our happiness upon the righteousness of another, namely, of Jesus Christ, remains unintelligible, has its ground principally in the fact that they have an erroneous conception of what faith is. They conceive that faith is equivalent to assent. They regard faith as a matter of the head, whereby no change takes place in the man himself, in the heart of the man. It is no wonder, then, if such persons ask with astonishment, whether this accords with the righteousness of God, that a foreign righteousness should avail as our own. Were faith in Christ nothing but an assent to the fact that Christ is this and that, and that his death has such and such significancy, then, assuredly, Christ remains to us a foreigner, and that his death should avail for us would be out of the question. But the faith which the Scriptures call justifying and saving is far different from a mere assent. There are, it must be confessed, a great many Christians who hold fast to a dead assent, and esteem themselves believers on account of this assent; but true believers have always protested, and will never cease to protest, against this error. To believe in the crucified

Christ is, rather, to make his expiatory death the foundation upon which one stands, the bread on which the soul feeds, the fountain from which it quenches its thirst; it is to hunger and thirst after righteousness, and yet to acknowledge one's own unrighteousness and to lay hold of Christ's righteousness and with the whole heart to rejoice in Christ's righteousness; it is with the whole soul to subscribe for one's self to that verdict which Christ, by his willing suffering of our death with us, on account of the sin of humanity, has pronounced; it is to make, with humble and yet trustful heart, the holy plea for the pardon of human guilt, which the first-born brother has offered in the name of his brothers, our own plea. To which a second element must be added. Christ, the same Christ who died for us, has risen, lives from eternity to eternity, is present with us, dwells, rules, works in the midst of us, accompanies the announcement of his word with touchings of our souls by his Spirit, apprehends our souls, — and if now thy soul in turn apprehends Him who apprehends it, that is faith. Or, to use the words of Luther in his treatise on the freedom of a Christian man, faith unites the soul with Christ as a bride is united with her bridegroom. The assurance is nowadays at times heard, that for the Christian faith and life it is essentially indifferent whether Christ has risen or not. That is about as though one should say, it is for marriage indifferent whether the bridegroom is alive or not. To him, however, who has once understood that faith is a living apprehension of the living Saviour, it is by just that understanding rendered also intelligible how Christ's righteousness can avail for the believer. Also this I can best express in the words of Luther. When the soul has by faith become Christ's bride, says Luther, " then to both, possessions, hap, mishap, and all things become common. What Christ has, is the believing soul's; what the soul has, becomes Christ's. If Christ has all possessions and blessedness, they become the soul's. If the soul has all vice and sin on it, they become Christ's." Even so, as no one doubts, that, as soon as the marriage is concluded, the married woman can regard all the property of her husband as her own, so also this can by no deep thinker be doubted, that he who by faith is in Christ and Christ in him is entitled to call Christ's righteousness his own. And experience confirms this right. For every man who in living faith lays hold of Christ has that witness in himself of which Paul, in Rom. 8, writes, "The Spirit itself beareth witness with our spirit, that we are the children of God." Thus it has been for eighteen centuries; thus it will remain. All events of the deeper soul-life, indeed, are intelligible only to him who has himself experienced them; so this deepest experience of the human soul, its faith-union with Christ, will remain to those who have not experienced the same unintelligible. But what to a Paul and a John, what to a Luther and a Calvin was the most blessed experience, we shall all do well to endeavor to experience. Therefore let us remember that word which our Lord spoke to the two who were the first in desiring to learn to know him, after the Baptist, pointing to Jesus, had cried, "Behold the Lamb of God, which taketh away the sin of the world!" namely, the word, "Come and see."

LECTURE VIII

THE AUTHENTICITY OF OUR GOSPELS

By CONSTANTIN TISCHENDORF, D. D.

PROFESSOR OF THEOLOGY AT LEIPSIC

CONSTANTIN TISCHENDORF, D. D.

BIOGRAPHICAL

Dr. LOBEGOTT FRIEDRICH CONSTANTIN TISCHENDORF, so well-known throughout the whole Christian world for his vast labors in biblical criticism and for his discovery of the "*Codex Sinaiticus*," was born at Lengenfeld, in Saxony, Jan. 18, 1815. His father was the village physician and apothecary. He studied at Plauen and Leipsic. In his school life he seems to have been remarkable for his diligence and poetical gifts. In 1836 he took a prize-medal for an essay, and another one for another essay in 1838. His first important work that brought him into notice, was his deciphering and publishing at Paris (about 1843) of a famous palimpsest, the "*Codex Ephraemi*." He published his first Greek Testament in 1841, the eighth large and critical edition of which was nearly completed at the time of his death, and in all twenty-two editions had appeared from his hand. Another one of his publications that has a wide circulation, is his little work entitled *Wann wurden unsere Evangelien verfasst?* This was translated into English and a large number of other languages. In 1844 Dr. Tischendorf made his first journey to the Orient, where, in the convent of St. Catharine, on Mount Sinai, he discovered forty-three leaves of the "*Codex Sinaiticus*." But it was not until his third journey to the same convent, in 1859, that he succeeded in finding the rest of that important work and in persuading the monks of the convent to make a present of the manuscript to the Czar of Russia. Accordingly the "*Codex Sinaiticus*" is now in the imperial library at St. Petersburg, although Dr. Tischendorf published three editions of it, one of the entire work and two of the New Testament part of it, and thus gave this codex to the whole literary world. His death occurred at Leipsic, where he was a professor, in 1874.

SUMMARY OF LECTURE VIII

THE authority of the life of Jesus depends upon the authority or genuineness of the Gospels—The evidence of this genuineness may be divided into internal and external, the external being the more important—The external testimonies may be classified as ecclesiastical, heretical, antagonistic, and apochryphal—Beginning with the Irenæan age, 170–200, we find, among the oldest external testimonies, the two earliest translations of the Gospels, the oldest Latin and the oldest Syriac—The Muratori Catalogue of the books of the New Testament is about as old (160)—About the same time appear two "Harmonies of the Gospels," one by Tatian and the other by Theophilus—Justin Martyr's "Apology" comes next—The Epistle of Barnabas is also a testimony of canonical rank—The Ignatian letters carry us up to a still earlier period (107 or 115)—The testimony of Polycarp and Papias is also important—The recently discovered prologue of the Gospel of John, and Irenæus' quotation from Papias, may finish these ecclesiastical testimonies—Of the heretical evidences, the doctrinal system of Valentine, who came to Rome about 140, may be referred to—Also Ptolemy and Heracleon, disciples of Valentine, are witnesses—Basilides carries us still further back—Marcion (came to Rome before 140) recognized, according to Tertullian, all the four Gospels, especially that of John—Of the antagonistic testimonies, the polemical treatise of Celsus, as quoted by Origen, is most important—Two writings belonging to the apochryphal testimony may be adduced, the "Testaments of the Twelve Patriarchs" and the "Acts of Pilate"—The result of all these testimonies is to show that between 140 and 110 the four Gospels were received throughout Christendom in general, and their canonical rank was acknowledged—As to the internal evidences it may be affirmed that although there are differences in the accounts of the four evangelists, these differences are far from being contradictions.

VIII

THE AUTHENTICITY OF OUR GOSPELS

BY CONSTANTIN TISCHENDORF, D. D.,
PROFESSOR OF THEOLOGY AT LEIPSIC

THE life of Jesus has become in Christian science the great question of the day. And this question engages the attention not only of professors, ecclesiastics, and other men, whose position brings them nearer to theological science; by no means, — the interest of it is shared also by the church, by the whole Christian world. Whence this interest, this significance of the question? That can be told without difficulty. For on the answer to the question, What must be said of the life of Jesus? depends in a very particular sense Christianity and the church, our faith, our salvation. But on what does the answering of the momentous question itself depend? The sources from which we derive the life of Jesus are our Gospels. On the nature of these sources, on their reliableness, their authority, therefore, depends especially the life of Jesus, depends the authority of the evangelical life of Jesus. Are our Gospels authentic or are they unauthentic? — so more definitely runs the question on whose answering the authority of the Gospels, and consequently also the authority of the life of Jesus, which they contain, is dependent. Let me, then, enter at once upon the examination, upon the answering of this question, though in the compass of an hour no full argument can be attempted.

The authenticity of the Gospels being disputed, our task is to search for proofs or evidences that they are authentic. These evidences are often divided into those which are external and those which are internal. The internal evidences have to do with the contents themselves of the Gospels. Accordingly, the opponents of the authenticity of these sacred narratives have designated many peculiarities of one or the other of them, individual details or passages, as incongruous with the character of the author. It has, for example, been said that the form of expression repeatedly used in the fourth Gospel, "The disciple whom Jesus loved," does not favor the view that John, who is to be understood by this disciple, composed the Gospel. To others, and myself among the number, this form of expression shows precisely the opposite. There is a peculiar delicacy in the evangelist's being content to make himself known by such an intimation. How could the like have occurred to the mind of a forger, of a pseudo-John? I mention this instance only to remark, that manifoldly the so-called internal evidences are made to conform to our opinions, nay, to our tastes, so that they can prove to one the contrary to what another finds in them. Entirely different is it with the external evidences. They rest upon facts which force themselves on us even against our will, which necessitate by their own weight a recognition of themselves, and that though modern skepticism questions even what is best established. It is easy to comprehend why, from the apologetic point of view, the external evidences are sought for by way of preference. It is because they, far more than the internal, are beyond the reach of skeptical caprice.

We shall, therefore, ourselves first of all notice the external testimonies to the authenticity of the Gospels. Where are they? We have to search for them in the earliest Christian literature, in those writings which followed near to, and some of them almost in connection with, the apostolic evangelical narratives. If in this literature we find traces of the existence and of the authority of the Gospels, then in them we have the proof of the Gospels' authenticity; for they prove their highest age and early repute in the church. Of far less consequence would it be, did such traces fail us; for it is conceivable that much might have been written in Christendom without any direct reference to the letter of the Gospels.

The literature to whose examination our attention is now to be given we divide into four classes: the *ecclesiastical*, the *heretical*, the *antagonistic*, and the *apocryphal*. The ecclesiastical is that which belongs to the faith and the bosom of the church itself. The heretical we can term also that of false teachers, of those errorists who, indeed, subscribed to Christianity, but at the same time adhered to their old philosophical ideas imported from heathenism or Judaism, and sought to blend them with Christianity. The third class embraces those writings which originated with different opponents of the Christian church. The apocryphal books of the New Testament, lastly, are writings which treat New Testament material arbitrarily and under the names of persons falsely represented as their authors.

Commencing, then, with the earliest ecclesiastical literature, we will take, as our point of departure, that of the Irenæan age, which may be located at perhaps from 170 to 200 (Irenæus, Bishop of Lyons, from 177 to 202), because at that time our four Gospels ruled so generally and unqualifiedly in the church that even those learned men of to-day whom we must call opponents of the Gospels' authority start from that point for their purposes. On the other hand, the immediately preceding decades of years cannot be thus passed over. Through these we are led, as could be sufficiently shown, — uncertainty being connected with only one or two decades of years, — by the two earliest translations of the Gospels, the oldest Latin and the oldest Syriac.[1] The former originated in Proconsular Africa, somewhere near modern Tunis; the latter in the country on the Euphrates. The two versions, to leave out of view the individual differences of the text, contain already precisely our four Gospels, — a circumstance which necessarily supposes the authority of these same writings in the mother church, which used the original Greek text. At the same time, perhaps about the year 160, was composed a catalogue of the books of the New Testament, which in principal part was discovered by a learned Italian of the past century, by the name of Muratori. In this catalogue the four Gospels are found, as in our customary order, at the head.[2] Lastly, not far from this same period, two writings, to be described as "Harmonies of the Gospels," make their appearance, the one from the hand of Tatian, Justin's (about 165) disciple, the other by Theophilus, before 180, Bishop of Antioch in Syria. The two works being designed to combine the four descriptions of the life of Jesus into one, could have been produced only after the quaternary number of the Gospels was completely recognized in the church.

---

[1] The version discovered some twenty years since, in the British Museum; it was presupposed by the so-called Peschito.

[2] To be sure, the first part of the fragment is lost; but since the Gospel of Luke is given as the *third*, that of John as the *fourth* Gospel, unquestionably as the first and second the Gospels of Matthew and Mark preceded.

But we go back at once to Justin Martyr, whose chief writing, with which we have particularly to do, a defence of Christianity addressed to Antoninus Pius, is very justly assigned to the year 138 or 139. In this book, as is conceded, use has been made of the first three Gospels, at least of Matthew. As to the employment of John, on which most depends, some learned men have expressed doubt. To me it seems unquestionable that Justin used John also. While this is shown by the many passages in which Justin employs John's peculiar designation of the Saviour as the Word of God, it appears with especial obviousness from a passage in the sixty-first chapter of his Apology. Here Justin writes, "Christ has said, Except ye are born again, ye cannot enter into the kingdom of heaven; but that it is impossible that they who are once born should enter a second time into their mother's womb and be born, is clear to every one." This expression must have been derived from John 3: 3–5, where to the words of Jesus on the second or new birth Nicodemus replies, "How can a man be born when he is old? can he enter the second time into his mother's womb and be born?" It would be inexplicable, should any one wish to raise such an objection as this, that the form of expression here used might accidentally occur in the writings of both John and Justin. And wholly unwarranted is the reference of this passage in Justin to Matthew 18: 3, — "Verily I say unto you, except ye be converted and become as little children, ye shall not enter into the kingdom of heaven."

Still another item from Justin I must use for our purpose. Justin tells us in the same Apology that the Memoirs of the Apostles, "called Gospels," or the Writings of the Prophets, were read every Lord's day in the assemblies of the Christians. This proves incontrovertibly that already at that day the Gospels were recognized as equally canonical with the Old Testament. That by these Gospels only our four, neither more nor less, are to be understood, is just as certain.

For one such attestation of the canonical rank of these books of the New Testament we are indebted to the Epistle of Barnabas. But this production is older by some twenty years than Justin's Apology, since, at the very latest, it cannot have been written subsequently to from 110 to 120. Here we read in the fourth chapter the words, "Let us, therefore, take care lest we be found among those of whom it is written that many were called, but few chosen." That by this Matt. 22: 14 (For many are called, but few chosen), is referred to, every one perceives at once; also, that it is an utterly fanciful shift to bring forward in place of Matthew the words in the fourth book of Ezra, "For many are born, but few shall be saved." Perhaps, however, you will ask, what is there in this reference that authorizes us to conclude upon the canonical rank of the Gospels as recognized at the time when Barnabas wrote his epistle? We are not only authorized, but required to do so by the expression, "It is written." This is the classical phrase by which the canonical writings of the Old Testament were indicated. Who does not remember that it frequently proceeded from the Saviour's own mouth? As soon as it was applied to the New Testament Scriptures, a New Testament canon sprang up side by side with that of the Old Testament. Just on this account many doubted that these important words were written by the author of the epistle, so long as only an old Latin translation, and not the original text itself, of the passage lay before us. But, fortunately, the original text has been found. It was discovered ten years ago in the ancient manuscript of the Sinaitic Bible. This decides that the expression, "It is written," belongs to the author of the epistle himself. Nor can it be objected, that the inference resulting from this decision must be limited to the Gospel of Matthew. No, it applies to all four Gospels; for there is not the least probability that one of the Gospels was regarded as canonical while the others were not so received.

Up to a still earlier period Ignatius carries us; for he wrote in either 107 or 115. Of the three different versions still extant of his letters, we must, for reasons sufficiently given in the texts themselves, assign the first rank to the so-called middle one, which consists of six letters. Besides, this version is supported even by the testimony of Eusebius (died 340), and by that which is still about two centuries older, the testimony of Polycarp. In these letters, which Ignatius composed on his journey from Antioch to his martyrdom at Rome, may be found (in the seventh chapter of his letter to the Romans) as follows: "I desire the bread of God, the bread of heaven, the bread of life, which is the flesh of Jesus Christ, the Son of God. And I desire the drink of God, the blood of Jesus Christ, who is undying love and eternal life." Are these, also, accidental expressions which anybody might have hit upon? No, they are an unmistakable reference to John 6: 41, et seq., where it is said, "I am the bread which came down from heaven. I am the bread of life. The bread that I will give is my flesh. Whoso eateth my flesh, and drinketh my blood, hath eternal life." It would be strange if testimonial force were attributable to only a strictly verbal reference. Precisely in this instance an exact verbalism was wholly aside from the purpose; besides, such exactness of quotation was certainly not needed, that the readers might be reminded directly of Ignatius' leaning here upon the evangelical narrative of John, whose disciple he was, as well as of his having in the same letter (chapter six) undoubtedly had in view a passage in Matthew.

Immediately after Ignatius' death the letter of Polycarp bears testimony to the first Epistle of John, as already Eusebius remarked. But that a testimony to the epistle is also one to the gospel, since the two writings must have had the same author, can only be questioned by a spirit of contradiction which is inimical to the truth.

And a testimony similar to that of Polycarp is borne by Papias in the five books of his expositions of the prophecies of the Lord, according to the statement of Eusebius. To this we may add the prologue to the Gospel of John, recently brought to light, which a Latin manuscript of the Gospels in the Vatican library, a manuscript of the ninth century, has drawn from a source at all events much older. In this we read, "The Gospel of John was written and delivered to the church while John was yet alive and by this apostle himself, as Papias of Hierapolis has recorded in his five books." The appeal very uncritically made to the silence of Papias respecting the same Gospel in the account of him given by Eusebius, who on his part had not the remotest thought of furnishing ancient testimonies to any of the four Gospels, is thus converted into its complete opposite. But we must not here forget the earliest testimony of all to the much suspected John, the testimony which Irenæus (v. 36, 2) extracted, as the connection shows, from this same book of Papias. No less important witnesses than the highest authorities of Papias, his "most ancient presbyters," who touched upon the rank of the apostles, depose this evidence, "Therefore, say they, the

Lord uttered the word, In my Father's house are many mansions." This we have on the authority of Irenæus, in whose work until but recently the passage was unaccountably overlooked.

These then are testimonies to our Gospels from the very bosom of the church. Their force as argument is so great that it can hardly be exceeded. Still it is of real importance to see the result we have gained on all sides confirmed. Let us therefore, according to our announcement, now pass to the heretics. What Irenæus says of them, " So well established are our Gospels that even teachers of error themselves bear testimony to them; even they rest their objections upon the foundation of the Gospels," — this we can still to-day most satisfactorily prove. First of all by the procedure of Valentine, who came from Egypt to Rome about 140. Notwithstanding the extreme arbitrariness of his doctrinal system, he appears according to Irenæus, as according to Hippolytus, Irenæus' disciple, to have depended decidedly on passages from the first three, the so-called Synoptic Gospels, and still more on John. Expressions such as the Only-begotten, the Word, Life, Light, Fulness, Truth, Grace, the Redeemer, the Comforter, pervade his entire scheme; besides, there are not wanting sentences which he has quoted literally and used in his sense. It is purely arbitrary and uncritical to suppose that on the part of the vouchers named there was in this matter a confounding of Valentine with the Valentinians, nis disciples and adherents. But it is true that the disciples follow their master's example, and corroborate the view that it appeared to Valentine an important matter to prove, even though it must be in the most artificial and forced way, the unison of his system with the Gospels, — especially with that of John, — as the holy, standard-giving, primitive writings of the church. This applies particularly to the two most distinguished disciples of **Valentine**, Ptolemy and Heracleon, the latter of whom wrote an entire commentary on the Johannine Gospel, of which Origen has preserved for us several fragments.[1]

Still farther back, to pass over all other heretics of this period, we find Basilides. He belonged, according to Eusebius, to Hadrian's age (117-138), and he also himself pretended to have received from Matthias, who was chosen to fill the traitor's place in the apostolate, certain secret doctrines. Basilides wrote, as Agrippa Castor, one of his contemporaries, tells us, twenty-four books of commentary on the Evangel, under which name the four Gospels were comprised in the second century. Moreover, Hippolytus points out several citations made by Basilides from our Gospels, two of which are from John. To destroy the force of this latter fact no artifice was left but the one employed in the instance of Valentine, — to substitute for Basilides himself, notwithstanding that Hippolytus distinctly names him, the Basilidians.

We must in this place refer yet briefly to Marcion, who before 140 came from Sinope on the Black Sea to Rome. In conformity with his antichristian prejudice against Juda-

---

[1] On the age of Heracleon comp. the 4th ed. of my little work, "Wann wurden unsere Evangelien verfasst?" (When were our Gospels written? Translation of 1st ed. published by Am. Tract Soc.) p. 48. There it is remarked, "This question (How old is Heracleon?) has been used as the masterpiece of modern falsehood invoked against Sacred Literature; and with unbelieving frivolousness it has been answered, He was the contemporary of Origen and Hippolytus." After Rich. Adalb. Lipsius had in three places of his pamphlet, "Zur Quellenkritik des Epiphanios" (1865), laid particular stress on the assertion that Heracleon was not known at all yet by Irenæus, Volckmar, Scholten, and others seized so confidently upon it, that they assigned him to the end of the second century. But the name of Heracleon is wanting only in the index to Irenæus' work; in the book itself it stands triumphant against the tendency theory of cutting down the ages of the witnesses.

ism, he rejected several of the New Testament writings, as well as mutilated and altered those he received. Tertullian, however, attests in several passages of his book against Marcion expressly, by appeal to an earlier work of the latter, that he originally had recognized all our Gospels, and particularly that of John. To overturn this assertion, some have not shunned to accuse Tertullian of having falsely imposed upon Marcion a knowledge of our Gospels, — an accusation which would be incomparably better suited to many learned professors of the present day than to that serious-minded, venerable zealot.

To the erroneous teachers we add a bitter, jeering enemy of the church, by name Celsus. His work against Christianity Origen has refuted at length, and so made the substance of it known to after ages. In this production Celsus first brought forward against the founder of our religion, and against Mary, Jewish calumnies. Then he declares he will now restrict himself exclusively to the Christians' own writings, to the "writings of the disciples of Jesus." This he did obviously for the reason that these writings were regarded by the church as of the highest authority. And he seizes upon passages from John as well as from the other Gospels. This even the impugners of our Gospels admit. Therefore some of them have declared against the commonly accepted age of Celsus, but by so doing have only made it a witness to the feebleness of their own position.[1] Origen says, in the first book of his refutation, that Celsus had been "dead a long while," and places him under "Hadrian (117–138) and later." This statement weighs more in the scale of honest reason than the vague suppositions of modern times. Absolutely nothing can be

---

[1] Comp., on this point, "Wann wurden unsere Evangelien verfasst?" 4th ed. p. 73 ff., and p. x., f.

discovered which is sufficient to disprove that Celsus lived about the middle of the second century. And so it is certainly of some importance that we have evidence from this period, given by an open enemy of Christianity, in favor of the highest esteem of our Gospels then in the church.

Of the Apocryphal literature, lastly, I will refer to but two writings. One of them bears the title, Testaments of the Twelve Patriarchs; the other, Acts of Pilate. In the former, which cannot have been composed later than about the beginning of the second century, our Gospels, especially John, as well as other portions of the New Testament, are presupposed. The other, which likewise came evidently from a Jewish-Christian hand, and indeed was designed to make the Jewish authorities, as well as Pilate, give evidence for the divinity of Christ, follows especially the Gospel of John in its representation of the proceedings at the trial of the Lord and of his death, though with the greatest freedom as to particulars. Already Justin, in his Apology to the Emperor, — 139, — cites this production as a generally received fragment of Acts. It must, therefore, at that time have been long extant, and have enjoyed peculiar respect among Christians. Inasmuch, however, as it supposes the Gospel of John more than the others, it requires the hypothesis that the former must have been already in existence about the end of the first century. As to the originality of the text of the Acts of Pilate still obtainable, notwithstanding all that may be alleged against it, I hold it to be fully credible that this same text goes back in the main to the very ancient form used by Justin.

And now what is the result of our research in the earliest Christian literature? It is this, — that already, between 110 and 140, our Gospels permeate and rule the entire church and its writings. All lives and moves in them.

Another fact attested expressly by Justin, as also by the Epistle of Barnabas, is that already in that day the canonical rank of the Gospels was recognized by the church. At what point of time and in what way this exaltation, this canonization, of the Gospels may have taken place, — on these points we have no definite information. But the Gospels were born authorities, and the recognition of them as of equal rank with the books of the Old Testament eventuated at the right time as it were of itself. Or did the Gospel of John, to select an instance, as it went forth from Ephesus, need first an ecclesiastical decree? If it came from that city immediately authenticated by the apostolic church, could any one have entertained a doubt regarding its origin, regarding its authenticity? But if it proceeded not from Ephesus, who in the world could have been persuaded that it was the work of John at Ephesus? After the centre of the Israelitish worship, Jerusalem and its temple, had fallen, the emancipation of the church from the synagogue was complete. And after, with the death of John, the last immediate disciple and apostle of the Lord was taken from the young church, and this church was dispersed everywhere, threatened and persecuted by enemies without and visited by different tendencies and dissensions within, then arose the most urgent need of finding in the Gospels, these sacred legacies to the community of believers, a succedaneum for the departed eye-witnesses of the life of Jesus, as also an authoritative rule of faith and practice for the church, that is, of elevating them to equal canonical rank with the sacred books which had passed over from the synagogue to the church.

But what, then, shall we say respecting the efforts of those who impugn the authority of the Gospels, whose cry of victory is based upon precisely the opposite results to ours? Are they vanquished? Oh, there always remains a convenient method of reply, a very ready way of parrying all our results. It is by casting suspicion upon all that the church and science have hitherto regarded as incontrovertibly established as to the history of the second century; it is by substituting for a sound an unsound historical investigation, by setting in the place of genuine science skeptical arbitrariness, criticism falsely so-called. A feature or two of this criticism we have already indicated. At one time it is denied, in spite of the greatest obviousness, that a Gospel quotation is made; at another, recourse is had for help to lost documents; one of these would-be critics rejects entire writings as ungenuine because not suited to his preconceptions, or, at least, decides that those very passages on which the question turns have been interpolated; another represents the witnesses as younger than they are; still another reverses the relations, as, for example, the author of the fourth Gospel has been made to borrow from Justin or from Valentine; in short, everything is undertaken that flight from the truth suggests. Now to all this no word seems more suited than that of Paul in his Epistle to the Romans (1 : 22), "Professing themselves to be wise they became fools."[1]

[1] Many particulars, here only hastily touched, or even wholly passed by, have been more thoroughly treated in the author's writing, "Wann wurden unsere Evangelien verfasst?" Leipsic, 4th ed., 1866, 1st ed., 1865. The translations of it, in their different forms, English, French, Italian, Dutch, Swedish, Russian, have appeared in thirteen different editions. But also treatises and extended articles against it, in German, French, English, Dutch, have not been wanting. They are noticed in part in the Leipsic edition. Unnoticed remains the Hollander Scholten's treatise, "Die ältesten Zeugnisse," which appeared in Bremen, rendered into German by an ecclesiastic of that city, and has been commonly announced by booksellers as "Scholten contra Tischendorf." There is nothing in it that could occasion the least change in my conviction. How fully it belongs to the old rationalistic and the so-called Tübingen stand-point the Hollander Hofstede de Groot has admirably shown in the German edition (Leipsic, 1868) of his apologetic writing, "Basilides."

However, we have not yet fully solved our problem. For, besides the external evidences, we set before us the examination of those which are internal. At least something from this wide field must not be wanting to our present discourse.

I mention, to begin with, an item which occupies, as it were, an intermediate position between the external and the internal evidences. In it, it has been imagined a historical testimony was discovered against the fourth Gospel. John celebrated the Christian eucharist with the churches of Asia Minor on the 14th of Nisan; in the fourth Gospel, however, it is stated that on the 14th of Nisan Christ died on the cross, while according to the first three Gospels Jesus ate, with his disciples at the same time, the paschal lamb in connection with the institution of the supper. Does not the feast custom of John, therefore, contradict the fourth Gospel? Not in the least. The alleged contradiction rests on the assumption that the Christian eucharist was joined, so to express one's self, on to the day of the institution of the Lord's Supper. But this supper appears rather, according to the teaching of Paul, that Christ is our passover who was sacrificed for us (1 Cor. 5: 7), to have been linked with the day of the death of Christ, as the true paschal lamb. It is the same with many other objections.

However, the assertion is not incorrect, that one evangelist gives this, another that. In Luke the birth of Jesus is announced to Mary, in Matthew to Joseph. The accounts of Peter's denials vary. Of the events at the crucifixion one Gospel narrates what the other does not. The same is true of the appearances of the risen Saviour. Generally, however, we miss in John very much that the other evangelists have recorded. The explanation of these differences is to be found, first of all, in the fragmentary character of our Gospels. It was not the intention of any one of the evangelists to compose a regular biography of Jesus. That in Jesus of Nazareth the Christ of the Lord had appeared, — this they all bring out in their biographical sketches, each according to his peculiar design. Moreover, many of these divergencies are far from being contradictions. And, for the right understanding of the fourth Gospel, it is peculiarly necessary to assume that John wrote with a full knowledge of the three earlier composed Gospels, and that not the least governing principle in his work was the supplementing of these. The oldest intelligence we have, which is a tradition preserved by Eusebius, respecting the composition of John's Gospel, supports this view. It is of not a little interest, though a process very greatly abused, to trace out the various particulars in this Gospel which allude to that relation.

Another specification brought forward is the great difference which a comparison of the first three Gospels with the fourth reveals in the teachings of Jesus. There we have the simple parables, here the long abstruse discourses. But cannot this difference be easily explained? The parables were addressed to the common people of Galilee; they were the popular element in Jesus' instruction; they most readily impressed themselves upon, and certainly were especially retained in, the memory. That they are found in the very foreground of the Synoptic Gospels harmonizes with the entire character of these Gospels. John, on the other hand, represents the Saviour chiefly in his intercourse at Jerusalem with the Pharisees and scribes. The discourses which he communicates lived in his personal remembrance; they are by no means of such an order that any one could so easily have delivered them. And, after all, is it not the same spirit that rules in both kinds of teaching? Rules there not in both a striving to lead from the near at hand, the natural, the simple, up to the spiritual, the high, the heavenly? John gives us the discourses on the bread of life, on the living water, concerning the good shepherd, about the true vine; does not all this agree with the parables? Besides, are not the long discourses found in the Synoptic Gospels, as in John, shortly before the last great events? and, in turn, are there not many of the Synoptists' expressions to be discovered also in John?

But particular stress is laid upon this,— that the person of the Saviour itself appears different in the narrative of John from the representations given of Jesus by the other evangelists. The latter portray him as the Son of man; John makes him to be the Son of God. As an objection to the credibility of our Gospels, this criticism has wholly failed. And as complete a failure is the supposition that in this designation is presented a foreign appropriation made by the author of the fourth Gospel. It is true, the use of the two designations was dependent upon the educational purpose which the Lord must have had in view with regard to his disciples and to the people. But even in respect to his person the most complete harmony is revealed in the different representations. To be sure, with John the designation of Jesus as the Son of God especially rules; but this forms the necessary basis for the characteristic representations of the Synoptics. How otherwise shall we understand such expressions occurring in the latter as these: "He that loveth father or mother more than me is not worthy of me;" "All things are delivered unto me of my Father; and no man knoweth the Son, but the Father; neither knoweth any man the Father, save the

Son, and he to whomsoever the Son will reveal him;" "Not every one that saith unto me, Lord, Lord, shall enter into the kingdom of heaven;" "Whosoever shall confess me before men, him will I confess also before my Father which is in heaven"? Is not this in perfect accord with John's representations of the Son of God, as, e. g., when we read, "He that believeth on the Son hath everlasting life;" "Who convinceth me of sin?" "He that believeth not is condemned already;" "I and my Father are one"? Just this agreement of the evangelists on the divine character of the person of Christ, notwithstanding all their many differences in details, is of the greatest consequence. And observe how much all these utterances aim at the person itself of the Saviour. Could a mortal have spoken thus of himself without committing blasphemy? I know no way of escape; if Christ was not what he claimed to be, the Son of God, then he spoke with blasphemous audacity. And how far from the representation, common to all the Gospels, of this sublime, heavenly personality, is the thought that we have here to do with a product of the reflection and fancy of the first Christian community. To attempt such an explanation of the Gospels is to wander off into the realm of the most unintelligible. It is an error which overleaps the bounds of both the possible and the wonderful.

But the reply will be made to me, with all this the contradictions of the Gospels are not solved. That such are in fact presented, though many have been arbitrarily and erroneously alleged, I do not deny. On the other hand, I do deny that the credibility of the Gospels, so far as the divine person of the Lord and his divine redemption are concerned, is affected by them. We have, of course, no right to affirm a mechanical inspiration of the evangelists which secures against every error; the character of the Gospels itself forbids that. The evangelists wrote their books from human points of view and under human relations; impenetrated with the Divine Spirit, they scientifically and to the best of their knowledge drew up their records. That here and there they do not altogether agree, proves that they wrote with a certain independence and far from all artificialness. Inasmuch as the Synoptic Gospels, after which came John, could not have been composed earlier than between the years 60 and 70 of the first century, as was the view also taken by Irenæus, who, first of the church fathers, wrote on this topic, nothing is more intelligible than the differences we find in many of the Gospel narrations as to each other. But does not this leave manifold opportunity for doubt? If that were not so, to me the nature of faith would seem to be injured. Would faith then have its full worth, if the possibility of doubt were wanting?

The faith of the Scriptures is faith in the Son of God. He who confesses that Jesus is the Son of God, God dwells in him and he in God. To this declaration of John (1 John 4) the church has to hold fast. No other than the faith of the Scriptures, obviously, can apply to itself the promises of the Scriptures. Salvation is promised to it. It must be a great act to which so much is promised. It is an act of God himself; for that is implied in the words of Christ, "No man can come to me, except the Father draw him." And it is an act of our own hearts; otherwise it could not be said, "He that believeth not is condemned already." The most learned man can make no one a believer. Faith must be the innermost product of the heart; it must be one's own property; only from within can proceed the decision in the most important concern of life. This decision must, however, be a victory over all motions of doubt; and the more we have to overcome doubt, the fuller and the stronger becomes our faith. With this, then, the structure of our Gospels is most fully in harmony. It is not an accidental make-up, but belongs essentially to our stand-point, to our need. No document is put into our hands which excludes all doubt, which from its own nature convinces everybody. We stand to the Lord rather to-day as did the Pharisees who referred his wonderful works to the devil. The question presents itself, whether this Pharisaic unbelief is not after all worth more than the infidelity of these times, which resolves the Gospel miracles into mist and vapor.

It is a pernicious error of the times to pay especial homage to the spirit of negation; as though apprehending and recognizing were not more noble than misconstruing and assailing. Erudition, indeed, has never had the key to the kingdom of heaven. "Blessed are the poor in spirit." This being spiritually poor is suited to man and woman, high and low, learned and unlettered. How else would the Gospel be a power of God to the saving of all who believe in it? Unbelief is as old as Christianity; besides, it will never die out. But in the midst of the world of unbelief there is a large, royal band of those who believe. Did we wish to number them all, the heroes of faith, from John and Paul down, we should find many whom history has recorded among the foremost representatives of our race. The Lord's saying, "He that believeth not is condemned already," will to the end of days retain its crushing weight. Let us, therefore, take that word home to our hearts which the Apostle Paul addressed to his most loved church, that at Philippi, "Work out your own salvation with fear and trembling."

LECTURE IX

THE IDEA OF THE KINGDOM OF GOD AS CONSUMMATED, AND WHAT IT TELLS US REGARDING HISTORICAL CHRISTIANITY

By J. P. LANGE, D. D.

PROFESSOR AT BONN

BIOGRAPHICAL

Dr. JOHANN PETER LANGE, the great Bible commentator and author of so many other literary works, is described as being small of stature, with a benignant face, bright eye, and vigorous constitution. He was one of the most fertile and original theological writers of the nineteenth century. He was born on a farm in the parish of Sonnborn, near Elberfeld, Prussia, April 10, 1802; died at Bonn, July 8, 1884. After attending the gymnasium at Düsseldorf, he entered the university at Bonn in 1822. There he was particularly influenced by Professor Nitzsch. For a year after leaving the university he was pastoral assistant at Langenberg to Rev. Emil Krummacher, brother of the celebrated Dr. F. W. Krummacher. Then he became Reformed pastor of Wald in 1826, of Langenberg in 1828, and of Duisberg in 1832. While at the last-named place he attracted attention by his brilliant articles in Hengstenberg's *Kirchenzeitung*, by his poems, and by an able publication upon the Saviour's infancy. In 1841, after Strauss had been prevented from taking his professorship of theology in the University of Zürich, Dr. Lange was called to this position. There he elaborated his extensive work on the life of Jesus, which was a reply to Strauss, and being widely circulated in German and English, had a marked effect upon the large subsequent literature on this topic. In 1854 Dr. Lange became a professor at Bonn, and in 1860 he was made consistorialrath. His great *Bibelwerk* he planned and superintended himself, engaging some twenty different scholars to assist in the literary labor. He himself wrote the commentaries on Matthew, Mark, John, Romans, Revelation, Genesis, Exodus, Leviticus, Numbers, Haggai, Zechariah, and Malachi.

SUMMARY OF LECTURE IX

THE idea of the kingdom of God as consummated is a spiritual highland, and still more formidable would appear our undertaking to draw from that idea conclusions regarding the present times and the ancient foundations of that kingdom—A great, instructive, corrective, and determinative efficacy is contained in a look to the ends and aims of life—*Proposition one:* The world is under the control of God—*Proposition two:* the end which God has in view regarding the world is the establishment of a dominion of perfected, free, personal, spiritual beings, united in love—*Proposition three:* the basis of the world at the creation must have been a plastic, impelling idea; also, in the general idea of creation Christ really comes before Adam—*Proposition four:* The Spirit, which overcomes the great antagonism between the rule of God over the world and the perfect freedom of souls, presupposes the sacred history and especially the life of Christ—All natural life unfolds itself in harmonious antagonisms; so also with the rich historical life of humanity as the basis and preliminary condition of God's kingdom—The antagonisms in history preceding Christianity may be specified as follows: the *individual*, the *psychological*, the *ethnological*, and the *economic*—In Christianity the individual antagonism perfects itself in the *organic*, the psychological in the *allegorical*, the ethnological in the *social*, and the economic in the *cosmical*—There are three kingdoms which God has in connection with our world: the kingdom of power, the kingdom of grace, and the kingdom of glory—Order of the moments in the consummation of the divine kingdom—At last heaven and earth will pass away as divided life-districts, to come together in the appearance of the city of God—The conclusions to be drawn from this consummation are particularly two, one concerning the superiority and reign of spirit over matter, and the other concerning a reconstruction of our present ecclesiastical social life.

IX

THE IDEA OF THE KINGDOM OF GOD AS CONSUMMATED, AND WHAT IT TELLS US REGARDING HISTORICAL CHRISTIANITY

BY J. P. LANGE, D. D.,

PROFESSOR AT BONN

THE theme of discussion which I have the honor to bring before you has been, in its essential thought, suggested to me by your honorable committee. In so doing, your committee has required of both speaker and hearer a somewhat formidable undertaking. The idea of the kingdom of God in its consummation is unmistakably a spiritual highland; the next hour, therefore, is to be occupied by us in a spiritual mountain ascent. We cannot, however, deny, that, in our times, the physical traversing of Alps is more the order of the day than is the spiritual. Yet this reflection will not disturb a select audience of a bold northern maritime city. More suspicious might a second task appear to us, which the honorable committee has connected with our first. From the kingdom of God as consummated, i. e., in any case, from the idea of the farthest and highest scope of our Christian faith, from

---

[1] The lecture here presented was delivered at Bremen in large part extemporaneously. Consequently, it accords strictly neither with the original sketch, nor with the oral discourse. The oral discourse, adapting itself to time and place, naturally touched upon many matters here omitted, especially many more scientific moments. On the other hand, meditation furnished many additions. In essentials, however, the present rendering fully reproduces the Bremen discourse.

the still greatly concealed consummation of the still concealed kingdom of God, we are to draw conclusions regarding present times, nay, regarding the foundation anciently laid of that kingdom.

And yet this design, seemingly quite too bold, is, closely inspected, a truly happy thought. The question of the goal of life diffuses, wherever it is earnestly asked, a peculiar light upon the ways of life at the very place where one is standing. The immediate consciousness of present endowments is, as an anticipation of the future, one of the most potent guiding stars of life. He who has earnestly fixed his eyes upon the true object of his life will surely find also the right way. The mother bows over her child in the cradle with the thought, he is to become a good, worthy man; this heart-thought becomes the light of the nursery, the tenor of the maternal prayers, the rule of the child's education. Above all things else, the haven, the end of the journey, is had in view by the mariner; and from this look ahead is shaped the certainty of the voyage under the motto, *Navigare necesse est, vivere non*.[1] Just so Israel by a great religio-ethical look forward to the end of the world's course became the blessed people of the future, and would have remained the first-born among the nations, had it kept its forecast untarnished. There is, then, in the look to the ends and aims of life a great instructive, corrective, and determinative efficacy. If we cannot possibly walk together longer, then it behooves us to make a last attempt with the question of the unity of aims. In the dispute concerning the ultimate ends, the mere exchanging of views ceases, here the ways differ and divide in ethical form. Among them, however, are distinguished, with respect to this form,

---

[1] The motto of the Bremen "Seefahrt," the building in which the lecture was given.

the Hierarchical and the Protestant extremes; the author of the Syllabus pronounces in advance all views dissenting from his system godless, while the absolute protest, i. e., the absolute skepticism of the second degree, in the livery of thoughtlessness, demands that even the most radical negatives, which dissipate all the common religio-moral aims of humanity, shall be urged upon the conscience of no one. According to the first extreme, Christ could have said to the tempter in the wilderness, perhaps already with the first temptation, " Get thee hence, Satan!" According to the latter extreme, he should have answered him even after the third and last temptation, which disclosed his devilish design as the negation of all real aims: I have a different view on that point. Christianity, however, in the question of aims, will have to do least of all with unseasonable diversions. Therefore, the Apostle Peter, the same who refuted the frivolous judges who said of the phenomena occurring on the first Whitsuntide, " These men are full of new wine," with the quite dispassionate words, " It is but the third hour of the day " (9 A. M.), — the same has characterized the deniers of the Christian end of the world, who with sweeping rejection say, " Where is the promise of his coming?" as simply scoffers walking after their own lusts. The justification of this verdict, however, is found in the self-contradiction of which these persons are guilty who, in the concrete apprehension of the advent of the Lord, deny the moral aim of the world. While they deny not only the specifically Christian teleology, but also in general all teleology, all ends and ultimate ends in the world, they run with excitement and passion after their own false ends, and thus show that they have done with making life a poor jest. As it has been often and justly remarked, that absolute doubters refute themselves, since they make of doubt a great tenet;

that absolute protestants refute themselves, since they make the setting aside of all dogmas the principal dogma, the abolition of all confessions the modern confession;[1] so, in an eminent degree, this holds good also of those who put before them the particular end of banishing all ends from acknowledgment in the world of thought and from the reality of the objective world. Thus even the false ends of egotism must testify to the inalienable existence of the true religio-moral ends grounded in the world's very constitution.

We now premise at once, that man is a social being; that mankind is a unit, and that this unit has a history, — a history, which is above that of nature, entirely distinct from zoölogy into which some would degrade it, a regular development from a definite basis, according to definite laws, to a definite end; that is the end of the world. But can we now go farther and say, The end of the world is the kingdom of God in its consummation?

Let me indicate some general propositions, the truth of which we must assume to be granted, as we cannot here discuss them without going aside from the subject immediately in hand, — the postulates, then, upon which our affirmation rests, The end of the world is the kingdom of God in its consummation.

Proposition one. The world is subject to God, to the true, personal, i. e., eternally self-conscious, absolutely free God, who is love itself. Because he is free and spiritual, he has created and upholds the world as correspondingly free and spiritual.

Proposition two. The end which this God has in view regarding the world is none other than the establishment

---

[1] **As**, indeed, even the negative thinkers in Paris style themselves Positivists.

of a dominion under his own government of perfected, free, personal, spiritual beings united in love.

Proposition three. The great antagonism which exists between the absolute rule of God over the world and the perfect freedom of souls, and exists seemingly as a contradiction, will be eliminated by the Spirit of God, who desires to impart himself to all, so as to unite all.

Proposition four. As the wind, the symbol of the Spirit, is not an empty air-current which drives restlessly through the empty ether, but the one, agitated life of the earth which relates to the infinitely fine organism of the earth's form, so the Spirit of God, who establishes the kingdom of God, is not a pseudo-spirit, who with Indio-Brahmanical jingle of phrases about spirit, and non-spirit, comes whirling in, but He relates to the one organism of mankind and to his revelation in the essential Word, hence also to the Head of this organism, the one concentration of the revealed Word, to Christ. The other Paraclete, it is therefore said, will not speak of himself, but whatsoever he shall hear, that shall he speak; he presupposes the sacred history.

Accordingly we affirm with the utmost confidence, The end of the world is the kingdom of God as consummated, i.e., the full actuality of the human, free, spiritual kingdom blessed in love, — a kingdom which God in his personal manifestation in Christ has founded, founded by creation and by redemption, to perfect it, by the sanctifying of men, to a blessed community of life and love under the rule of the Word, in the freedom of the Spirit, even to its coming glorious appearance.

Still, we are to speak not merely of the consummation of this kingdom, but also of the value of its idea in the explanation of the relations of historical Christianity.

Yet as soon as we approach our entire problem, we encounter obstacles which must be removed in a preliminary way, to wit, modern obscurations of all the foundations of the kingdom of God. In other words, we shall have to ascend gradually through the hill-country before we come to the highland proper. This hill-country is the beautiful riches potentially in that humanity which is destined to be the bride of Christ. As all fulness of life, these riches spread out in definite antagonisms, which are each the exact counterpart of the other.

We shall therefore speak, first, of the bases of the kingdom of God in the great antagonisms of human life; secondly, of the kingdom of God itself in its different fundamental forms as related to the form of its consummation; thirdly, of the leading questions of our day which from this luminous goal receive their proper irradiation. Inasmuch as the bases of the kingdom are, in the first part, to be set in the light over against modern obliterations, I pray you not to regard a somewhat protracted sojourn in this division as delay.

All natural life unfolds itself in harmonious antagonisms; in the antagonism of form and matter; of root and top; of male and female; of soul and body. Accordingly, the rich historical life of humanity also, as the basis and preliminary condition of the kingdom of God, presents itself in a fulness of antagonisms. And here already we must, alas, depose, that all these antagonisms, and therefore also all these questions, antecedent to our question, are, without exception, injured, yea, manifoldly obliterated, by a method of thought which boasts of being modern, albeit it has long since passed through its old and musty age in ancient India.

Yet we shall have to confess, also, that an extreme orthodoxy has shared largely, has even been a principal in the guilt of this obliteration.

As such antagonisms, which in primitive history precede Christianity, I mention the *individual*, the *psychological*, the *ethnological*, and the *economic* antagonisms. With Christianity itself, again, four new antagonisms, which, indeed, previously existed, appear with perfected definiteness, in a certain measure, as the higher powers of the first antagonisms. The *individual* antagonism perfects itself in the *organic;* the *psychological* in the *allegorical;* the *ethnological* in the *social;* the *economic* in the *cosmical antagonism*.[1]

In part strange designations! They will, however, I trust, become intelligible enough by the elucidation, — perhaps will seem at times only too intelligible.

By the *individual* antagonism I understand, that with the truth of the human individuality, *according to which man is raised above the conception of a representative of his genus*, the endless difference of individualities in quantity and quality is already postulated, and then, as a consequence thereof, appears also in the great antagonism of creative spirits and receptive communities. But here says a new religion-founder of the latest agitation save one, "I am a man; about me are men; behind me, before me, mere men; Christ was also a man." We cannot altogether deny the serene man's assertion; but this is to be remarked in passing, between man and man there is a difference, as there is between the mighty cedar and the dwarf-fir on the heath; between the heaven-reaching palm, and the little holly in the forest. And in this connection the question might be put, why has the old doctrine of the elect been

---

[1] The physiological, elementary antagonisms might have been discussed previously, viz.: soul and body, spirit and nature, freedom and necessity, first and second life; but this would have led too far.

left out of notice so much of late in theology, on account of its old, hard, discouraging, but also outworn form? It might so happen that a dialectically clever man, who himself believes strongly enough in the elect of his party, even now charges the old doctrine of election upon the reformers, instead of inquiring whether a kernel of truth has not, perhaps, been sticking in the shell which burst long since.[1] It might even be that to-day many theologians, with all compliments for the comparative greatness of the absolutely elect of the elect, are endeavoring to take the crown of that peerless greatness from him, while just now the philologists, the poets, the profane historians, are crowning anew with enthusiasm their elect.

The second antagonism, the *psychological*, expresses the fact that man, as a spiritual being, develops his life in the reciprocal action of a double form of consciousness, the reflecting consciousness turned toward our earthly days and the earth, and the more noctural, visionary, intuitive consciousness, which is directed toward the universe; therefore, also, toward the manifestations of a higher world.

This fact, of which Socrates in his mysterious tutelary genius, his δαιμόνιον, had an experience; which Plato designated by his divine μανια, by the frenzy or ecstasy of poets and philosophers; which Josephus knew of; concerning which philosophers like Krause and Hegel, and poets like Atterbom, have expressed dark hints, — this fact authors such as Perty, and as the deceased prince of Neuwied, have denominated the place, or rather the pole in the human soul-life, by which the same becomes an

---

[1] "Jaxthausen is a castle on the Jaxt," said the little son of Götz von Berlichingen, from the school-book, without imagining that he was at the time himself in the castle.

organ for revelations of a new and higher world, for new revelations of God himself, above the universal revelation through creation and the inner human life. One of the leaders of the latest theological agitation, however, the well-known Dr. Schenkel, would, to be sure, inform us that not the reason, not the will, not even the susceptibility, relates to Deity, but only the conscience, the isolated conscience. This is to be designated as the need of truth, and this need is an organ, and this organ is, so far as is possible, an organ for the reception of higher influences. In this so-called organ, then, stands the moon in her last quarter, like a little gray cloud in the clear day, over against the real sun of revelation, i. e., the consciousness of Christ, as the approved ability to behold the Father in his providence, all eternity in time, all heaven in the phenomena of the universe, and so also to authenticate the sharpest judgment regarding the things of the world.

We have, consequently, found the elect man and the all-comprehending revelation-organ of the same, a wholly unique genius-life, in which the height of humanity and the depth of divinity can come together in one, — and only in the depth of divinity can such a life have its foundation. For it is a modern weakness of thought, when in these days the human is manifoldly made the primary determining principle for the divine; as though it were easier for man to become God than for God to become man, easier to ascend up to heaven than to come down from heaven. Even the incarnation of God, or of the Son of God, required a great historical mediation through the people of God.

Thus we come to the third antagonism, the *ethnological*. Two ridges run parallel to each other through the history of the old world to Christ. It is the antagonism of Shem and Japheth, the antagonism of two kinds of blessing, the blessing of a stable worship of God and the blessing of a restless spiritual conquest of the world; yet *not to be confounded with the very similar antagonism of Seth and Cain.* The idiosyncrasies of the Hebrew religious turn of mind and of the Greek radically human turn of mind are as far apart as the east is from the west; e. g., in the immediateness of the Hebrew, in the mediateness or the mediation-talent of the Greek language, in the symbolism characteristic of the one side, in the mythology peculiar to the other, in the divine content with the Hebrews, in the classical human form with the Greeks. But just because of this extreme difference the two tendencies were suited to each other; they must become one in Christianity. But if an injudicious friend of the Holy Scriptures desired to criticise the Greek forms, or even the ecclesiastic classical forms, after the pattern of the Hebrew forms (e. g., Homer after Job), that would surely be denominated presumptuous ignorance. And yet the whole development of the Hebrew theocracy, including its New Testament consummation, is still manifoldly criticised (especially by Strauss) exclusively after ideas which have been derived from the Greek or the Greco-Roman antiquity. Certainly the second onesidedness is not better than the first.

Also the fourth antagonism of the old time is overborne by the most manifold obscurations and obliterations; it is the *economic* antagonism. According to the Sacred Scriptures the history of the revelation of salvation branches off into the history of the Old Testament theocracy, as the typical prefigurement of the New Testament real Kingdom of God, and into the history of the founding of this kingdom upon the groundwork of the patriarchal period; or into the period of the people of God in their minority, who had by a written law and ceremonial picture-language to be educated for faith, and into the epoch of the appearance of the people of God attained to majority, for whom the law had become spiritual life, and the picture-language living word. Now we know that, in consequence of the great migration of nations, and the water baptism of nations, this relation has in the church been repeating itself, and that with the Reformation a period of majority began a second time. Accordingly, our Evangelical Christian people should now move as securely upon the new stage, as the Christians of the apostolic times moved upon the stage of manhood; since they, with victorious clearness, struck through the extremes, the legalistic Ebionism of the Judaizers on the one hand, and the antinomian libertinism of the Gnostics on the other. But how many vacillations appear here on our stage: Tractarians, Ritualists (Germany, too, has, alas, its Ritualists, who are indirectly working into the hands of non-ecclesiasticism), Confessionalists of the most diverse classes, pure representatives of the Statute, and on the other side numerous Neo-Gnostic forms of unmannerliness, libertinism, social insubordination, which claim first of all to be real freedom and majority. The index of maturity, however, is the full conservation of the pure content of the experienced pedagogical training relieved of its shell, and the free use of discipline as a prophylactic to relapsing into minority, and the conservation of freedom is respect for the freedom of others, for the right, for the abandoned stage itself; while modern Gnosticism, which puts before us the prospect of a new knowledge, but in the mean time serves us with mere lawlessness, is even now threatened with a complete relapse under tutelage, as could be shown by documents, with the names of places, persons, and tendencies.

The first clearly New Testament antagonism is the *organic*, the *consummation of the individual*. Here the entire greatness of the antagonism with the entire intimacy of the union is expressed. Christ the shepherd, his people the flock; Christ the foundation-stone, those who are his living stones of the spiritual temple; Christ the vine, they the branches; Christ the bridegroom, the church the bride; Christ the head, the church his body. Even this harmonious antagonism between the highest authority and the highest liberty is seldom kept pure in its ideality. Not to speak of those who would, with hierarchical mediations, because of the greatness of the antagonism, break through this intimate and indissoluble connection, — in how many ways, even on our own grounds, is this sacred union injured! And if we complain especially that the dignity of Christ, the God-man, the Redeemer, is so manifoldly detracted from and disparaged, yet we would not forget that the dignity of man is also, in many ways, still disfigured by dwarfed and distorted forms of living Christianity. Yet would any one have the entire intimacy of the spiritual union with Christ, let him manifest it by keeping pure the entire difference, the entire sublimity of Christ; and would he glorify this sublimity, then he should remember that even Christ himself would see himself glorified in his members. But how much the true knowledge of human dignity is conditioned by the true knowledge of God, — this the latest times have taught. First the idea of a personal God was obliterated, then the picture of Christ, the God-man; at present many are already on the way to a denial of the truth of human nature.

A second antagonism has its force even in the Old Testament, but first attains its full significance in the New, the *allegorical, as a higher power of the psychological.* It is the difference between faith itself, or the truths of faith, and the temporary conceptions in which they are clothed. The distinction rests upon the law of the development of all life. It is truly remarkable how uncertain and fluctuating are the ideas of the law of life-development even yet. The idea which, e. g., Hegel had of the development of all life, and particularly of the history of philosophy, is at present, although his thoughts on development have been in themselves abundantly appreciated, an idea long since condemned in philosophy. But the Hegelian error, that every development of life starts from the poorest form, and by its poverty, by its contradiction, produces the antithesis, with this to gain a richer form in the synthesis, — this error the Tübingen theologian Bauer, in unfortunate dependence upon the school-philosophy, has applied to the apostolic age, and from the sad heritage of it comes a great part of the present boisterous opposition to the Bible. The whole method is the posthumous offspring of a defunct philosophy, a cast-off philosopher's mantle, and so the court-dress of the "modern theology." A consequence thereof is the utter confounding of the temporary conception of faith with the eternal content of faith. But Christ has clearly indicated for us the law of development, in his beautiful parable of the growth of the seed (Mark 4 : 26–28). First the seed, then the blade, the stalk, after that the ear, then the full corn in the ear. Here, now, is the law of all development, clear; the forms change, the substance, the essence, remains specifically the same; the only alteration consists in the fact that the seed reappears in the harvest, not poorer, but richer; not that perhaps from many sound grains is left in the end only one little mother-grain, but that the seed cast into the ground reappears with much fruit. Yet for many even this little parable seems to be too high a school. With the invariableness of the essence some would have the forms to be also invariable, either by inventing a constancy of the same forms, or arresting the formation of forms, even crowding it back into the middle ages or into the seventeenth century. These choke and smother the living essence with dead forms. Another class, on the contrary, would have the essence to vary constantly with a morbidly increased change of the forms, so that with the lawless play of form the essence itself is dissipated; e. g., we are to believe that Christianity, as early as during the first three centuries, changed its peculiar form two or three times. Again, the confession-obligation, which once was a free, self-obligating of the body of believers, and made of it a spiritual phalanx over against all the hierarchical powers of the world, we are to-day to regard as but a despotic fetter and hierarchical statute. So also the moral discipline to be used by the church, which once proved itself the salt of the earth and made of morally sunken cities widely illuminating places of piety and culture, is to be in these times rejected as working only hyprocrisy.

But as the promise of salvation in the Scriptures passes through many perishable forms, and remains always the same in substance, only becomes continually richer, continually more distinct and definite, so the fulfilment of this promise, Christianity, also passes through the ecclesiastical times and their forms, only continually more richly unfolded. Now as to the distinction between faith and the conceptions of faith, upon which the law of ecclesiastical development rests, we cannot be mistaken in affirming that many wholly mistake and obliterate this distinction, grounded, as it is, upon the antagonism between the temporal conceptions and reflections and the internal experience and intuition of man directed towards eternity. And herein the neological theology agrees perfectly with the dead orthodoxy, that it holds the temporary conceptions of faith to be the real faith itself. We know, on the contrary, that in the old covenant the rainbow had a sacramental import, then the stars of heaven, afterward circumcision and the passover, until the sacrament appeared in the New Testament form; that also in the church faith has passed through manifold conceptions. For faith itself the sacrament has by all its changes in form become constantly richer and more beautiful, while the people either no longer know any sacramental certainty of the hollow conception or adhere to antiquated school-forms and church-forms, which have made temporary investures of the sacrament. So the word of God is the living unity of the letter and the spirit. The word is letter, says one party, therefore it must be understood absolutely according to the letter; the word is letter, says the other party, therefore it must give place to the free wordless spirit. Thus one of the parties puts the whole accent of the idea of faith upon the letter, or, in other words, upon the momentary exegesis of the letter, exchanging the living word for a dead letter; the other does the same thing, substituting for the dead word a vague fancy of spirit.[1] But faith itself has never accented its passing conceptions. The ark of Noah has disappeared; the essence of the ark has remained in the church. The altar with the sacrifice has disappeared; the essence of the sacrifice, the eternal propitiation in the death of Christ, has

---

[1] Moreover, persons of the one party often become those of the other, as with a turning of the hand.

remained. Elijah let his mantle fall, the pious Hezekiah destroyed the brazen serpent, Jehovah twice suffered his temple to be consumed by fire; all this change of form impoverished not, but in each case enriched, faith itself. When, now, a dead legalism accents the perishable forms, it is, at least for the most part, honorable narrowness; if, however, they are accented for the purpose of characterizing faith itself as perishable, this cannot, at least frequently, be so honorably intended; among other things an unmistakably bad consciousness is therein operative. But could a poet complain that the cast-off integuments of his development are pulled about and beaten, much more has faith a right to protect itself against the violence which pulls and tears at its cast-off vestments, as if they had to be arranged as grave-clothes for itself. So one tears at the clerical and theocratic church-regulations of the sixteenth century; another at the overstrained doctrine of inspiration prevalent in the seventeenth century;[1] a third at the ascetic forms of piety in the eighteenth century. Faith itself, however, has at all times sought its essentiality as little in its vestments as if it had clothed itself in pure ether or the aurora.[2] I mean to affirm this, however, not merely of universal religious ideas, but of the real full faith of the kingdom of God. An illustration will make the entire distinction clear. The Christian believes still to-day, with the Holy Scriptures, in heaven and hell. Now, the mediæval Christian found heaven above the firmament,

---

[1] Vid. Rothe: Zur Theologie. Besides, the object of the fantastic knighthood is to the utmost disfigured, as if the theological doctrine of inspiration in the seventeenth century had gone even beyond the Montanistic, and made of man a mere machine. Such a caricature is then charged not merely to the theology of the seventeenth century, but also to the church of present times.

[2] Comp. Rom. 10: 6 ff., Deut. 30: 12, 13. Also the different representations of *Scheol*.

hell in the interior of the earth. These conceptions have fallen, cries one to us; consequently there remains at most a sort of heaven and of hell in the human breast. But faith is to-day as certain as in the middle ages of its conviction that all the inner relations in God's world come likewise to appearance; that, therefore, at some time a separation between matured sanctification and matured obstinacy will occur, and that internal happiness will find likewise its home, and internal unhappiness also its place. The local particularities, however, in themselves considered, cohere with passing conceptions and reflections which rest upon temporary views of the world; they have never been the concern of revelation and faith. But the newer cosmology knows much more (with the anticipating words of the Lord) of the many mansions in the Father's house than did the old; also of terrible world-wastes. Nay, we can say generally, as it regards the conceptions, faith in the midst of the new knowledge of the world is much less at a loss for apparel, and, indeed, true royal apparel, than in the midst of the old. So with respect, also, to the personality of God, to heavenly appearances, to the union of divinity and humanity in Christ, to the atonement, and to the universal spread of the gospel.

Also concerning the *social* antagonism of the Christian world, the antagonism between state and church, in which the *ethnological* antagonism of the Hellenic and the Israelitish culture is reflected, much uncertainty and obscurity are promulgated, although it is a favorite theme of the day. No wonder; for the judgment regarding this antagonism coheres with the most diverse and passionate interests. Still the old mediæval forms of the consolidating of the two establishments, though in principle subverted, stand before our eyes in the antagonism of the Occidental Papacy,

V

which would like to be also Cæsarism, and the Oriental Cæsaro-Papacy; the one form supporting its threats by romantic enticements, the other its craft by great acts of violence. Even in the Protestant world there are ecclesiastical or pseudo-ecclesiastical ideas which would enslave or reduce to a mere diminishing shadow the state, political or pseudo-political ideas which would enslave or even utterly destroy the church. In opposition to these come views which aim at rending completely asunder state and church, without being clear on which side the common possessions, marriage, the school, the oath, and others, are to fall.

But respecting these preliminary questions, the views of men engaged in the same latest ecclesiastical agitation also differ widely. According to one voice, the state is wholly to absorb the church, in that it takes up Christianity wholly into itself and becomes the consummated kingdom of God (Rothe); according to the other, it is to surrender even its specifically Christian character, thus opening the way for the culture of the Mohammedans and the Japanese (Bluntschli). According to one opinion, the historic Episcopal power of the state over the church is to be retained, that by the help of the state the ecclesiastical confessor may be forced to confess his want of a confession; according to the other, the state is to let the church, with the foundation of its Christian principles, drift. We hold, nevertheless, that both establishments are from God, and that not only all consolidations, all reciprocal enslavements, are contrary to their nature, but also all separation proper, such as is had in view by many; since here, also, the question respects a harmonious antagonism, therefore a sound reciprocal action between an independent Christian state and an independent Christian church. Now, without regard to exact definitions, according to which one might describe the state as the religion of a national fellowship, the church as the fellowship of an international religion, the problem of each is still to be described to the extent that the church has to care especially for the Christian religious dogmas, the state *especially* for the Christian moral or *humane* dogmas. It is true, the announcement has recently been made that the day of dogmas is past; but that was, certainly, not a dogma of true science. Even the saying of a famous theologian, that dogmas are the church's own, and stricken with decay, while on the contrary the development of the morality of the state free from dogma stands in bloom, rests upon a remarkable lack of memory. The first New Testament dogma (recorded in Acts 15) was a *moral* dogma, and down till within the fourth century linguistic usage termed the *moral* maxims of the church, as well as the *religious*, dogmas. It was entirely in accordance with the law after which the antagonisms, in their misunderstanding and unwisdom, on both sides strain themselves, that the Christian spirit in the state began to promote the humane maxims as soon as the church began to promote its religious maxims at the expense of the humane, albeit according to the sound relation the two lines condition each other throughout. So far, too, it could go then, in the second half of the mediæval period and later, that societies of one-sided ecclesiasticism were formed, and, in opposition to these, societies of one-sided though always Christian humanity. When at the end, however, men would array the ecclesiastical system against Christian humane maxims, especially against freedom of conscience, religious toleration, universal human rights, that is a completely spoiled church construction; and when, on the other hand, ultra human conceptions are marshalled in boisterous bands against the right of the ecclesiastical maxims, that is likewise wild masonry in the temple of humanity. Here, therefore, it specially behoves us to set free again a thoroughly harmonious antagonism from its ruinous disfigurations, and to expect confidently the glorious results which a free union of church and state, of the living ecclesiastical Christian faith and the unfeigned Christian humanity, will produce.

The last antagonism which we have to mention is the *cosmical*, as the *higher power of the economical*. All the more important religious systems of mankind have each embraced a beginning and an end of the world, another life as well as this, — time and eternity. But Christianity, in keeping with the universality and depth of the Christian spirit, is specially conformed to such an all-embracing view of things. It was reserved for the modern progress after the appearance of the Hegelian philosophy, to limit the view of the world essentially to the earth. And so in the realm of theology, also, many have begun to restrict themselves religiously to the limits of the world, as defined by the latest wisdom; to restrict themselves with the history of a humanity which can know neither a beginning nor an end of things; to restrict themselves, with the soarings of the intellect and the yearnings of the heart, to the hopes of this present earthly life. We know, indeed, that the material light has free course from star to star; but to the nobler, immaterial lights, this free course is to be barricaded; the earth is to be a pagoda of the soul in a rocky cavern; the history of the world a seclusion in the midst of the universe, and the starry heavens a scattered collection of heathen offerings which never come into association with each other. Manifestly, even the spectrum analysis could not console us in the experience of such infinite impoverishment. Let us, then, rejoice that our Christianity, with the antique world-pictures of "anticipative peoples," is in advance, also, as to the proud distinction of uniting heaven and earth, time and eternity. Besides, we need just so much space and just so much time for the full expansion of the kingdom of God.

The kingdom of God itself the older theologians divided, not without grounds, into the Kingdom of Power, the Kingdom of Grace, the Kingdom of Glory. Still, it must be remarked that each of these kingdoms properly separates into two kingdoms; the kingdom of power into God's rule over entire nature, and his rule over the whole rebellion of such intelligences as, in the misuse of freedom, have gone astray; the kingdom of grace, into the typical prefiguration of the real kingdom of heaven, or the Old Testament theocracy, and into the real, i. e., spiritually potent, New Testament kingdom itself; the kingdom of glory, into the realm of the triumphant church in the other world, and the union of that world and this in the final consummation. Accordingly, a world made the perfect organ and the transparent symbol of the kingdom of God is the appearance of the kingdom of glory. But the rule of the Divine Omnipotence and Wisdom over heaven and earth, the spiritual world and the corporeal world, is the antecedent condition to the founding of the kingdom of grace. The power-realm of God is called the kingdom of power, because the personal Spirit of God bears sway over the same, and because he, with invincible might, bears all things, comprehended in a single plan, on towards a single end, which is the end of the world, — doing this by virtue of a perfectly harmonious motion of the world, in which he himself reconciles the conflict between spirits and forces. The belief in this power-kingdom is a fundamental religious article in which the most different views of the world, so far as they are religious, agree; only they define it differently. In this belief, the Old Testament witnesses to the All-Ruling, and it is a true hymn on the kingdom of power, when the one hundred and forty-eighth Psalm speaks forth the unanimous, actual, conscious and unconscious, willing and unwilling, praise of all creatures to the glorification of God. In this spirit the apostolic church, in a sublime prayer, glorifies the universal rule of God, even over the conspiracy of all instruments of darkness against the Lord's Christ and his people. Of a truth against thy holy servant Jesus, both Herod and Pontius Pilate, with the Gentiles, and the tribes of Israel, were gathered together, to do whatsoever thy hand and thy counsel determined before to be done. (Acts 4: 24, et seq.) But the being of God, as it is Love itself, could not be satisfied with a kingdom of power, with the rule of Omnipotence over the regular circuit of the stars, over all circles and circlings of life in nature; as little could it be satisfied with a rule of the Highest Wisdom over the revolt of opposing intelligences, with the fact which the poet has expressed by the words, *ducunt volentem fata, nolentem trahunt,* — the willing are led by the fates, the unwilling dragged. And the more reason was there for founding a higher kingdom, a kingdom of realized freedom and love above the realm of necessity, inasmuch as the power-kingdom itself was designed only as the basis thereof, and as over against the first appearance of the kingdom of light and pious freedom the beginnings of a kingdom of darkness and the false freedom of rebellion presented themselves. It cannot content the holy God, who holds his own personality pure, and desires to mirror and glorify himself in a kingdom of personal existences, everlastingly to extend the almightiness of his rule over the power of the rolling worlds, and to let it triumph over the impotence of rebellious intelligences; still less to move intelligences in the play of only a seeming freedom after the nature of a concealed destiny. Not so much the rolling spheres or the overthrow of evil world-powers is it that he is concerned about, as about the hearts of men; and only then has he reached his aim when the impelling power of his love has become in them the innermost self-impulsion; when his freedom has become their freedom, his mind their mind, his will their will; when they stand in a true bond of love with him, one in him and one with each other; and when the necessary harmony of forces is taken up into the service of a free harmony of souls.

This is the motive, the work, and the aim of the kingdom of grace. The realm of love which God has through Christ established in the inner being of mankind is called kingdom of grace, because it is based upon a harmonious manifestation of justice and love, upon an infinitely generous spiritual administration, which so arranges that from the verdict of justice goes forth the saving work of love. This kingdom is, first, in a legal and symbolical form, prefigured in the Old Testament theocracy, in which God reveals himself as the King of his people, of the land of this people, and as Director of all its destiny. And this prefigurement serves the special purpose of introducing and mediating the realization of the actual kingdom of God,— a realization by the centralization of all verdicts of salvation in Christ. Therefore, also, the antecedent signs and works of salvation in the history previous to Christ proceed from antecedent verdicts, and the centre of the world's history is a verdict of God upon the blindness of the world, which, by the atoning compassion of Christ, has been spiritually complied with, and by love's triumph transformed into the salvation of humanity. To be sure, the old Socinian word, no man can suffer for another, has been, of late, proclaimed again with variations, as if it were the newest wisdom.[1] Yet the propounders would surely have needed but to look about them a little to see how one man can suffer not only by, but also on account of, and even for, another, suffer even punishment. Thus, had they not chosen rather to make a modern school-book — with which the fettered egotist will by all means hold to the end of days — agree with their own wishes and preconceptions, they might have beheld numberless reflections of the mystery of redemption in mundane history itself. To be sure, moreover, the idea of repentance has been changed, for the first time, by the later theology, into the idea of atonement. And we will acknowledge that no man was ever truly redeemed who did not, by repentance, sympathetically receive, in his own bosom, Christ's atoning suffering of the verdict. This realm of grace in which the will of man is made one again with the will of God, wherein every visitation of God in condemnation is to the upright changed into a redemption, is a true kingdom, a royal kingdom of Christ. For, as all powers and forces of evil in the other world and this instinctively co-operate in one rebellion against the Messiah, for which reason it is proper to speak of a kingdom of darkness, although those leagues between Herod and Pilate, Pilate and Caiaphas, Caiaphas and the Jews, are always but temporary coalitions; so, much more is the kingdom of grace, or even the inner, invisible church of Christ, a kingdom wherein all powers of good, all pious, spiritual works, all open testimonies and all secret sighs, work together to a single end, — that God may through Christ become fully revealed in the appearance of his glory over all the world, and in the whole world itself.

And that is, then, the conception also of the kingdom of

[1] Schwalb, Der Alte und der Neue Glaube. Manchot, Ueber den Opfertod Jesu.

glory, or, what is the same thing, of the kingdom of God in its consummation. The ideal and dynamic foundations of this consummated kingdom are laid in the counsel of God, laid as deep as is eternity, and as firm as is the will of God. All the seeding of it took place in the redeeming work of Christ, and the first fruits of the harvest are being in ever increased richness brought home in a country which the exaltation of Christ has made the land of glory. The Scriptures speak in the sublimest figures of the future in which this kingdom, the heavenly Jerusalem, shall descend to the earth, and the hope of residence in this magnificent city, still more of its appearance, has always most profoundly moved, waked, purified, comforted, cheered, all Christian hearts; in a thousand songs, winged words and similitudes, it has poured itself forth. But we must not here abandon ourselves to this feature of agreeable prefigurement, if we would keep sight of our problem. Therefore, we ask, how have we to conceive of the end of the world's course, or of the kingdom of God as consummated?

Nothing is more to the purpose than that, first of all, we express the expectation according to the usual balance of the thesis and the antithesis in the synthesis: When the kingdom of God's power has become one with the kingdom of God's grace, then the kingdom of glory is realized; in other words, when all forces of the Christian world and all relations of this world have been converted fully into a unitary organ of spirit, of the Spirit of Christ, of the Love of God. To this idea of the world's end, moreover, the true philosophy of spirit surely will not object. But what holds good of the kingdom of glory in its entirety holds good also of its individual citizens. "There is a psychical body," says Paul, "and there is a spiritual body." This can mean nothing else than that the body of the perfected man is to be wholly a spiritualized body, a transparent image of the pure soul, a permeated organ of the soul. And this, then, is also what the apostle calls the glorious liberty of the children of God, in which their whole creatural sphere shall be transferred from the round of necessity to the cultus of an imperishable existence.

Entirely the same view is implied in the Scriptural idea of glory. It is the revelation of the governing spirit in the symbolic lustre of the appearance. The glory of Jehovah is the luminous image of his revelation in angelic form, together with a manifestation of the holiness of his being and his dominion over all the world (Is. 6). The glory of Christ is, in its first form, the perfected human future-picture of the eternal Logos before the throne of God (John 17); in its second form, the spiritual beaming beauty of Christ before the eyes of his disciples (John 1); in its third form, his proper exaltation and transfiguration, with which the circle of his power is illuminated from and by the centre of his spiritually perfected personality. Thus the glory of Christians also is determined; it is the whole personal sphere of their lives, illuminated and shone through by the personal kernel of their lives.

The sum and the living unity of all these spiritualizations, however, is the kingdom of glory. He who contends with sin — the sin in the world — can have no less hope, or he rolls the stone of Sisyphus up the steep, which always rolls back to the depth. He who contends with evil, struggles with death, can have no less hope, or he suffers the torments of Tantalus, in his impotent endeavor.

The order of *the moments in the consummation of the kingdom of God*, Paul has definitely indicated. The resurrection of Christ is the consummation of this kingdom, in principle (1 Cor. 15: 23; Eph. 1: 19). The ontological truth, that spirit has absolute power over nature, the personal spirit over its corporeal sphere, has here been realized as a truth of history. With this fact the Spirit of glory, as the resurrection-germ in believers, corresponds (Rom. 8; 1 Pet. 4: 14). This resurrection-seed will become the harvest in the first resurrection (1 Cor. 15: 23), which belongs to the beginning of the cosmical consummation. The end, then, is the conclusion of the one day which is as great as a thousand years. In this altogether organic period of transition from time to eternity, Christ will destroy all powers of sin and of the old world (1 Cor. 15: 24-25); then, as the last enemy, death, — as the essence of all evil. Finally there appears yet a wonderful change of things. The official work of Christ in redeeming and renewing has been accomplished, and his antecedent mediatorial reign now passes over into the consummated theocracy, the immediate rule of God in the glorified world by virtue of the omnipresence of the Spirit (v. 27-28). In this kingdom of the immediate intercourse of all souls with God, Christ has, without detriment to his peerlessness, divided his inheritance with his brethren (Rom. 8: 17), or rather has made it the eternal joint possession of himself and his people.

Would we now have this picture of the future of Christian humanity made clear to us in *its individual features*, then we must return to the fundamental forms of its potentiality, which were sketched in the first division. For in the consummation nothing more or less than the *whole potentiality* of whatever in the world is determined for Christ and his salvation will come to full development and appearance, the Alpha become the Omega; so that at the end of the world is needed only a single stroke from above and all the fundamental forms of Christian humanity stand in clear light and complete harmony.

Especially must the dynamic differences of individuals be fully realized in the kingdom of God, be realized simply on account of truth. They must be realized, indeed, with the precondition that the pure consummation of the differences between the central geniuses of humanity and the multitudes influenced by them results in the closest union of all in true equality. We must here remember, to understand the watchword of the day, *Suffrage Universel*, that every subsequent time has a certain office of revenge upon a guilty past. In times gone by, from the obligations of the true elect, the spiritual princes of the race, rights and privileges of the traditionally elect have been made. As a consequence of this guilt, we find ourselves in the age of retribution, and the revenge is — *suffrage universel*. But we need only look a little westward, to see how this watchword, i. e., the abrogation of all census, all concrete conditions of life, can put the noblest spirits of a nation in the background. We need only notice the virulent commotion in the ocean of popular life, to see how this abstract equality is designed to create a privileged caste underneath, over against the privileged nobility above, retiring from the scene. And with such threatening signs in the political horizon, where the abstract right of voting may have become a temporary expedient, the agitators would even in the church, by the suffrage of the masses in the individual churches and in the national churches, call into being a new reformation! But even if the political spirit may, because of its being in a transitional stage, allow itself to employ majority-action, the ecclesiastical spirit can never, never so do. That the funeral piles and the inquisitional dungeons show; especially, however, is it declared in the origination of the name of Protestants at Spire in the year 1529. Verily, this generation of confessors will not pass till the Lord comes, even though continuing for a season as a little church of the Anastasia at Constantinople in the time of the Arians, and even so would it stand as an insuperable reproach to every enacted or enacting majority-felony. The final prospect, however, is simply this: Christianity unfolds the forces, sanctifies the forces, distinguishes and estimates the forces, and puts every one in its place; is this accomplished, then is the organism of humanity accomplished in the kernel of humanity.

But then will also the antagonism between the reflecting consciousness and the visionary consciousness be balanced, as with the perfected spirits in the other world it is already balanced. Should this expectation be considered doubtful, we can point to its similitudes in history itself. Ordinary talent only reflects; genius thinks and works intuitively. The small philosophers are reflection-philosophers; the great speak of ideas, of immediately apprehended ends, of intuitions. In the province of revelation, however, human intuitions are visions accomplished by the Spirit of God, and Christ the Lord has comprehended in a single intuition the two worlds. The whole visible universe was to him a parable of the invisible; all eternity he saw projecting into time. But Christ's apprehension is the anticipation and foreshadowing of the apprehension of all believers.

Thus, too, the expectation that Shem will become one with Japheth; Israel one with the Hellenes; the holy earnestness of piety with the beauty of the purest culture; that, therefore, the church, which already in the time of Hermas (in his Shepherd) had the appearance of an old woman gradually beautifying herself, is to become Christ's beautiful maidenly bride, freed from all the spots and wrinkles of false piety, — this expectation also belongs to the consummation of the last times. About the restoration of Israel, individual theologians, particularly Dr. Baumgarten,[1] have, indeed, in a literal interpretation of Scripture, made wonderful announcements, how the Israelites are in the evening of the world to have again legal privileges, and renew, in a higher way, their former cultus; perhaps slay with glorified knives glorified oxen, and observe glorified sacrificial feasts, and the Gentiles with them. Christianity is above all such fancies. Legal privileges and Jewish customs are, as connected with the consummation of the kingdom of God, entirely out of the question; by no means, however, dynamical rights, i. e., the right to work according to the measure of force. And in such a purely dynamic equilibration, Israel, too, will come to the complete fulfilment of its mission; yet equally so the Japhetic potentiality of the world. The essential thing of this union, however, will be, that the culture of humanity and the culture of religion are perfectly reconciled with and vivify each other; that the beautiful comes to appearance in the full truth of the holy, the holy in the full lustre of the beautiful.

But if the consummation is above the becoming, then the equilibrium of the antagonism between the legally mature and immature divisions of the kingdom of God appears to fall away in the time of the consummation. And we shall surely decline the prospect which some ingenious men have devised, that the mediæval Church of Pedagogics and the Church of the Reformation will be united in a higher unity. With the liberty of the children of God, the law's tutelage

---

[1] Comp. the article "Ezechiel," by Baumgarten, in Herzog's Realencyklopädie. vol. iv. p. 304. "Per tot casus, etc.. — in Judaismum."

was done away already in the apostolic age. But even at the end of days, the reaction of the Christian kernel of humanity upon the whole creatural world will not be done away. Above all, however, must the Christian spirit of freedom always prove to be more than the spirit of a religiously beautiful and elegant training in the church itself. Arbitrariness, which still so often deports itself to excess as higher evangelical freedom, will disappear; and, as the antitype to that lay-obedience to the hierarchs, whose day is past, a heavenly, free obedience to the voice of God will find full realization in life. Suffice it, then, for our prospect, that we think of the life of the perfected as truly festal, but not idle, still less aimless.

The central point of all Christian hopes is formed by the expectation that the conjunction of the head with the members, the conjunction of Christ with the church, will yet be made perfect. And with reason, for only in the head can the members find themselves together. This coming together is, in truth, a fundamental article; but an article of faith which is intimately connected with our belief in humanity, in humanity as an organic whole. Thus is disclosed the outlook to the second appearing of Christ.

With that, however, the great macrocosmical parables or types of the revelation-world, or Christianity, will be fulfilled according to their eternal meaning in their perishable form, according to the saying of the poet, " All the perishable is only a parable." As yet it has not been made evident what the tree of life in the garden signifies, the infinite healing virtue in the holy enjoyment of nature; what the ark signifies, the symbol of all salvations of the higher life by the floods of the ocean; what the stars of heaven signify for the seed of Abraham; and so with other past and passing symbols. But, surely, at the end of the world, these envelopes will be spoken of with greater respect; as nowadays many speak of their kernel. Would we behold an illustration of this spiritual resurrection of all truly religious elements in the life of men, we need but notice the work of present philology, in its interpretation of the mythological systems as symbolism. The heathen mind turned the symbolical religion into mythology; the matured Christian mind finds again on the basis of the mythology the symbolical thoughts.

As to what farther concerns the social antagonism, we have repeatedly remarked, that state and church are to become one in the kingdom of God. The state is not to be merged into the church, for then it would follow that from the beginning the world was designed to be disembodied by a one-sided priesthood at the altar, or, indeed, to be divested of its many-colored lustre by a one-sided monachism. But as little is the church to be merged into the state; for, in that case, the heaven-yearnings of the heart would be enslaved by the manners of the world, the individual by the community, the inner life by the appearance. Let us, however, conceive of all prayer-forces and all action-forces reconciled in a people of kings and priests; truly, there rises a picture of life, rich and great, far above all conceptions pertaining to this present life.

But not only state and church, also heaven and earth, are in the kingdom of God to come into unity. This expectation of the future transformation of the earth into a heavenly establishment, of the conjunction of the spiritual kingdom in the other world with that in this, nay, of the uniting of that world itself and this, is to many a mere fancy,—to every earnest Christian, though, a great hope, an assurance of faith, a certain prediction. We shall not, however, stop with this. The common anticipation of the most important peoples is, after all, as fully related on the one side to reason as on the other side to belief. As for the requirements of reason, they in truth stand thus, originally. From the first the thought of the anticipating spirit has complained that the course of the world should continue on aimless. From the first it has moreover appeared to the human intellect an intolerable barrier, that earth and heaven should, to all eternity, communicate only by means of the elementary light. The human intellect in its youth, rich in anticipation, was too great to prepare itself for an exclusively terrestrial state. This view of the world, Christianity, in the light and fire of revelation, has purified. And so to us the end of the world appears not merely as the human, but also as the cosmical, realization of the internal universality of Christianity. Heaven and earth will pass away as divided life-districts, to come together by a great metamorphosis in the appearance of the city of God. Yet the fundamental tone of this new world remains the idea of glory, of the perfect lordship of spirit over nature, the perfect appearance of spirit in nature, the perfect revelation of spirit through nature. From this clear, luminous goal, gleams of light fall backward upon the whole course of humanity. Of this significance of the world's destination, in regard to the fundamental questions of historical Christianity in its antecedent condition, in its nature, and in its present state, something is yet to be said.

We deduce a conclusion, first, from the Christian end of the world in regard to the Christian ground of the world, the creation. If, at the world-termination, the entire new world is to come to appearance as a perfected harmonious organism, then also the basis of the world must have been, or rather must have become and remained, a single plastic, impelling idea. Quite likely some one will say now, — that is the original cell, which, with the help of infinite time and favorable circumstances, has opened to the extended fulness of the actual world. But we come with our conclusion from the destination of the world back to neither the *world-egg* of the Indians, nor the *Chronos* of the Greeks, nor the *magic caldron* of the Celtic goddess Ceridwen, in which the gifts of beauty and mind were brewed from the vapor of matter. That world-egg, the Indian has doubtless, by this time, himself come to regard as a figment; Chronos, as the god of infinite time, has been deposed by his son Zeus; and the great magic caldron, with the contending forces and circumstances, popular superstition long since put aside in the Shakespearean witch-kitchen. The inference drawn from a world which, in its material consistence, is thoroughly spiritualized, impenetrated with spirit, adapted to spirit, shone though by spirit, nay, is made the organ of a personal life-kingdom, leads back necessarily to a homogeneous producer, to the Logos, wherein Spirit itself, as the omnipotent, personal formative principle, is first, and the breath of the Word, the originating appearance, matter, is second. For that matter, which at the end of things has to prove the servant of all servants (servus servorum), — that this at the beginning was a lord of all lords, the father of spirit, appears to us as simply an absurdity. Such a self-denial as is ascribed to this all-the-world's servant, that he "who perfects all this grandeur" has always made himself subject to all things, nay, has hid himself behind all things or forms of life, — so completely hid himself that no man ever has seen or can see so much as a single atom (for the elements, as such, are a long way from being atoms and molecules), — far surpasses the Christian measure of self-denial. Aristotle and Plato were likewise unable to understand how matter could have proceeded from spirit, its life and its plastic energy; but they were, nevertheless, too clear thinkers to attribute to that unconscious something lying behind phenomena, and to be apprehended only by the touch, any mastery. Had matter conjured up the beautiful world, then we should have respecting the world no other prophecy than the prognostic of the gambler, Lightly come, lightly go! He who, therefore, would bring spirit ultimately to absolute rule can only rely with hope on the assurance, In the beginning was the Word.

Now, if the creation, as likewise the basis of the eternal spiritual world, was in principle consummated with the existence of the first man, then we could not expect to find any miracle, that is to say, any absolutely new form of life, in the history of the world. The grain of the harvest, as the new miracle in the ear, will admit of reference to the first miracle only, to the seed which lay at the basis of the harvest; yet during the whole period of its development the seed has disappeared as completely as if it were lost. Accordingly, those who do not recognize in the history of the world, or in the life of Christ, an epoch entirely homogeneous with the epoch at the beginning and the epoch at the end of the world, of equally heavenly height, have to tax their ingenuity in many ways to ground the notion of miraculous events inside a purely periodic course of the mundane life; conceive they, then, of the work of Christ in a Jewish-Christian fashion, as a legal reform, or in a Gentile-Christian fashion, as a new school of life. But as the Old Testament justly postulates a great turning-point, a new miraculous epoch inside the history of creation, over against the genesis of light, the genesis of the first man, the concrete spiritual light-bearer; so the New Testament also supposes an equally, and even a more important turning-point within the history of mankind, — a turning-point which forms the basis of the redemption of humanity from its bondage to sin, in abnormal development. The Apostle John has denoted it by the expression, "The Word was made flesh;" the Apostle Paul by the expression, "The first man is of the earth, earthy; the second man is the Lord from heaven." By the earthy man, he understands always, not a sinful man, but human nature in its psychical, corporeo-spiritual endowment, from which the spirit could have unfolded as naturally as the red flower unfolds from the green stalk and leaf; which, however, through abnormal self-determination, entangled itself in the bonds of a false demoniaco-spiritual carnality, and so developed downward to death. Yet the second man, since he is in his advent mediated, received, but not produced, by the first humanity in its higher features, signifies the human endowment in its *realized and universal* potentiality, a quite heavenly new birth, which is in its nature already the principle of regeneration for the whole Adamic world. The antagonism between Adam and Christ is the antagonism of the merely pure and the purified, absolutely potential, spirituo-corporeal endowment. Hence it is as incorrect to say, Christ took the paradisaic human nature, as to say he sanctified in his person the sinful human nature. Rather does he enter upon his way with a sanctified nature, and on just that account is he able to experience by his perfect sympathy, and overcome all the temptations of humanity. To such an epoch in principle, to such a seed of the thoroughly spiritualized and deified human life, the world's destination, as we have apprehended it, refers. We go back, therefore, from the idea of a world ruled by Spirit, and consequently filled with God, first of all, not to Adam, but to Christ, the God-man and personal Author of the whole new world, as he is not merely Redeemer of the old world, but also Renewer of the old world and Finisher of the new. But then this conclusion follows: As unique and as high and as miraculous as was the creational foundation of the world, and as the new world in its entire periphery is to be; so unique, so high, and so miraculous must have been also the life of Christ in the midst of the providential history, or the history of the world. When I draw a line from the miraculous summit of the creation to the miraculous summit of the world's consummation, it must touch the crown of the life of Christ; in other words, whatever is detracted from the life of Christ, that is detracted from the hope of all mankind as to the consummation. If, however, any one should deem a single life too limited to form the basis of the new world, he forgets that it is the nature of humanity, even over against the manifoldness of the world, to concentrate and creatively to regenerate itself in a few great personalities; that, however, the one humanity, over against the one God, had to sum itself up in one human Head, in one Head in whom God imparts and surrenders himself to it, and in whom it is to impart and surrender itself to him.

Finally, we come to the question, what the idea of the kingdom of God in its consummation has to tell us regarding our own times. Let us notice, in the first place, the universal mundane life. If it is certain, then, that we await new heavens and a new earth, wherein dwelleth righteousness; wherein Spirit in all its glory rules over and through nature, things, matter; wherein the Personal World has completely appropriated to itself the impersonal world, — then we can regard even the restless conquest of the world by science, industry, mechanics, and action for the service of the spirit in general as only a beautiful way of the future. Looking, however, sharply at the goal, we cannot fail to perceive the danger that the means will be, as it is, made the end; that countless personalities will, as they do, in struggling with the impersonal, lose themselves deep in the impersonal. Materialism is the name for the extreme degree of this aberration in its theoretical and practical form. But when we remember that matter is destined to be the rich attire of spirit, as humanity is destined to be the bride of Christ, we could wish for the present times, instead of a coarse cultus, a finer culture of matter. Why, if matter is to be accounted a beneficent deity, is it in so many ways, then, made a fiery Moloch, which with more and more frightful signs consumes houses, ships, and men? Surely, in place of the fantastic deification of matter, there must come in infinitely greater respect for its spiritually fine laws, according to which medicines can be changed into poisons, and poisons into medicines. And now as to the dignity of spirit, true spirit is personal spirit, the bloom of the soul-life and heart which are open to God and his heaven, and not a tissue of thought-creations which have separated themselves from love, from the hearth of the personal life. In these days, however, such is the false spiritualization of the spiritual life that many find more of divine revelation in the pulsing of a nightingale than in the pulsing of a choice human heart, and, in the end, more in the characteristic of a stone than in the singing of the nightingale. But if Japheth could disrupt the connection with Shem, his spiritual conquest of the world would become a wild and disorderly hunting of external observations in an endless labyrinth of unique particulars, or analytical notices. But the prospect of the consummation of the kingdom of God assures us, that, in the kernel of humanity, the tendency of the spirit to abide in God will be made prevalent over its tendency to traverse the world.

We close with a look at ecclesiastical relations. Obviously, from the prospect which believing Christendom has of an organic and free consummation of the kingdom of God, there is to be in our day, or the not distant future, a reconstruction of the ecclesiastic social life. It is true, the fulness of the developed intellectual life, of personal faith, of moral endeavors, is a spiritual power which can no longer be confined within the old massive or stiff and uniform forms, be they called popedom, Cæsaro-papacy, or state-church and pastoral tutelage of the spiritual life. The spirit must have more vent, — forsooth, the true spirit, not the pseudo-spirit which would conjure up a new vox Dei from the voting of the masses, which with its ecclesiastic ideals has sunken below the level of the state; — as this must, indeed, recognize under moral conditions religious freedom, but with every recognition of a religious community must also inquire into its statutes, and can never connect itself with an unbound community which will know of no obligatory principles, but only of unfettered opinions. For it is desired to make the variable, infinitely seducible majority-vote of all religious, moral, and intellectual idiots the guardian of all that in the Christian life of faith, knowledge, and sentiment has become ripe in our age; and this organization of the Christian spiritual life from below up is to be the new Reform, the Reformation of the Reformation. Still, even such a tendency, as it announces itself in the Protestant Union, may have given to it by the state its share of vent and motion. Wholly new, however, and more than naïve, is the expectation that the church founded upon the Evangelical Confession is to surrender its confession-obligation, or rather its confession-right, is to abandon its old storm-proved ship on which it is sailing to meet the coming of the Lord, in order to drift aimlessly away upon a loosely constructed raft. But as this expectation is only an idle whim, and as from respect to the persons we must suppose they can no longer recede, the programme of the immediate future is indicated. The state must set the church at liberty, and not with base ingratitude for the services received from it; in any case, with honest perception of its rights. The state must help it to a constitution corresponding to its principles. Then, on the right and on the left, a broad channel may be set off; here the church bound by authority, there the overfree tendency of a society loosed from the authority of the Scriptures, confessions, and church-regulations; the middle and deep ground-current of the church of the evangelical confession will remain powerful enough to move festally on to the ocean of the Christian consummation of the world, a consummation in which the majestic glory of Christ is to appear in the closest connection with the moral beauty of his church. When, therefore, we hear, in our day, the loud and over-loud watchword in the church, FREEDOM, FREEDOM! we join in, YES, *freedom, freedom for* YOU; *but freedom also for* US!

LECTURE X

CHRISTIANITY AND CULTURE

By REV. JULIUS DISSELHOFF

PASTOR AND INSPECTOR AT KAISERSWERTH

REV. JULIUS DISSELHOFF

BIOGRAPHICAL

REV. JULIUS DISSELHOFF, author of the last lecture in this volume, was born at Soest, November 20, 1827. He is reported to have died during the past year, or in 1896. His lecture on "Christianity and Culture" shows him to have been a very widely informed scholar, with no little special knowledge respecting the topic considered. He was also a careful and judicious critic all along the line of the different factors having to do with culture; and with peculiar ability does he show how these factors produce different results when influenced by Christianity and when not so influenced. His address is a fitting conclusion to the others in the volume, inasmuch as it exhibits the last great battle between faith and unbelief—the battle of culture joined with religion and of culture wholly separated from the influences of at least all revealed knowledge of God and the hereafter.

SUMMARY OF LECTURE X

THE subject is so extensive, preliminary discussions must be omitted—By Christianity we understand a religion that is positively biblical, and by culture the development of the human powers as far as they have reference to this life—The word culture relates to the term *cultus*, as of like root with it—The culture of the Egyptians, Babylonians, etc., attracts us not, because their cultus does not attract us—It was first in Greece and Rome that men began to call upon deity as a free personality—The admired classical culture of these two ancient peoples has its root in their religious cultus—But in the very bloom of this ancient culture a barbarism is seen, principles which are the contradiction of culture—Neither the Greeks nor the Romans had a correct idea of personality, or of marriage and the household relation, or of the State—Singing and music were scarcely known among these peoples—In their architecture matter is not conquered by the spirit; and in their sculpture the despotic power of fate appears to the beholder, or in it is concealed very often a corrupting influence—In ancient poetry there is found nowhere a reconciliation of the person—These ancients did not have even the suspicion of a real science of history—Roman jurisprudence neither gave rights to other peoples nor could save Rome from moral barbarism—The fundamental condition of cultured life was not held fast by either Plato or Aristotle—Only in Christianity do we have the true conception of personality, the divine and the human—Christianity alone provides rightly for marriage and the family, for genuine political organization, and for the relation between labor and rest—The various factors of civilization as affected by Christianity during the last one thousand years—Schiller, in his poem entitled "The Walk," puts forward the idea that all our present civilization must end in barbarism, and thus become rejuvenated; but we know a better remedy and a better preservative power, namely, Christ, who is the Life and the Light of men.

X

CHRISTIANITY AND CULTURE

BY REV. JULIUS DISSELHOFF,

PASTOR AND INSPECTOR AT KAISERSWERTH

CHRISTIANITY and Culture, — that is the subject which is now to come before us. It is so extensive, that, to make the most of my time, I must ask permission not to detain you with preliminary discussions. Only be it in a word remarked, that I understand by Christianity a *religion positively Biblical*, and by culture the care and development of man's essential powers and gifts, so far as they have reference to this life. The unfolding of individual talents, as it is only a partial, will ever be a one-sided and imperfect culture; the harmonious unfolding of all human talents to one whole can only be regarded as genuine culture.

My lecture will be occupied chiefly with facts, — facts which speak eloquently in the way of demonstration. I might, accordingly, state the question thus: —

What does universal history teach us respecting the influence of Christianity on Culture?

You all are sensible of the importance of this question as related to the present; for in it two views of life struggle for the victory. One, the Christian, adheres to the conviction, that only by the self-revelation and self-impartation of God in Christ can humanity attain its end. The other, the so-called *humane*, emancipates itself from the revelation of God in the Holy Scriptures, and asserts that humanity unfolds itself of itself even to consummation. At the same time, this doctrine of humanity claims that it alone civilizes man, defames Christianity as an enemy of culture, and gives it the advice to be transformed into harmony with the spirit of the times, by the advanced views of the century.

From the troubled party-confusion of the present, let us flee to impartial universal history, and, as humble, truth-loving disciples, hear her decision on that assertion and accusation of *humanism*.

Our preceptress must lead us, first, into the history of the culture antecedent to Christ, so that, having learned what man was able to achieve by himself, we shall be prepared to estimate the influence exerted on culture by Christianity.

The word *culture* refers us to the word *cultus*, as of like root with it. The language-forming popular mind, then, which has made or appropriated these two words, considers cultus and culture to be cognate. In other words, the voice of the people declares that the right care or service of deity, and the right care of human endowments and relations, are vitally connected.[1]

Those peoples which have no cultus. with whom the consciousness that deity and humanity are essentially related, are reduced to a minimum, perhaps to fetichism or belief in spectres, — such peoples have no culture. All peoples, on the other hand, which lead a civilized life, are also cherish-

---

[1] The Scripture narrates, it is true, that, in the race of the God-forgetting Cainites, beginnings of culture, city-builders, pipers, and harpers made their appearance; but it causes to be seen, likewise, with what barbarism of the spirit this culture was united.

ers of the organic connection existing between man and deity.

The culture of the oldest historic peoples, the Egyptians, Babylonians, Assyrians, and Medo-Persians, attracts us not, because their cultus does not attract us. They were servilely given to the worship of the powers of nature, which, with unbroken, despotic might, ruled over them. Bondage, despotism, is also the character of their culture, whether we view their social and political institutions, or the architecture and sculpture they have left.

Not until in Greece, and still later in Rome, the rudest cultus of the powers of nature was overcome, and men began to call upon deity as a free personality, did there bloom in all fields of human life a culture from which we at this day learn. It is an undisputed fact, that the admired, classical culture has its root in a religious cultus; that especially the life-connection between deity and humanity is the source of the classical art. Take deity away, and Homer and Hesiod, Pindar and Herodotus, Aeschylus and Sophocles, are phantoms; and that power which built the Parthenon, cast the image of Pallas Athene, and chiselled that of Jupiter Olympus, is cut through, veins and nerves. It is a fact, as universally admitted, that the culture of classic antiquity flourished only so long as the life of the people was pervaded by reverence for personal divinity. When piety disappeared, — and it had to disappear, because the ancient gods were not truth and life; when philosophy overthrew the old popular religion without being able to put in its place a better; when thus God-estrangement, eclaircissement, and pyrrhonism attained rule, — then entered into the cultural life a process of decomposition that rapidly and irremediably bore the Greek, and also the Roman, body-politic on towards putrefaction, which an Aristophanes in Greece, and even a Horace in Rome, plainly and strongly enough have declared.[1] The particular features of this picture of corruption, it is not the province of my lecture to describe. Besides, they are in part so repulsive and unclean, that I should here have to cast the veil over them. But the fact must be emphasized, that the Greek and Roman popular minds were not in a condition to produce an abiding culture, nay, that at the very heights of their cultures internal decomposition announced certain death,—which thoughtful historians, like Thucydides and Livy, by no means concealed from themselves and their contemporaries.[2]

Still more. Even the bloom of the ancient culture we behold affected with unculture, nay, even with barbarism. It is on the whole only a commencement of culture, or, better, a beautiful and noble attempt towards culture. Only by those who are not acquainted with it, and who substitute for the facts their own fancies, can it be

[1] The real pulse-stroke of all the comedies of Aristophanes is the conviction that the departure from faith in a personal deity and the predominance of rationalism was the poison which spoiled in the kernel all the relations of Grecian life. It is well known with what energy he exposes and satirizes the internal barbarism of his brilliant age; it should, however, never be forgotten that he looks upon the decay of piety as the source of the decay of culture. As familiar is the ode of Horace (lib. III. 6) in which the same view obtains. Comp., also, Odes, lib. I. 35, 33–38; III. 5, 29; II. 15, etc.

[2] Thucydides portrays, e.g., III. 82, 83, the internal corruption of the Athenian state in his splendid day. "The ordinary meaning of words was changed, and associations were formed, not to gain the benefit of established laws, but for selfish purposes in opposition to those institutions. The assurance of mutual fidelity rested not so much on the divine law as on the common participancy in crime," etc. The inevitable fall of the Athenian state which Thucydides foresaw, he ascribes not to assaults upon it by wars, but to divine agency (II. 64). Livy says of his day, that the Roman state suffered from its own greatness; that long already the energies of the excessively strong nation had been destroying themselves; that the Roman people could endure neither its vices nor their remedies; that the desire reigned by excess and sensuality to go to ruin and to ruin everything. (Preface.)

admired to deification. Very much did the Greek and Roman culture lack of being true and complete. There were, in the ancient life, principles which are the contradiction of culture. Let us consider, first of all, the human personality. According to the ancient view, only the man is the full and real man. The woman stands far below him, so far that even an Iphigenia, who is willing to sacrifice herself for her country, justifies her act of love by saying, "For one man is better than ten thousand women, that he should see the light." The entire one half of mankind is, then, theoretically put down and hindered from bringing to development the germ which is in their natures. Neither is every man a real, full man, but only the free man. The slave is, not merely as to his external and social position, but in his nature, a less important being. And, again, not every free man is the full man, but only the Greek and the Roman. All others are barbarians, even though they worship the same God, and possess the same civilization. On this point, the classical culture was unable to rise higher than that of the Chinese, to whom we are "red-bristled barbarians," or that of the Esquimaux, who call only themselves *innuit*, i. e., man. Because full worthiness does not dwell in the woman, she is consequently not the equal of man; and so there can be no true conjugal love, no true marriage, no real family-life.

The most ideal womanly figure of classic antiquity is the Antigone of Sophocles, who, from obedience to the eternal law of Zeus, does not fear death. But how triflingly even she judges of marriage and the family-relation, of wedded and of parental love, may be perceived from the following words (v. 896 et seq.): "Never would I for a child that I have borne, nor for my husband, were he dead and turned to dust, have undertaken such a risk, the state opposed. One husband dying, I another might have found, and, my child lost, another from another man."

From what has been already said it follows that the ancient state could never give to two classes of its members, the woman and the slave, the cultivation to which each is by essential nature adapted. As little could it attain, as a whole, the culture to which the political community is summoned, since on principle it shut out from its fellowship other popular communities as barbarian, using them only as means for its egotism. It made itself a despot, the peoples slavish instruments of its purposes. While in Rome culture seemingly flourished, the circle of the world groaned under the tread of the Roman tyranny. What we call in state-life barbarism, was the principle, the maxim, of the state.

I take you to the province of ancient art. Its form is in many respects to this day law for us. But it is far distant from the goal. Singing and music, according to our ideas, were hardly known. Were Roman and Greek singers now to strike up their art in our hearing, we should, I fear, not stay long, and be able to ascribe to these peoples scarcely the elements of a musical cultivation. I pass by Greek and Roman painting, because I have had no opportunity of becoming especially acquainted with it, and therefore am not qualified to pass judgment on it. But before the most celebrated remains of ancient architecture I have admiringly stood. In the ruins of the temples at Athens, Ephesus, and Baalbeck, impressions of glory and harmony flooded me which I am unable to put in words. I was as if overpowered. However, as finished and agreeable as are the proportions, the matter, the marble, is after all not conquered by the spirit. Every column stands isolated by itself; when the eye has coursed up its finished form to the capital, then between column and column lies the horizontal line of the marble architrave, like an unbroken barrier, to arrest the flight of the spirit and precipitate it back to the earth. Still more sensible is the barrier behind the row of columns, where the eye falls upon the wall of the temple proper. Marble block rises above marble block, and forms a dead wall. And in the temple, — a dark room, four marble walls, — scarcely an attempt to breathe into the internal structure an idea.

Touching the perfection of form in the ancient sculpture, as, e. g., in the groups of Niobe and Laocoön, or the statues of Apollo Belvedere, the Mediceau Venus, etc., on whose beauty I at several times and leisurely was permitted with the deepest interest to gaze, I need not lose a word. But the artists of the line and our own feeling tell us that in those groups the despotic power of fate, which makes of man a repining slave, still oppresses even the beholder; and those statues attest to us that the cultus of beautiful form can produce beautiful forms, but they also show that this cultus only poorly conceals a corrupting cultural life.

The ancient poetry exhibits to us a noble struggle for personal freedom and free unity with deity. But internal reconciliation is nowhere found. The free life in a God who is holy love, and who guides the life of the individual and of the community, throws not its transfiguring rays upon the creations of poesy. Deep, internal dissension comes clamorously forth. Even an Antigone, who, as we have already mentioned, obeys deity rather than human statutes, could not find peace in her divinity, but ends in despair. From all the classic poetry, again and again, breaks forth the old sigh which Homer represents Zeus himself as uttering over " unfortunate man " (Iliad, xvii. 446) :

"For the race of mortal men,
  Of all that breathe and move upon the earth,
  Is the most wretched;"[1]

or the hopeless creed of Achilles, with which the Iliad closes (XXIV. 525):—

"The Gods ordain
  The lot of man to suffer, while themselves
  Are free from care."[2]

Lastly, a few words respecting the ancient science. Of a real science of history, of a history of mankind, the ancients could have had not even a suspicion; for they knew no human race which is a unity and summoned to development, a race which branches out into peoples that serve the general development according to the measure of their gifts. They knew only Greeks and Barbarians. The fundamental condition of a science of history, consequently, was wanting to them.

The Roman jurisprudence is certainly a noble production of culture. But it neither gave rights to the non-Roman peoples as over against their oppressors, nor was able to save Rome itself from moral barbarism. As with us many visit the comedy for a pastime, so at Rome the rich and the poor, males and females, streamed into the amphitheatre, and delighted their eyes with the horrible spectacle as wild beasts lacerated and ate slaves and condemned persons, and among them many Christian men and women, — a horrible amusement.

And the philosophy in fine? How little even the deepest and most ideal, the sharpest and clearest thinkers of Greece were able of themselves to apprehend and hold fast the fundamental conditions of cultural life, Plato and Aristotle show incontestably. Plato, who has been called the *divine*,

[1] Bryant's Translation, XVII. 537-539.   [2] From the same, XXIV. 661-663.

sees, precisely at that time when in him and Aristotle the Greek philosophy had culminated, that his nation, if it continued living under the old relations, was lost. In his political philosophy he proffers his nation the safety-anchor. And what is the safety-anchor? The forces in which the bloom of Greece consisted, such as poetry, indeed all art in general, is banished, or is deprived of its living soul. On the other hand, matters antagonistic in principle to culture are immortalized and held forth as the sources of salvation. There is established a qualitative difference among men; marriage and the family relation are abolished; a man is no longer to have his own wife, and the father and the mother no longer their children; but the women and children belong to the whole political community (v. 8, 9, 12). Weakly and physically defective children must be put out of the way (III. 15; v. 8, 9). Whereby not only the human, but also the free male personality is totally annihilated. For the model kings in the model state, deception, as a holy, wise, and necessary means of ruling, is made a duty (III. 3, 21; v. 8, et al.). Valiant young men who have served their country well, receive as a reward for their deeds, on the state's account, unlimited permission to indulgence in the foul, shameful passion which forms the most disgraceful stain in the Grecian popular life (v. 14).[1]

Aristotle combats, it is true, Plato's theory about the community of women and children; but the original root of barbarism, want of esteem for the human personality, he also makes the corner-stone of his political system. The male is by nature better, the female less important. There are men who are as far inferior to the free man as the body is to the soul, or the animal to the man. These are the

[1] Compare on this point Schleiermacher in his translation of the Republic. p. 35, and what Plato narrates in his Charmidas, 10, 155, of Socrates. Touching the latter, also Xenophon's Memorabilia I. 3, 14; I. 6, 13.

slaves. The slave has participancy in reason only to the extent that he can be sensible of it; but he does not possess it. The use of slaves and animals is but slightly different (Arist. Politics, vol. I., chap. 2: 12-14). The slave has not the least reflective ability; even in the moral virtues he has only share enough to keep him from neglecting his work, through intractableness or indolence (chap. 5, 6, and 9). Still more barbarous and destructive to all free personality are the state laws which he advances regarding marriage; to which, however, I cannot here, except in this general way, refer (chap. 14: 1, 2, 10). The number of children that may be born is determined by the state; weakly and crippled children he, like Plato, would have put to death (chap. 14: 10).

You perceive, from even these few traces, that with the two greatest philosophers of antiquity an utter confusion regarding the nature of culture reigns. Historically approved groundworks of it are pronounced pernicious; especially by Plato, roots of barbarism, on the contrary, are declared to be means of salvation. Withal, it must be expressly observed that what has been communicated is not accidental, incidental remarks, but principles and aims of their philosophical systems.

Let us now, having acquainted ourselves with some of the barriers to, and defects of, the culture previous to Christ, at least in their general outlines, pass to the consideration of the cultural power that lies in Christianity, and the culture which has actually proceeded from Christianity.

It seems to me to be wholly incontrovertible, that a view of the world which cannot look through the forces which are absolutely inimical to culture, is still less able to overcome them, and therefore can never call into existence a complete and sound culture. Real and abiding culture will be developed only when its original enemy has been recognized as such, and with inexorable earnestness combated till entirely subdued. But are there, then, within humanity, forces which are absolutely inimical to the complete, harmonious culture of the human endowments?

My hearers, let there pass before your eyes all the innumerable and utterable horrors which not only in one, which among all nations, which not only in one, which in all ages have occurred; let it be told you by the incorruptible mouth of history that precisely the times of a partial brilliant culture, like those of Pericles and Aristophanes, of Cæsar Augustus and his successors, of the Medici, and of a Louis XIV. and a Louis XV., carry in their bosom unculture and barbarism, and all that debases man, and tramples his honor in the dirt; let it be attested by the present that the seats of a partial culture, the great cities, are to-day yet also the breeding-places of human degeneracy; still more, conceive that, like the omniscient God, you could, with one look, and without being hindered by disguise, see all the secret and open offences, the host of selfish desires, the endless progeny of hellish thoughts in mankind and in human hearts and heads,—would you then ask, Are there, then, within humanity, forces which are absolutely inimical to the complete, harmonious culture of the human endowments? And if now, in face of such testimonies of universal history and your experience, certain of our poets and philosophers would sing and prove to you that sin is the necessary starting-point, and all those facts and states a necessary, reasonable transition-point in the human development; or, if you hear how so-called *humanism* refers those black, disgraceful spots in humanity, not to a positive apostasy from God, but with weakening effect to an imperfection still adhering to human nature, in spite of which man will, of himself, without redemption, attain to full development, — must not this be to you an irrefragable proof that the human reason cannot, by its own light, apprehend that mysterious but actually-existing power which is hostile to culture, and therefore has neither the will nor the ability to lay the axe at its root? Both these are found in Christianity alone, and, indeed, in positive Biblical Christianity. Look into the history of the later philosophy and theology, and of *humanism* in general. As soon as you see the spirit of the times, or even of an individual, be he the sharpest and deepest thinker, or the naturally most noble, most amiably-disposed person, deviating from the Scriptural revelation of God touching the nature of sin, he becomes, in his scientific view, immediately more yielding and lax towards sin, the mortal enemy of sound culture, concludes a philosophical compromise with it, or overlooks it, or at least underrates its power, and the worm remains in the bud or flower, and eats it Only Biblical Christianity knows no compromise with sin, no pardon to this destroyer of mankind and its development, only deadly earnest combat till complete victory is gained. Neither does Biblical Christianity allow itself to be dazzled by a brilliant partial culture, but looks with calm, clear eye at the death-germ concealed therein, and says decidedly and earnestly, "Ye must be born again. That which is born of the flesh is flesh; and all flesh is as grass, and all the goodliness thereof as the flower of the field." But it adds, "Ye *can* be born again!" and actually and truly provides the means whereby man and human society may be delivered from the dominion of the power inimical to culture, and thoroughly renewed.

This is not to be understood as affirming that the bearers of Christianity would be, at once, wholly and forever freed from that corruptive power; rather are we taught by experience that, both in single Christian personalities and in Christian communities, sin, the root of barbarism, has, alas, very often in a terrible way broken out anew. This, however, is not the fault of Christianity, but of the want of attention to it. While Humanism on the heights of her development makes it a rule — as one can nowadays easily see — to boast of her strength, beauty, and elevation, and cries out to everybody, So high I have come by my own strength, never shall I be made low! Christianity makes it a rule to admonish her adherents to continued humility, to earnest search for knowledge of the sin still adherent and always asserting its existence anew, to incessant repentance and self-abasement. The first of Luther's articles — those ninety-five from which the renovation of Christianity has proceeded — runs, "Whereas our Master and Lord Jesus Christ says, Repent, etc., he would that the whole life on earth of his believing ones should be a constant or incessant repentance." As soon as the Christian community should forget this, and mind not the corruptive power still inherent in itself, it would be ruined by this, as were the states of antiquity. The Romish Church is the proof. Before the Reformation it was still penetrated by a consciousness of an internal corruption; the cry for a reformation in head and members was as yet not to be suppressed. But since the Tridentine Council every recognition of internal sin and impurity has disappeared; no expression of repentance on the part of the church as such, only boasting of infallibility, of perfection. But since then the states in which the Papal Church has been able to unfold its power without restriction have been very nearly ruined.

There are many sad defects in our Evangelical Church.

There is much that is rotten in the predominantly Evangelical States. But as long as our church remains conscious of its internal evils, and truly and honestly confesses and contends against them; as long as the Protestant peoples truly observe their national fast-days; as long, in a word, as we have the real sources of corruption disclosed for us by Christianity, — so long will our history furnish the proof that Christianity is the salt of the earth.

Or does human history show us another power which can preserve from putrefaction, and thoroughly cleanse, sanctify, form anew? Perhaps reason and science? "Possibly," says Hamann, "philosophy could do us no other service than to set our passion in a methodical, forced, and affected play" (vol. II. p. 195). And the same Mephistopheles, who terms reason and science the highest potency of man, flings, nevertheless, into the face of the god of humanism, in cold blood, the affirmation that man uses the appearance of the heavenly light, reason, only

> "To be more beastly than any beast.
> Saving thy Gracious Presence, he to me
> A long-legged grasshopper appears to be,
> That springing flies, and flying springs,
> And in the grass the same old ditty sings.
> Would he still lie among the grass he grows in!
> Each bit of dung he seeks, to stick his nose in." [1]

In *each bit of dung!* And can the impartial history of mankind, and especially the history of philosophy and science, say to Mephistopheles, — Thou liest! Must it not rather change the ironic "possibly" of Hamann into an indisputable surely. Nothing else, indeed, can be done. Philosophy does not make man, but man makes his philos

---

[1] Bayard Taylor's Translation, p. 15.

ophy. Man is not a product of his reason, but reason is one of the faculties of man. As is the man, so is also his reason, his philosophy. The reason is an expression, a revelation, of the human existence. If this, the fountain, is pure, then is also the emanation pure; if the fountain is turbid, then also the emanation. The emanation cannot cleanse the fountain. Man purifies the reason; not the reason man. Man preserves the reason from sin and error; not the reason man. First, then, must man's essential being be redeemed from the power inimical to culture, and then a redemption also of the reason can be expected. Or is a sickly root to be cured by attempting to cultivate on the tree a bough? Only Christianity seeks to sanctify the kernel of the human personality from within, and thence to carry purification through the individual faculties of the human life, such as understanding, reason, imagination, talent for art, etc.; while the non-Christian wisdom endeavors, by beginning with the individual faculties,— reason, talent for art, and the like, — to improve the central natures of men.

In the same measure, then, in which it is true that only Christianity takes cognizance of and overcomes the enemies of culture, in that measure is it true that Christianity is the groundwork of culture; and in the measure in which it is true that all other views of life do not take cognizance of the enemies of culture and their real nature, still less overcome them, in that measure is it true that they cannot be regarded as suitable for the groundwork of a sound and enduring culture. With these general considerations, let us turn yet to the principal phenomena of the cultural life. As such I designate the free, spiritual personality, marriage and the family-relation, the state, and again, within these domains of life, science and art.

We begin with the conception of personality. The ancient philosophy, in order to hold fast the unity of deity, surrendered the living personality of the same, and did not find it again, even through Plato, still less through Aristotle. From that time down to the present, the philosophy which has not been rooted in the Christian revelation has been so little able to attain to an understanding of the Absolute Personality, that it has declared the same to be an absurdity, a self-contradiction, or else has degraded the Absolute Personality to the pitiable figure of the impotent, dead, mummy-like Deistic and Rationalistic God. Nay, even the theology which has not been firmly rooted in the Biblical revelation has abandoned the personality of God. Remember, for instance, Schleiermacher. If there is no *absolute* personality, there is also no *relative* personality. In pantheism, man is an emerging, and again disappearing wave of the great life-substance; the system knows only necessity, not freedom, not personality. According to materialism, man is a product of matter; his thoughts and feelings are the secretions of bodily functions. How can free, spiritual personality be here spoken of? To flat rationalism, man is — pardon the expression — an understanding-chest; to the higher rationalism, a thinking existence, whose reason is able to fathom and criticise all things. The wonderful mystery of a full, living personality is reduced to a logical phantom. Even the theology which is wiser than divine revelation in the end lets the human personality go, as is evident enough from its doctrine respecting the life eternal. Only Christianity brings us to even a far-off understanding of the Absolute Personality; only Christianity, therefore, is in earnest about the relative personality of man. " Let us make man in our image, after our likeness. So God created man in his own image, in the image of God created he him." Man, then, according to the Christian view, is a free, spiritual personality; for he is the image of the Absolute Personality. And now consider what an important relation the *personality* sustains to culture; that it is so much the bearer of culture, that without it culture seems inconceivable. Remember, further, that all great historical epochs of culture have had their starting-point in the relatively creative power of personality, their promotion in the force of personalities, their culmination in the glory of a personality; or that even in the aberration of a personality the most energetic powers have concentrated themselves to one-sidedness, to distortion, to ruin. And as the sure result of your reflection the conviction will force itself on you, that a view of life which obliterates the essential conception of personality is, in its inmost nature, inimical to culture; that, on the contrary, Christianity, whose inmost impulse is the knowledge and care of personality, must be called Guardian and Friend of culture. This would still more plainly appear, could we enter into the spirituo-moral sanctification and unfolding of the human personality. We admire the masters of art, who, as with poetic license we express ourselves, breathe life into blocks of marble; but what are all these masters compared with the personal Originator of Christianity, who breathes his life into lost human nature, and makes of it actually and truly living images of God! But this consideration would lead us from the realm of culture into that which is specifically religious; hence we relinquish it, and only refer to the familiar words of the man who makes the development of the human race to commence with sin: —

> "Religion of the cross, only thou bindest together in one
> Crown of humility and strength two gifts of the palm."

Certainly, the religion which in such a way exerts a cultural influence on the human personality, and indeed according to the admission of one who was not its friend, has a sound and fruitful culture-producing power.

The essential thing in the human personality is the image of God, and indeed not merely in the free man of a select race, but in all men, also in the slave and in the woman. Moreover, the God who, with the creation of man, breathed into him his living, spiritual breath, also implanted in apostate humanity his only-begotten Son, the express image of his person, that by him every man might be freed from sin and renewed from glory to glory. Every man who is led back by Christ into life-fellowship with God is a child and heir of God; stands before God as a king. Christ, the first-born Son of God, so loved, so highly esteemed every man that he laid down his life for him, and is not ashamed to call him his brother, and says to all the children of men, "*Whatsoever* ye have done unto one of the least of these my brethren ye have done unto me; and *whatsoever* ye did not unto one of the least of these ye did not to me." So Christianity looks on man, and by this view alone is the unculture and barbarism connected with the establishing by classic antiquity of a degrading difference between people, between man and man, between man and woman, overcome. As an irrefutable maxim in the consideration of the human personality within Christianity the saying of Paul now holds good, "*Here* there is neither Jew nor Greek, neither bond nor free, neither male nor female; for ye are all one in Christ Jesus (Gal. 3: 28). And *ye* have put on the new man which is renewed in the image of him that created him; where there is neither Greek nor Jew, circumcision nor uncircumcision, barbarian, Scythian, bond nor free; but Christ is all, and in all" (Col. 3: 10, 11). Here we have the noble, vigorous root from which alone true culture in the consideration and treatment of the human personality has grown, and can grow. A man who will not be continually influenced by the spirit of Christianity cannot possibly apprehend in the perishing and lost the dignity of the human personality. He will, first in the treatment, and then also in the consideration of the human personality, approximate to the ancient barbarism. A partial culture does so little against this, that it looks upon him who lacks this partial culture as inferior, erects barriers, and lapses into a squeamish caste-existence. For knowledge puffs up, only love edifies.

Only by woman's being put on a complete equality with man, in the points which concern the essential being of the human personality, is it possible for man duly to esteem woman, and in the full sense of the word love her, i. e., give himself to her, and for the woman to become really the helpmate of man. Only on this condition also is a true marriage and a true family-relation possible. Only by Christianity, therefore, is woman placed in the position that rightfully belongs to her, a position where she can develop the whole power of her womanhood. Only by Christianity has the man as well as the woman received the incalculable blessing of a true matrimonial family-life. The philosophers of the later antiquity beheld with amazement the wonderful transformation which Christianity had effected in woman, marriage, families.

Libanius, a mortal enemy of Christianity, the tutor of Cæsar Julian the apostate, who pronounced his pupil John Chrysostom the most excellent of all, when he had heard the boy's story about his mother Anthusa, broke forth in the words, "What women these Christians have!"

Marriage and the family are the bases of culture. He

who undermines them is a traitor to mankind and its healthful development. Something of this even a Horace saw. He confesses (Odes, Bk. III. 6) : —

> "Fertile in sins, the times of late
> Have rendered, first, the marriage-state,
>   Then race and home, unsound.
> From this polluted fountain-head
> The direst influence has spread
>   O'er land and people round.

> "What has unspoiled by time remained?
> The age which to our sires pertained,
>   More vicious a degree
> Than our grandsires, has given birth
> More vile to us, who'll curse the earth
>   With offspring worse than we."

No civilization which is not grounded firmly in God's word can keep marriage and the family-relation pure and steadfast. In the times of the most brilliant partial culture, just these fundamental conditions of genuine culture suffer most; as you have just heard from the mouth of Horace, and as the history of a Louis XIV. and his times tells you. The aberration of men's heads and hearts goes so far that the chief supports no longer are recognized as the chief supports. That is barbarism in principle. And this barbarism reigns in our day, in our midst. The past century is considered to be the blooming-period of our poetry. And precisely this century has given us a marriage-legislation by which marriage is in reality abolished. "Because the matrimonial relation," says Hamann, "is the precious foundation and corner-stone of all society, the misanthropical spirit of our century reveals itself most largely in the marriage laws."[1] One who

---
[1] Versuch einer Sibylle über die Ehe, vol. IV. p. 227.

refuses to be judged wholly by divine revelation laughs low or loud, and proceeds to prove, by his reason or his æsthetical taste, that the ground-pillars of culture are not the ground-pillars of culture, that at all events they can be eaten into by subjective lusts,—as can be plainly seen by way of example even in Schleiermacher's letters about Frederick Schlegel's sad "Luzinde," in æsthetical garb in Goethe's "Affinities" and "Stella," and in later times, open and blunt, in the pleasure-and-authority doctrine, as well as in public demands of the well-known Her von Kirchmann,[1] formerly president of the Court of Appeals.

He whose eyes this does not open must read the thousand wretched romances which for a century have been devoured by our people, and whose chief service has been to undermine the Christian view of marriage and of the family-relation; or he must look behind the screens of the more than heathenish so-called free love in America;[2] and, if all this does not suffice, then he must cast a glance into the fearful orgies of our large and small cities, and into the sentiments of millions of our cultivated and uncultivated cotemporaries on matrimony and the relation of the sexes,—to see with horror what it is a shame to speak of. Did Christianity not stand here, as a preacher in the wilderness, and scatter a little small salt, the decaying foundations would long since have fallen in, and the abyss of barbarism have swallowed us up. But Christianity is in this region also a salt which can save our culture from universal and absolute rottenness. Still truly Christian marriages and families stand before the eyes of poor ship-

---

[1] Æsthetik auf realistischer Grundlage (Berlin, 1868), vol. I., p. 99 ff. 108 ff. The same Kirchmann, moreover, condemns in the sharpest terms the "Luzinde" which Schleiermacher deifies as the ideal of woman's love for man, vol. I., p. 313. So fall even great theologians when God's word is no longer a lamp to their feet.

[2] Comp. Volksblatt für Stadt und Land, 1869, no. 4.

wrecked people as saving ideals. Think of Kinkel. With Christianity he has absolutely broken. "Let," he cries, —

> "Let old women vex themselves,
> Will they then, 'bout heaven;
> Free men, though, we are, and will
> Not to that be given."

But this same Kinkel sees a quiet parsonage, in which Christ is guest and has sanctified marriage and the household-relation, and sighs : —

> "Blessed peace! all world-embittered,
> Wounded, flees my heart to thee,
> Trembles with foreboding of that
> Rest in the Eternity."

> "Yes, my heart, with ease thou couldest
> Thus the world's affairs resign;
> And thou wouldest beat more calmly,
> Were such outward quiet thine!"

We enter upon the domain of the political life. To him who admits that esteem for the human personality, that marriage and the family-relation are the groundworks of human society, — to him it is clear beyond a doubt that only Christianity can produce, sustain, consummate genuine political organizations. To him who does not admit the maxim named it is as impossible in this field to say another word, as in the field of mathematics to one who refuses to accept the multiplication-table.

But let us notice other fundamental relations which condition the life of the state; and, first of all, the divisions, necessary to organic life, into rich and poor, high and low, etc. What is naturally good and necessary the power hostile to culture has transformed into fatal contradictions.

As in the atmosphere the inequalities of temperature strive by storms to equalize themselves, so in the popular life it has, down to the present, stormed, and will continue to storm, in order to equalize the rough, unendurable inequalities. In the non-Christian cultural life there is no means by which the same may be effected. This even thoughtful heathen perceived. Aristotle remarks that most counsel for the quieting of the people aimed at a correct disposition of the relations of ability; for thence generally arose tumults. "But," says he then, "much rather is it needful to equalize the desires than the possessions. For men commit wrong not merely on account of necessary wants, such as hunger and thirst, but also for their gratification, to still their desires; nay, the greatest sins occur on account of excessive lusts, not on account of necessary wants. The baseness of men is an insatiable thing; it asks more and more to infinity; for boundless is the nature of desire, for whose satisfaction the great mass of people live." (Politics, vol. II., chap. 4, § 4, 5-11.) So far philosophy. Only Christianity is rich and strong enough to equalize the pernicious inequalities. The essential difference between man and man, between people and people, it has in principle overcome. Every man, every people, recognized in his or its worthiness, receives through Christianity a possession and enjoyment, an end to aim at by which the whole man can be satisfied, and sees thereby the fundamental condition of development met. In truth, Christianity is so far from wishing to abolish all earthly differences and make all things even that it supports as a divine regulation the division of society into classes, such as rulers and subjects, rich and poor, gentle and common. But while it always accents the idea that this difference is only temporal and accidental, not an essential one, rather that the real kernel of the human personality is of like worth and summoned to a like end; it incites the one to labor and earnest combat to obtain for himself in a justifiable way the external earthly position which renders possible and facilitates the internal progress, and teaches the other not miserly to keep to himself the advantages lent him, but to recognize the former in his struggle. "Let the brother of low degree rejoice in that he is exalted; but the rich in that he is made low." This is the only possible equalization; every other attempt at it will fail.

Another fundamental relation in the state's life is that of justice and duty. In the *humane* state, theoretically only justice reigns so much that it is called the justice-state.[1] It is utterly impossible for justice alone to bind the state together in a unitary organism. Justice divides to every man his own, and punishes him who reaches beyond his own. Granting now that justice could succeed in accomplishing the impossible and thus did divide to every man his own, and restrain every man from grasping that of others, still every individual would be, only a little isolated whole by himself, an atom. Who shall bring the atoms together into one great living whole? It is said, Duty, which even the justice-state requires. Were men numbers or logical conceptions, then it would be possible to execute such an equilibristic feat, in which duty and justice keep up between them the balance. But, now, men have strong desires; especially are they full of the selfish desire to claim very much as justice, and to regard very little as duty, for themselves. Who shall restore the equilibrium? Only the conqueror of the selfish desires, Love, can do that. And, indeed, not the hollow phrase

---

[1] Der Rechtsstaat.

of love; but the essential love which is grounded in Christianity, or, better, in Christ. When this love, born of God, the giving of self to the whole and to individuals, a principle that cannot be extorted by any Jus, forms no longer a power in the popular life, then will also the modern state, as did the ancient, fall into atomic fragments, and bleed to death on the internal contradiction between required justice and duty not performed.[2]

Permit me to refer yet to a fundamental condition in the popular life, to the relation between labor and rest. In the stir and whirl of the present, when restlessly and gigantically progressing industry, in union with as violent a passion for enjoyment, is urging on humanity, already urged half-to-death, more and more, Christianity calmly stands, and wearies not in attesting that only the right observance of the Sabbath can save individuals and peoples from being ruined by work and pleasure. In North America first, and secondly in England, this restless activity is at the highest. Were it not that in these countries Sunday is still celebrated, perhaps as a state-custom, who knows but that they would have already exhausted their energies? That with us mails and roads, in many places manufactories also, and on numerous large estates agriculture, find no rest even on the Sabbath, contributes not to the promotion of culture. To assail the Sabbath is to assail a jewel of culture, a foundation-pillar of the popular welfare.

A deadly enemy of Christianity, the so-called Social

[1] Two of Shakespeare's principal plays, "The Merchant of Venice" and "Measure for Measure," show that state laws fail to preserve the state, private justice to protect the private life of the citizens, and penal justice to compel in the right way the public life; that, if the life of the state is to prosper, other forces, grace and love, and indeed such grace and love as come from God's grace and love, must rule in it.

Democratic party, has perceived this at least, and is clamoring loudly for freedom from labor on Sunday. But transplant the noblest date-palm into northern soil, and it remains there not the date-palm. Sunday is blessing-bringing Sunday only in the maternal soil of Christianity. In the Social Democratic camp it will become the day it is already everywhere in apostate Christendom, — the day on which the most sins occur, and culture is the most deeply sapped.

And now ask the present world around you, Who are they that still place themselves in the midst of the waves protectingly about this popular and cultural palladium, the Sabbath, the true equalizer of labor and rest; the disciples of positive, Biblical Christianity, or the men who make of Christianity half an echo and half a marionette of the times-spirit?

I have thus far spoken on the principles of Christianity and of the state; I must now invite you to question universal history. Which are the states, still existing, whose mother is not Christianity? There are in reality only two. The Chinese empire and the Turkish! For neither culture does any adversary of Christianity have an itching.

All the other states of our day were founded and have been, and are still, sustained by Christianity. Dating our present state-formations no farther back than the times of Charlemagne and Alfred the ·Great, we have lasted already a thousand years. Greece and Rome were after a thousand years no more. Their citizens were just as wise, just as rational, just as energetic, just as patriotic, just as æsthetic, just as juristic, just as diplomatic, just as rhetorical as we are. That no one will dispute. The enemies, too, of our peoples and states are equally as powerful and numerous as were theirs. But still we are not yet in the grave; on the contrary, the assurance is given us that the nineteenth century is the blooming-period of mankind. Has a mightier industry, has the enormous progress of the natural sciences, prolonged our life beyond that of those noble, ancient peoples? That one would hardly like to affirm. Well, then I know of nothing else that they had not, and that we have, save Christianity, whose principles are the sources and fortresses of sound political principles.

And still Christianity continues to demonstrate its people-improving and state-forming potency. The heathen mission is a child of positive Christianity. This has an internal and necessary prompting to restore the dignity of the human personality in all men, thereby to establish an existence worthy of man, marriage, and the state. They who accept Christianity only after having deprived it of its soul, feel not this prompting. They resign to selfish culture the cultivation of the savage peoples. We see, to be sure, that traders carry powder and brandy and moral pest into the lands of the heathen, and increase the original barbarism, if only thereby they become richer and gratify their desires. Is that culture? Whence, then, shall those peoples receive culture, if not from Christianity? "Could, indeed," an eminently scientific man asks the *humane* culture, "could, indeed, our literati and academicians so much as land on the coasts of savage, hostile peoples, except they brought with them the resignation with which an apostle comes who is ready to become a martyr? Or should," he adds in the most profound irony, "or should this mission of civilization wait a while, until the islands had received European governments, and one could unpack and set up the beautiful instruments under the protection of cannon?"[1]

---

[1] Nitzsch: What Evangelical Christianity has done among Cultureless Peoples, according to Facts from the Missionary History of the last Half-century. (A Lecture.) Berlin. Wilhelm Schultze. 1852.

He then notices what Christianity has in our times made, e. g., of the South Sea Islands, of New Zealand, of the Karens; confesses, "Without a miracle such an establishing of culture is impossible!" and refers to the expression of Karl Ritter, who calls the transformation, effected by evangelical Christianity, of the New Zealand cannibals into peaceful men, "a true miracle of our day." He, an ornament to science, openly declares, what to be sure we all know, that not science, not the doctrines of universal religion, but the peculiar facts of Christianity worked this cultural miracle.

Where Biblical Christianity is lastingly injured, there the states also suffer severe injuries. Since the Tridentine Council, Romish Christianity has set itself in intentional and persistent opposition to essential points of Biblical Christianity. Who but a blind man can to-day deny that the purely Catholic States are also those which present the saddest aspect!

"In Italy," — so, in the midst of the triumphal procession of King Victor Immanuel, an eminent statesman, who concerned himself personally very little about religious matters, said to me, — "in Italy not the financial trouble is the one full of despair, but the wide-spread undermining of the state's religious and moral foundations." Is there any need of saying much as to Spain? And has it proved the salvation of France that under Louis XIV., brilliant infidelity, moral frivolity, egotistic absolutism, on the one side, and the stiffest Romanism on the other, combined by the destruction of Jansenism to put down the last powerful reaction of Biblical Christianity inside the Catholic Church?

And look at our German fatherland. When did its national honor lie deepest in disgrace? From what cause came the day of Jena, and what followed it, upon us? And by what means have we risen from the disgrace? The displacement of Christianity from the popular life by French immorality and stupid rationalism,—that it was that overthrew our national life. The new Christian breath of life has saved us.

I leave this domain, to conduct you to that of science and art. Our noblest and most peculiar treasure is language. The centre-point of science is, therefore, the science of language. Christianity has brilliantly proved its language-forming power. Let us stop, first, with our mother tongue. The present form thereof has its vigorous life-root in the Lutheran translation of the Bible. A departure from the spirit breathing in this for a long while corrupted our language. A new and better epoch begins with Klopstock's Messias. By Klopstock, and still more by the Lutheran Bible, Goethe and Schiller had their language formed.

Compare with the German language which has proceeded from our Bible the language which our philosophers speak, e. g., a Hegel. We can and we will rejoice in our German language more than many peoples can in theirs, but certainly not in the Hegelian or the abstract philosophical in general, which long since — and it deserved it — became a derision.

That Dante, and especially his Divine Comedy, born as it was of Christianity, has in like manner become the father of the Italian language, as Luther of ours, I will at least in a word mention, to remind you then of a fact which in the whole history of culture stands alone. The Bible is now translated into one hundred and eighty-two languages and dialects. In not yet one hundred years about one hundred languages have been raised by Biblical

Christianity to Scripture-language; and with this Bible language the foundation for wider culture in all departments of science and art is laid. That is a phenomenon in the realm of the spirit which all the gigantic advances and discoveries in the realm of nature do not equal. And this miracle of language-forming has been wrought, forsooth, neither by Romish, nor Rationalistic, but solely by positively Biblical Christianity.

This also is a fact, that the places of the higher scientific as well as the popular education have originated in the spirit of Biblical Christianity. The materialistic and industrial sense of our day is pressing boisterously towards the dominancy of the so-called real-schools. It remains to be seen, whether a full-rounded, complete culture will proceed from them; they do not yet, like the classic schools born of Christianity, belong to history. But it can be already seen that the gymnasia and the classical training cared for by them can be defended successfully against the assaults of industrialism and materialism only by genuine Christianity.

If we look beyond the bounds of Europe, at those peoples whose culture is far inferior to ours, we find it is again Christianity that brings to them also the scientific institutes. "Have, then," asks the man of science to whom I have already referred, "the European governments and academies only a far-off merit for the founding of the scientific and educational establishments of Serampore, Malacca, Calcutta, Eimeo, etc., compared with that of the missionaries and the societies which send them?"

The individual branches of science, too, are largely indebted to Christianity, even those many of whose representatives are to-day the most ungrateful heirs of the scientific treasures of their great predecessors, — I mean the natural sciences. From the womb of positive Christianity have been born men like Copernicus, Kepler, Haller, Newton, whose labors and discoveries belong, in any case, to the foundation and corner-stones of the present physics. The heart-throb of their scientific endeavor was the incitement to fathoming the works of God. And since this incitement is an inmost impulse of Christianity in general, that impulse must prompt, and continually, to the investigation of nature. The sins which have been, and will be, consciously or unconsciously committed under the name of Christianity must not be attributed to this itself. Its only concern is that what actually exists be most fundamentally searched into and found out; for only what actually exists, not the human notion of the same, is the work of God, a way-mark to God and a herald of his glory. The natural science which in these days calumniously opposes Christianity takes its chief weapons, not from the actually existing, but from its thoughts, conclusions, hypotheses, about the same; and persuades the credulous multitude, that its ephemeral hypotheses, which like waves displace each other, are the facts themselves. This fallacy, which surely does not promote true science, Christianity contravenes. Moreover, it relegates natural science within its bounds, namely, within the realm of nature; reminds it earnestly that there is another, independent, higher realm, that of the spiritual life, whose laws cannot be apprehended through the laws of nature; saves natural science from the foolish, unscientific delusion, that it is the only and the great science which can pass valid judgment on all things, even on the spiritual life; takes it out of its isolation and fitly joins it, at its rightful place, into the great organism of the universal science of mankind. Had not Christianity at times rendered natural science this service, consciously or unconsciously to the latter, it would long since have entirely sunken down to the materialistic lack of science.

While I remind you, only as it were in passing, of what enrichments the knowledge of lands and peoples has experienced through the Christian missions, I direct your attention to the science of history. Only by the Christian, fundamental view of a development, under the divine government of the world, of the human race, which has its starting and its ending point, has a science of history become possible. Christianity alone names to us a definite germ and a definite termination of development. Every non-Christian view, which retains the idea of an organic development, makes of it an unending process, an endless screw, which contradicts the nature of a development. "Not all events," says Hamann (I., 55), "can be explained by titles and reasons of state." There are divine purposes operative in human affairs. They are the very soul of events. When these are unknown or overlooked, then, to use again the language of Hamann, must "our history look leaner than Pharaoh's kine; however, fairy-tales and court-papers supply the lack in our historians" (II., 279). " Can one know the past when he does not even understand the present? And who would form correct conceptions of the present without knowing the future? The future determines the present, and this the past, as the design nature, and use the means" (II., 217). From these simple words of the Magus of the North it is clear why only Biblical Christianity can write the history of mankind.[1]

[1] Even a Hegel sets up the Machiavellian doctrine, that in politics ethics do not hold good, in blunt phrase as the crown-point of his philosophy: "The history of the world is outside of the stand-point of righteousness and virtue" (VIII., 424). In the work of Kirchmann. referred to above, this view is praised as the highest wisdom, and it is taught that mankind moves, properly speaking, neither forwards nor backwards, — consequently, no development, no history, exists. Vol. I., p. 139 ff., 160.

We come to philosophy. If he only is a philosopher who constructs the universe exclusively from his reason, according to his intellectual ability, then, it is true, Christianity is the death of philosophy. For it is a fundamental presupposition of Christianity that as effort by the law only brings us to a knowledge of our unrighteousness, so the reason's search only reveals the impossibility of coming by that means to a knowledge of the truth. The history of philosophy is old enough to show this. Had not Christianity exerted an influence on our philosophy also, and breathed into it some elements of truth, the impotency of philosophy to find the truth would be much more generally seen. Our later philosophy sets itself up as a master over the facts, instead of humbly subjecting itself to them and being taught by them. That is not science, that is presumption. True science begins with self-knowledge, with the knowledge of one's limitations and of the recognition due to other powers. Of this modesty the non-Christian philosophy knows little. On the contrary, it is the natural impulse of Christianity conscientiously to regard the facts of life, both those of the relative, the human life, and those of the absolute, the divine life. Life, universal Life, is our instructress, not a dismembered expression or faculty of life, like Reason, — whose soundness, besides, remains to be proved.[1] Only the philosophy, therefore, which has germinated from the totality of normal life can also lead to the consummation; while a philosophy which has come from a dismembered faculty of life must necessarily prove one-sided. If this is correct, then it is clear also that only from Christianity can that philosophy which is a mirror of

---

[1] "The soundness of the reason is the cheapest, most arbitrary, and most shameless pretension, by which the very things to be proved are taken for granted, and all free investigation is excluded more violently than by the infallibility of the Roman Catholic Church." Hamann, vol. IV., p. 324.

the truth grow; because only Christianity looks upon the normal, the redeemed and sanctified life in God and from God as the root of a normal knowledge. The vigorous germs of such a philosophy we have; I need only mention Hamann and Baader. Their unfolding, the future will bring.

It is left yet to show the influence of Christianity on art. I commence with architecture. Visit the marble temple of Theseus at Athens, — the single completely preserved ancient temple, — then hasten to Constantinople, and enter the Hagia Sophia. While the interior of the antique temple shows scarcely the attempt at a dominion of the spirit over matter, — the expression of an idea by the structure itself, — the interior of the church of Saint Sophia is, notwithstanding the Mohammedan disfiguration, the clear and grand testimony of the stones that the people of God have a house of God on earth. In our Gothic cathedrals, architecture has celebrated its triumph. Every part of the building is in itself the victory of the spirit over the material, of heaven over earth; every part cries, Upward! And every one of the innumerable individual existences adjusts itself readily as a living member in the totality, and the totality comprehends the language of all the separate parts in one great and mighty accord, in the words, "Set your affection on things above, not on things of the earth!"

This impression is strengthened by the art of painting; specially the art of painting on glass. It shows us in the transfiguration of which the colors in general are capable, symbolically and representatively, the powers which liberate us from the earth and carry us up into the transfiguring light of heaven.

This brings me to painting in general.

"Only on ecclesiastical themes," says Schnaase,[1] "can this art acquire a satisfactory, permanent style; without them, it becomes unsteady and vacillating, and at last declines to a mere play of talents, to an idle means of tickling the senses. Of this the artists themselves are sensible, even those who are little touched by religious motives."

Imagine that of the number of our pictures which pass as masterpieces all those were destroyed which represent persons and occurrences of Biblical and of ecclesiastical history, or in general Christian states of soul,— what would you have left? The unanimous reply to this question shows most forcibly how extraordinary must be the formative power of Christianity in this province of art. I will not by enlarging weaken the impression of this simple fact. Allow me in but a word to point out the internal reason.

Only the Biblical Christian view of history, as a progressive revelation of the being and will of God, brings unity and entireness into the same; and only such a view of history can produce pictures of imperishable worth.

Again, the revelation of divine glory in the human face, the transfiguration of the human lowliness into the divine elevation, love and sacrifice even to death, victory in defeat, calmness and resignation in suffering, the beginning of bodily transfiguration from spiritual purity and mildness,— these and similar phenomena of life will, according to their natures, always form the principal subjects of earnest, representative art; because they offer the most beautiful, most living, most speaking forms. And they all are truly and in their completeness to be found only in Christianity. This finds its application in principle to sculpture also. Christianity has broken through the narrow barriers which this art had with the ancients, and endeavors to breathe

[1] Ueber das Verhältniss der Kunst zum Christendom.

even into stone and metal something else than bodily beauty and purity of form. The Christian ideas must speak also from the marble. And though, it is true, success has not yet been reached in fully reconciling that with the laws of the plastic art, yet Lorenzo Ghiberti, in the reliefs on the so-called Gates of Paradise; Michel Angelo, in his Moses and The Descent from the Cross; Peter Vischer, in the statues and reliefs on the Sebaldus Monument; and in our times, Dannecker, in his colossal Statue of Christ; Thorwaldsen, in his Christ and the Twelve Apostles, — have made victorious attempts at plastically representing all the fulness of the human spirit pervaded by the divine.

Follow me into the realm of music and singing.

The two most powerful instruments by which art calls forth sounds are the bell and the organ. Both are children of Christianity, live with it, and with it would perish. The bell, it is true, has, like the sea, only one sound, but a sound full of majesty and power, full of alluring clearness and mysterious depth; and in company with its sisters, it sends forth from the heights over the activity of the world its mighty accord, which is full of heavenly peace, and allures to heavenly peace. The organ is the most complete musical instrument that we have or can as yet on the whole conceive of. Force and mildness; the thunder and roar which rends the hearts of rocks, and the still small voice of Jehovah; the deep complaint of the anguished conscience; the exulting praise of the redeemed spirit, and the still, uniform quiet of the forward-struggling pilgrim; and again the glow of sacrificing love, the storming of the combatant in the realm of the spirit, and the victor's song of triumph; the fervent confession of the individual soul and of the entire communion, and all else that rests in the Christian heart and in the Christian people,— this rests also in the organ and streams forth from its wonderful mouth.

They who long since tore Christ from their hearts cannot resist these messengers of Christ, — the tone of the organ and the sound of the bell,— but must with tears confess their calming, saving power, as is a thousand times to be read in our tales, legends, popular songs, and even in the poems of our infidels. When a man like Bürger would denote the highest and most beautiful, he says, "High soundest thou, song, like organ tone and sound of bell." And even from the lips of a Faust the tone of the organ and the bell's sound draw away the poisoned cup.

What shall I say of singing and music? How long would the most decided worldlings who have an organ for music remain, think you, at concerts, should they hear nothing but what the worldly sense has produced, and be required to miss all that bears upon itself decidedly or approximately the Christian character? Christianity is the kernel of our music; Christianity has raised it to the highest pitch it has in general as yet attained. I need only mention such men as, in the south, Palestrina,[1] and in our north, Händel and Bach. Since Beethoven styled Bach the "first parent of harmony," and Mendelssohn Bartholdy turned the hearts of the children of art to the fathers, even apostates from Christianity have been praising the creative father. Many men, whose judgments are considered good authority in this department, call him the greatest of musicians. Think you of Händel, then you must not forget that the bloom of his music belongs to the period of his later development, after he, at Aix la Chapelle, physically by the bath, spiritually by the Spirit of Christ, had been as

---

[1] Palestrina's teacher was Claude Goudimel, the Reformed creator of the psalm-melodies, who fell a martyr, on the night of Saint Bartholomew, in Paris.

it were born anew. Not the single Christian individuals who are called Bach and Händel produced the Bachian and Händelian music, but the spirit of Christianity. Without Biblical Christianity, Bachian and Händelian music is inconceivable.

Tarry yet a moment with the choral. I do not here speak of what incalculable influence the same has on our spiritual and ecclesiastical life; I only pray you to consider what position it occupies in music. Many words are unnecessary. The masters of art bow themselves before the choral. And who produced this pearl of art? Positive Biblical Christianity.

At last I lead you to the crown of all art, to poetry. Taking our stand preliminarily with the last century of German literature, and from that point surveying the whole earlier development of culture, we are greeted by the fact, that, so to speak, all classical and world-historic works of a poetical character have sprung from the Christian spirit. Right at the beginning of the history of our German literature stands the Heliand, a work in which the most original, strongest nationality is in so entirely living and genuine a way pervaded by the spirit of Christianity, that it must be called as primitively Christian as it is primitively German. Quite as clear a mirror of German Christianity are the chief poets of the first flowering-time of our literature. Our two great popular epics, the Nibelungen and Gudrun, come as to their original legendary content from pagan times; this has, however, like the whole German people, been regenerated to a new life by Christianity. Both epics busy themselves with the fundamental presuppositions of Christianity, with the first article of the Christian faith.

After brief joy and glory, which springs not from divine soil, ensues long sorrow and great barbarism. That sings the Nibelungenlied. The reverse the song of Gudrun; after long and deep sorrow, which is endured in communion with God and leads to God, ensues great joy and profound peace for princes and peoples. To understand the character and fate of Chrimhild, as also of Gudrun, notice the power which attaches these two women to their husbands. With Chrimhild it is the noble and strong glow of natural affection; you know how Chrimhild becomes disfigured by it to a Megaera. With Gudrun it is the divine regulation which binds wife and husband for always together. Only by the strength of this divine regulation did she so endure the severest trouble that precisely from the depth of disgrace her glory beams forth most brightly.

The jewel of our art-poetry is Wolfram von Eschenbach's Percival, the real harbinger of the German Reformation. Percival is the German, the German people. He is seized with a longing, which on natural principles cannot be explained, whose origin and end he does not at first himself understand. But he has to follow it, even though to do so seems foolish. Nothing on earth satisfies the craving, not man's power, nor man's deeds, not fame, not glory, not woman's love, nor any earthly charm. But as urgent as is this longing, it is nevertheless of itself unable, though pressed near thereto, to perceive and grasp the object by which alone it can be satisfied. This natural yearning for God and heaven must also experience the descent into hell, — the hell of repentance; thus it comes to the goal, in the kingdom where God in Christ dwells among men and communicates to them his living and sanctifying energies.

Perhaps the most beautiful, most amiable embodiment of a German sort is Walther von der Vogelweide. The kernel-point of his life is life in God through Christ. From this as the centre, his feelings, meditations, thoughts, volitions,

— all are ruled and sanctified. His love for women and friends, for home and country, roots and culminates in the love of God and Christ. It is only needful to remember that song, where he, a young man, in the midst of blooming nature, sat meditatively on a stone, leg crossing leg, chin and cheek buried in his hand, and reflected on the one thought, how a person ought to live on the earth. Three treasures should be together in one shrine: honor, good, and

> The third is God's grace and faithfulness
> Than this both the others are worth less.

In Italy, somewhat later, Dante Alighieri sang his Comedy,[1] which after-generations have called the *divine*. The plastic strength, the beauty and grandeur of the forms; their clearness and transparency; their manifoldness, and again their organic unity, — is surpassed by no work of a poetic description. What Dante himself says of another of his poems holds good, in the fullest sense, respecting the Divine Comedy: that to all who pass by and understand not its meaning, it says at least, Just see how beautiful I am! And in fact all hearts are bewitched by the beauty and elevation of the poetic art in this Comedy. And it is a genuine child of Christianity.

Over three hundred years afterward, Milton, in his Paradise Lost, considered from the starting-point throughout, poetically shaped the Biblical Christian view regarding the development of our race. Milton passes without dispute as the first poet of England, i. e., the first after Shakespeare; and the strength and music of his verse, in general the classical qualities of his poetic language, the

---

[1] That is, village-song. Far from the City of God lives the man on the earth, in a miserable village, as if banished, and sings of the way to the Eternal City of Home and of its wonders.

Englishman prizes as an inexhaustible fountain of art-refreshment.

But what position does Shakespeare himself, this hero-poet who is above all comparison, take towards Christianity? He is to be styled its secular prophet. For all the Shakespearean dramas, without exception, call to us: There reigns in humanity a corrupting principle which inheres in even the noblest phenomena, and spoils them at the very time of their bloom; in the whole human race is to be found no power which could redeem from this corruption. In the most terrible way is revealed in the history of individuals and of peoples the condemning and destroying righteousness of God. The recognition of this fact, which leads to repentance, is the necessary precondition and even the beginning of the Christian view; for only by the knowledge that man and the human race have in themselves no power of effecting redemption is the eye opened for the grace of God, which hovers over the tremendous chaos of human sin, and, in the blood-soaked field of ruin, in a wonderful way, plants new life-germs, that spring up, bloom, bear fruit. To be sure, this last point is not brought out by Shakespeare with that manifoldness and extensiveness with which the first is; but it is clearly and decidedly intimated. Human sin, then, and divine grace, the cardinal points of Christianity, are also the cardinal points of Shakespeare's dramas. Withal, Shakespeare holds fast intrepidly, as positive Christianity does, the foundations of society, the sacredness of marriage, of the parental authority, of the state ordinance, of the divine majesty.

"*The man belongs to us!*" Shakespearean poetry is without Biblical Christianity inconceivable.

Concerning Shakespeare's great cotemporary in Spain, Calderon de la Barca, I must employ more condensed expression. From every production of this man breathes his genial poetic vigor; that is readily conceded by all art-critics. When he makes the Biblical Christianity, still concealed, though buried, in Roman Catholicism the animating power of his art, then he rises to the heights of art; as soon, however, as he puts into fixed forms designedly and exclusively the specifically Romish view of Christianity, then he makes — that one still always feels — truly horrid caricatures. Even a hasty analysis of the chief Shakespearean and Calderonian dramas, which would bring to view what has been said, the shortness of the time forbids.

Such of the tragedies from the so-called classic period of the French poetry as are yet to us in some degree palatable, the Esther and Athalie of Racine, owe their flavor to the salt and vigor of the Bible. By the by, I will here mention, — it may be interesting to you, at all events it is characteristic, — that even those of Voltaire's dramas which possess a trace of life and poetry, the Zaire and the Alzire, are pervaded by Christian life-emotions.[1]

But let us now return to the poetry of our fatherland, with which we began. Scarcely had Biblical Christianity been by the Reformation shelled from mediæval Catholicism and revivified, when immediately sprang up, in our German Evangelical hymn, a new vigorous branch of art, which to this day has continued bearing so many and such refreshing flowers and fruits as hardly another. In our genuine hymns with their choral melodies, art has become the common property of the people. Had we them not, then we should have scarcely anything really and truly national that is understood by all grades of education alike, and alike satisfies all. With reverence stand even

---

[1] Of the Zaire it is said in the preliminary remarks, "On l'appelle à Paris tragédie Chrétienne."

the historians of literature — as Gervinus — before the classic hymn. The educating, hallowing, ennobling influence which it has on our people is incalculable. And this spiritual song, the child of positive Biblical Christianity, becomes the most insipid, miserable abortion as soon as Biblical Christianity is deserted. Witness the ridiculously pitiable figures which the rationalism of the past and present century has made of the old hymns of the church, or the dead, hung-with-bells phantoms and mummies of so-called hymns which the spirit-of-the-age Christianity has produced. Not only a man like the minister Stein, but an exclusive artist like Winkelmann, is overpowered with indignation, when compelled to see the abuses which the tastelessness of infidelity has inflicted on the hymn.

It was the hymn that, in the saddest times of our people, saved German poetry from entirely perishing, until the so-called second blooming-period dawned. This also confessedly proceeded from Christianity, from Klopstock's Messias; and could the poet have represented Biblical Christianity purer and stronger, less marred by his feelings and pathos, his poem would have won for itself as a work of art a wholly different significance, — that is unquestionable. Now the Messias closes the old time in which Christianity was the predominant view; it showed itself, however, incompetent to subdue the new *humane* development which sprouted up in the midst of Christianity. The chiefs of our new poetry are children and promoters of this development without God; nevertheless, their principal works are witnesses for the Christian view, though in a different way. I select only Goethe's Faust and Iphigenie. The former, Faust, once living in God, then apostatizing from him and developing himself from the forces of human nature, sinks down to unreason in the witch-kitchen and vulgarity on the Brocken. Iphigenie lives and moves steadfastly in deity, is led and ruled by it, obtains through deity the victory over herself and over falsehood, and becomes thus the foundress of peace and reconciliation.

The dramas in which Goethe does not allow himself to mirror the objective truth of history and life, but presents his own views, are not really works of art; e. g., Stella and the second part of Faust. The unchristian subjectiveness which he would make good or plausible has, in these productions, killed his poetic genius. That reveals, to him who is willing to see, the culture-inimical, more definitely the art-inimical power of un-Christian and anti-Christian wisdom. Much more unmistakably and affectingly does this appear with Lord Byron and Heinrich Heine. Both are men of eminent talent for art. Both have sung imperishable songs, and, indeed, only when they permitted themselves to be brought by the spirit of discipline to an objective apprehension.[1] Both, however, intentionally resisted the Spirit of discipline which proceeds from the Father and the Son, and so committed a shameful suicide on their poetic geniuses. Heine's art sank below mediocrity. Of Lord Byron says a man who himself breathes not the air of Christianity, he is like an eagle that, on broad-extended wings, mounts up to the highest height, —

> "Yet not thus does he strive to reach the sun;
> He looks with sharp eye round for — carrion.
> Nowhere gleams there of hope one single ray;
> 'Tis only hell, no heaven in the lay."[2]

Restless, wild, demoniacal, like Byron's life, is Byron's art.

[1] It is only necessary to think of Heine's poem beginning, "Du bist wie eine Blume," or the one entitled "Frieden."
[2] By Zedlitz, Todtenkräuze, s. 81 and 82.

Here we may stop. We have wandered through the principal domains of culture. The retrospect which we have cast over more than a thousand years' history shows incontestably what creative and preservative power Christianity has exercised in all cultural realms; while the apostasy from Biblical Christianity, whether it happen on the side of superstition or on that of unbelief, undermines the bases of culture. The more thoroughly and conscientiously the study of history is prosecuted, the more will the general and meagre outlines which I have in this lecture been able to sketch become transfigured before your eyes into living and loud-speaking figures. Notwithstanding this testimony of history, the prevailing current, forsooth, which neither proceeds from divine revelation nor is willing to be guided by it, is blind and presumptuous enough to praise itself loudly as the only fostress of culture, and to put Christianity in the pillory as the foe of culture. Alas, very many of our cotemporaries, who pronounce belief in the living God and in his voice in nature, history, and revelation, to be unscientific unreason, believe this palpable lie, surrender themselves to the *humane* superstitious belief in erring humanity, and would persuade us that this superstition and its doctrine are science. What shall we do? Shall we turn from belief in God to superstitious faith in infirm humanity and to disbelief in God? Shall we, as not a few advise us, so doctor up Christianity as that by its inoculation with the culture of infidelity and superstition we poison it? Far be it! We will not spoil the salt of the earth. For if the salt has lost its savor, wherewith shall one salt? We are willing to see and admit that much superstition and infidelity, much of the flesh and the world, has found way into Christianity, and that thence many and grievous sins even against culture have flowed, sins which enemies have charged to Christianity itself. But the remedy, surely, cannot be to take up yet more poison, I mean yet more superstition and infidelity into the Christian life-blood, but to cleanse this from all that is unchristian or contrary to Christianity, and to build up ourselves on our most holy faith.

"Ye shall know them by their fruits." Let the un-Christian and anti-Christian development exhibit in more than a thousand years' history the fruits of its culture.[1] Already from the materialism of science and life, from the morass of foul literature, from the religious, political, and social cry of the times, arises a strong smell of corruption. The hidden, but, alas, even frightfully large and deep cloacæ we will leave closed. God forbid that they should ever be opened. The noble plant of culture would, in their pestilential atmosphere, suffocate.

But let us ask the apostles and prophets of this God-estranged development, what they themselves hold as to the future of their culture. Schiller may speak, who for the last ten years has been by many half-deified. Although he stands in the midst of the Christian era, although he has modelled his language after the language of the Lutheran Bible, yet to him Christianity is an abandoned, childish stand-point. There was never any especial need of Christianity to come so far as mankind has come; for what it has

---

[1] I must once more cite Herr Von Kirchmann, standing as he does on the height of the times, that one may know what his contemporaries think about culture and training. "By culture and training," it is said in the above-mentioned work, vol. I., p. 106, "is to be understood not so much an increased knowing or a greater morality as a susceptibility, altered with respect to the crude man, for the causes of pleasure and pain. . . Cultivation belongs to the realm of pleasure, and has nothing to do with morality. . . Neither does cultivation increase the sum of pleasure or of happiness; but it alters only the kinds of pleasure, of which happiness is compounded. The crude man, nay, the beast, can be as happy in degree as the cultivated man, but not in kind."

acquired and by fighting gained, it possesses of itself and by itself. In his century, as it is said in the Artists, man already was "the ripest son of Time, free through Reason, strong through Law, Lord of Nature, which loves his bonds." Art and science have brought man so far. Art will lead man to the consummation.

> "At last what has as poetry been nurst,
> Shall as a happy inspiration burst,
> And flash once more in glory, — on that day
> Man comes to truth, to which now tends his way."

This is about the view of entire *humanism*. Whether for the words "poetry" and "happy inspiration" some other catch-terms or modes of expression are adopted, is immaterial. Nevertheless, this false doctrine of humanity, which superstitiously clings to its fancies, is troubled with disbelief in its own gods. Read Schiller's Walk. The glowing picture of the seemingly most beautiful, grandest cultural life rises before you. Art, science, laws, the state, — all are most luxuriantly blooming.

> "Then melt before the startled gaze the works of night,
> Delusions old, — o'er all now pours the morning light.
> Man, happy, breaks his bonds."

Happy man, indeed! In the same verse, in the same breath, in which Schiller describes man, on the summit of culture, in the light of *humane* truth and freedom as so happy, he must after all confess that this culture is rotten, hopelessly lost. For when it is at the highest, then the rein of Shame is snapped; wild Desire shrieks for freedom; all staggers; there is error even in the bosom of God; Truth, Faith, Fidelity, are displaced by Falsehood; the holy insignia of Truth are usurped by Deceit; Justice and Law have become vaunting spectres.

> "For years, for centuries, may the mummies there
> Mock the warm life whose lying shape they wear,
> Till nature once more from her sleep awake,
> Till to dust the hollow fabric shake
> Beneath your hands, Avenging Powers Sublime,
> Your heavy iron hands, Necessity and Time.
> Then, as some tigress from the grated bar
> Bursts sudden, mindful of her wastes afar,
> Deep in Numidian glooms, Humanity,
> Fierce in the wrath of wretchedness and crime,
> Forth from the city's blazing ashes breaks,
> And the lost nature it has pined for seeks.
> Open, ye walls, and let the prisoner free!
> Safe to forsaken fields back let the wild one flee!"[1]

The picture is true. The God-estranged culture leads, as history narrates and Schiller sings to us, to corruption and wretchedness, and ends, though individual branches of the culture continue for a time to excite the admiration of the world, at last in universal barbarism. But to believe with Schiller that a *return to forsaken fields* will save the lost humanity and its rotten culture is to pay homage to a more than heathenish and popish superstition. We have need of another Saviour for our persons as well as for our culture. We know the Saviour and the culture that he has achieved.

Surrounded by the facts of impartial history as loud-speaking witnesses, and well aware of what mankind possesses in Biblical Christianity and its culture, we are disturbed by neither the pretension nor the calumny of the

---

[1] Edward Bulwer Lytton's Translation (The Poems and Ballads of Schiller) pp. 213, 214.

Spirit of the Times, though its prophets and priests are many. We know that Christ is the Life, and the Life is the Light of men, and remain mindful of the injunction, "HOLD THAT FAST WHICH THOU HAST, THAT NO MAN TAKE THY CROWN.

GENERAL INDEX

Acts of Pilate, 292.
Adhemar's theory of the eccentricity of earth's orbit, 98.
Africa, accounts of circumnavigation disbelieved by Herodotus, 77.
Airy, on the earth's oblateness, 85.
Aix la Chapelle, residence for a time of Handel, 385.
Alexander the Great, his expedition to the East, 77.
Angelo, Michael, his "Moses" and "Descent from the Cross," 384.
Antelope with one horn, 83.
"Antigone, The," of Sophocles, trifling judgment regarding marriage, 353.
Apollo Belvedere, statue of, 355.
Apostles' Creed, 50.
Architecture, influence of Christianity upon, 382.
Argyle, Duke of, "Recent Speculations on Primeval Man," 99.
Aristophanes: his observation on piety, 124; on putrefaction of ancient Greek culture, 352; his times, 359.
Aristotle: accented the unity of God as a requirement of reason, 125; his mistaken ideas of culture, 357, 358; taught the personality of Deity, 364; his views of relation between rich and poor, 371.
Atheism: described, 21-23; protest against, 29; argument on which it rests, 32.
Athens, Ruined temples of, 354.
Atomic theory, 86, 94.
ATONEMENT, THE SCRIPTURAL DOCTRINE OF, 253-275.
Atterbom, recognized the intuitive consciousness of man, 312.
Auberlen, *Die Göttliche Offenbarung*, 85.
Ausland, German magazine, referred to, 79, 80, 82, 99, 101.

Baader: approaches Christian view of the Trinity, 61; indicated the germs of a Christian philosophy, 382.
Baalbec, ruined temples there, 354.
Bach, the "first parent of harmony," 385.
Baco de Verulam, opposed the Copernican system of astronomy, 80.
Baffin, the discoverer of Baffin's Bay, 78.
Barbarians, the Greeks knew only themselves and barbarians, 356.
Barca, Calderon de la, his poetry as affected by Christianity, 389, 390.
Barnabas, Epistle of, 293.
Barrow, Sir John, 78.
Basilides, heretical teacher of second century, 290.
Basler Missions-Magazin, 80.
Bauer, on resurrection of Christ, 217.
Beethoven, 385.
Bell, The, a child of Christianity, 384.
Bernoulli, opposed Newton's system of gravitation, 80.
Berzelius, one of the authors of atomic theory, 94.
Bessel, made investigations of earth's oblateness, 85.
Bible, the Sinaitic, 287.
Billed animal discovered in New Holland, 82.
Blood, discovery of its circulation, 83.
Blumenbach, a noted physiologist, 72.
Braniss, on Christianity and philosophy, 61.
Brewster, David, referred to, 80.
Brocken, journeys to the, 76.
Bryant, translation by, of Homer, 356.
Buddhism, contains materialism, 24.
Büchner: a leading German materialist, 24; quoted, 155.
Burger, appreciation of the organ and bell, 385.

399

Burmeister, author of "History of Creation," 91.
Burton, an African explorer, 79.
Byron, killed his own genius by resisting Christian discipline, 392.

Cæsar, Augustus, corruption at work in grandeur of his times, 359.
Cæsarea-Philippi, place where Jesus disclosed his Messiahship, 253.
Cassini, opposed Newton's system of gravitation, 80.
Castor, Agrippa, a contemporary of Basilides, 290.
Celsus, early opponent of Christianity, 291.
China: visited by Marco Polo, 78; early history of, recently explored, 99; one of the only two non-Christian empires yet remaining, 374.
Chinese, to them Western peoples are only red-bristled barbarians, 353.
Choral, the, influence of Christianity upon, 386.
Chrimhild, a character in poem of Gudrun, 387.
Christlieb, Dr. Theodor, his lecture, 19.
Cicero, his question touching the universal belief of men in the divine, 23.
Cochineal, an insect, 82.
Cold, as a disease not yet fully understood by physicians, 87.
Colebrook, a Himalaya explorer, 78.
Columbus: great faith of, 72; not appreciated by his own generation, 78.
Commune, atheism of the, 22.
Cooley, a London geographer, 79.
Conscience, discovered first by Christianity, known by Romans only as consciousness of guilt, treated by Plato as an exercise of the memory, 129.
Confessionalists, the, different classes of, in Germany, 315.
Conservation of force, opposed yet by eminent scientists on ground of unexplained difficulties, 86.
Copernicus: needed faith to make his astronomical discoveries, 72; one of the "heroes of science." 152.

Cosmogonies, the Etruscan and Persian, specify that the world was created in six thousand years, 92, 93.
Council, The Tridentine, 361, 376.
CREATION, THE DOCTRINE OF, AND NATURAL SCIENCE, 69–104.
Creed, the Athanasian, its peculiarities and defects, 50–52.
Cremer, Hermann, D. D., his lecture, 109.
Cross, lines upon "Religion of the," etc., 365.
CULTURE, CHRISTIANITY AND, 349–397.
Culture and cultus, 350.
Croll, James, theory respecting the eccentricity of the earth's orbit, 98.
Cuvier, testimony respecting the *Perca Scandens*, or flying fish, 82.
Czolbe, a prominent German writer and materialist, 24.

Daimachus, ancient authority on India, 77.
Dalton, the atomic theory of, 94.
Dana, American geologist, 99.
Dannecker, his statue of Christ, 384.
Dante, "Divine Comedy" of, born of Christianity, 377, 388.
Darwin: has a remnant of belief in a living, personal Deity, 73; draws his weapons from the Lyellian quietism, 94.
De Brahe, Tycho, opposed the Copernican system, 80.
Des Cartes, opposed Newton's system of gravitation, 80.
De Groot, supports Tischendorf as to origin of Gospels, 294.
De La Hire, the cochineal an insect, 82.
Deism: its conception of God, 26, 27; protest against, 30–32; truth in, 35, 36; see also 158–163.
Delitzsch, on the Trinity, 59.
Disselhoff, Rev. Julius, his lecture, 349.

Earth, oblateness of, 85, 86.
Earthquakes, in South America, and one which destroyed Lisbon, 97.
Ebionism, a legalistic tendency, 315.
Egypt, earliest history of, too recent to agree with the Lyellian chronology, 90.

Electricity, obscurities regarding, 87.
Empires, duration of ancient compared with modern, 374, 375.
Epicureans, were materialists, 24.
Ephesus, temple ruins there, 354.
Esquimaux, think only themselves to be *innuit* or man, 358.
Eucharist, celebrated in Asia Minor on 14th of Nisan, 295.
Eusebius, testimony respecting Ignatius' letters, 287.
"Ezechiel," article by Baumgarten, 334.

Fabri, Dr., *Briefen gegen den Materialismus*, 103.
Faith, the Christian, great question regarding it now, 20.
Feuerbach: an atheist, 22; strong advocate of materialism, 24.
Fichte, J. H., on the Trinity, 61.
Fischer, Phil., on the form of the earth, 86.
Fish, the *Perca Scandens*, or *Anabus Cuvieri*, climbs trees, 82.
Fons totius Deitatis, 52.
Fossil human remains, classification of, 91.
Fossil skeletons of strangely formed animals, 90.
France, ineffectual schemes for saving of, 376.
Fuchs, Rev. M., his lecture, 147.

Geoffroy, says cochineal is an insect, 82.
Germany, in deepest disgrace after battle of Jena, 376, 377.
Gervinus, historian of literature, 391.
Gess, W. F., D. D., his lecture, 253.
Ghiberti, Lorenzo, his reliefs on Gates of Paradise, 384.
GOD, THE BIBLICAL CONCEPTION OF, 19–63.
God: a spirit, 38, 40; holy love, 40, 41; a Father, 41, 42.
Goethe: on power of religion, 19; on pantheism, 25; on deistic view of the world, 159, 160; his "Affinities" and "Stella," 369; his "Faust" and "Iphigenie," 391; his "Stella" and second part of "Faust," 392.

Göppert, transformed vegetable and animal substances into stone coal by application of extreme heat, 98.
GOSPELS, THE AUTHENTICITY OF OUR, 281–300; oldest Latin and oldest Syriac translation, 284; the Synoptics and John, 296–298.
Gothic cathedral, the triumph of architecture, 382.
Grau, Charles Darwin, and August Schleicher, 79.
Grim, definition of *Aberglaube*, 75.
Gudrun, The, an old German poem, 386.

Hagia Sophia, church or mosque in Constantinople, 382.
Hamann: on service of philosophy, 362; on marriage relation, 368; on explanation of events, 380; on pretended soundness of reason, 381; indicated the germs of a Christian philosophy, 382.
Hamilton, a Himalaya explorer, 78.
Handel, his music as affected by Christianity, 385.
"Harmonies of Gospels" by Tatian and Theophilus, 284.
Hartwig, G., *Gott in der Natur*, 83.
Harvey, his discovery of the circulation of blood discredited, 83.
Hase, in *Hutt. rediv.*, 75.
Heer, Oswald, his theory of differently warmed spaces through which our solar system passes, 98.
Hegel: his conception of God, 26; on doctrine of Trinity, 61; on soul as organ for revelation, 312; on development of all life, 317; on ethics not holding good in politics, 380.
Heine, destroyer of his own genius, 392.
"Heliand, The," old German poem, 386.
Heraclitus, God the universal measure of the world's becoming, 39.
Herbertists, declared "the King of heaven must be dethroned," 22.
Heracleon, a disciple of Valentine, 290.
Herodotus, rejected reports of circumnavigation of Africa, 77.

Himalayas, the snow limits of, 78, 79.
Hippolytus: on Valentine, 289; on Basilides, 290.
Hodgson, discovered one-horned antelope, 83.
Homer, represents man as most unfortunate, 356.
Holsten, visionary theory of, of Jesus' resurrection, 223-239.
Horace: on putrefaction of Roman life, 352; on corruption of marriage and the family, 368.
Humanism, 361.
Hutton, James, one of the earliest geologists, 88.
Huxley, draws weapons from Lyellian quietism, 94.
Huyghens, opposed Newton's system of gravitation, 80.
Hymn, the evangelical, its remarkable character and influence, 391.

Jansenism, destroyed in France, 376.
Japanese, theory which would admit their culture, 322.
"Jaxthausen, a castle on the Jaxt," 312.
Jenner, his discovery of vaccination discredited, 83.
Jericho, near this city Jesus disclosed the purpose of his dying, 255.
JESUS CHRIST, THE PERSON OF, 181-206.
John, a Dane who made observations on the *Perca Scandens*, 82.
John, prologue to his Gospel recently discovered, 288.
Josephus, knew about the intuitive consciousness, 312.
Joshua, his appeal to the people, 63.
Justin Martyr, his apology, 285.

Kepler: needed faith for his astronomical discoveries, 72; one of the heroes of science, 152.
Kilimanjaro, a snow-crowned mountain in Equatorial Africa, 72.
Kinkel, a German poet: on the hereafter, 370; on the quiet of a Christian parsonage, 370.
KINGDOM OF GOD AS CONSUMMATED, THE IDEA OF THE, AND WHAT IT TELLS US REGARDING HISTORICAL CHRISTIANITY, 305-344.
Kirchmann, Herr von: public demands regarding society, 369; his views on the nature and object of culture, 394.
Klopstock, his "Messias" the dawn of second blooming period in German poetry, 391.
Kraff, an African explorer, 79.

L'Aigle, fall of aërolites near, 81.
Lacepede, authority on the *Perca Scandens*, 82.
Lalande, his atheism, 48.
La Mettrie, a French atheist, 22.
Lange, J. P., D. D., his lecture, 305.
Language, influenced by Christianity, 377.
Laocoön, shows despotic power of fate, 355.
La Place: his atheism, 48; calculations on earth's oblateness, 85.
Lavoisier, needed faith to make his chemical discoveries, 73.
Leeambye River, 79.
Leibnitz, opposed Newton's system of gravitation, 80.
Leonhardt, W., feels force of argument against Lyellian quietism, 99.
Libanius, on excellence of Christian women, 367.
Liebig, his faith and chemical discoveries, 73.
Life-principle, whether there is a common one is matter of dispute, 87.
Linnæus, his faith and discoveries in zoölogy, 72.
Livingstone, his reports concerning identity of Leeambye and Zambesi rivers discredited, 79.
Livy, on elements of decomposition in highest Roman culture, 352.
Louis XIV. and Louis XV., brilliant times of, still carried barbarism in their bosom, 359.
Lücke, correspondent of Schleiermacher, 150.
Luthardt, Chr. E., D. D., his lecture, 181.
Luther, on relation of believing soul to Christ, 274, 275.

Lytton, Edward Bulwer, his translations of Schiller, 395, 396.

Magnetism, animal, 83.
Mallet, Dr., remark of touching the "light troops" of unbelief, 73, 152.
Manschot, *Ueber den Opfertod Jesu*, 328.
Marcion, heretical teacher of second century, 290.
Marco Polo, his reports respecting the East disbelieved, 78.
Marriage, influence of Christianity upon, 369.
Materialism: described, 23, 24; protest against, 29; truth in, 32, 33; see also p. 152.
Mayer, J. R., author of famous heat hypothesis, 86.
Meadows, G. P., "The Chinese," 99.
Medical "school of skeptics," 87.
Medici, the, their brilliant times and barbarism, 359.
Megasthenes, ancient authority on India, 77.
Meinecke, in Neumann's *Zeitschr.*, 80.
Menken, Godfrey, on necessity of the atonement, 259, 260.
Mephistopheles, in Goethe's "Faust," on value of reason, 362.
Mesmer, his doctrine of animal magnetism discredited, 83.
"Messer Milione," nickname for Marco Polo, 78.
Milton, his "Paradise Lost" molded by biblical Christianity, 388.
Missions, Christian, their influence upon heathen peoples, 375, 376, 378.
MIRACLES, 147-176.
Möbius, K., *Das Meerleuchten*, 81.
Moleschott, J.: noted materialist, 24; drew weapons from the Lyellian quietism, 94.
Monotheism, biblical, 33.
Montholon's "Memoirs of Napoleon," 185.
Mosaic record, the, and natural science, 100-102.
Müller, *Die Natur*, 83.
Müller, John, a physiologist, 73.
Müller, John, great historian, made Christian by considering unique position of Christ, 198.

Muratori catalogue of books of New Testament, 284.
Murchison, does not accept conclusions of the Lyellian quietism, 99.
Music and singing as influenced by Christianity, 384-386.

Names applied to God in the Scriptures, 42.
Napoleon, his different views of Christ, 184, 185.
Naturalism, older name for deism, 27.
Necho, an Egyptian king, 77.
Neo-gnostic forms of unmannerliness appearing nowadays, 315.
Neptunism, doctrines of formation of earth by action of water, 89.
Neumann's *Zeitschrift für allgem. Erdkunde*, 83.
Newton: faith of, 72; one of the "heroes of science," 152.
Nibelungen, The, old German poem, 386.
Nile, countries recently discovered at source of, 79.
Niobe, the statue and power of fate, 355.
Nitzsch, what Christianity has done for cultureless peoples, 375.

Oetinger, the "Magus of the South," assails shallow dogmatism of the skeptics, 84.
Organ, the, a child of Christianity, 384.
Origen, on date of Celsus' death, 291.

Painting, as influenced by Christianity, 382.
Palestrina, eminent Christian musician, 385.
Pantheism: described, 24-26; protest against, 29, 30; truth in, 33, 34; see also 152.
Papacy, Occidental and Oriental, 321, 322.
Papal Church, its ruinous power, 361.
Papias, account of him given by Eusebius, 288.
Paschal lamb, the, 257.
Paul, his quotation from Greek poet, 124.

Pearson, quotation from, 27.
Percival, the jewel of German art-poetry, 387.
Pericles, the times of, 359.
Personality, the absolute and relative, 364.
Perty, recognizes the intuitive consciousness, 312.
Petermann's geography, 79.
Peysonnel, on coral, 82.
Philosophy, as influenced by Christianity, 381, 382.
Phlogiston, Stahl's theory of, 94.
Piato, Fernan Mendez, his discoveries disbelieved, 78.
Pilate, question of, "What is truth?" 76.
Plato: acknowledges need of revelation, 116; man the measure of all things, 117; his mistaken ideas of culture, 356, 357; teaches personality of God, 384.
Plutarch, on superstition, 124.
Plutonism, doctrine of formation of earth by action of fire, 88.
Poetry, as influenced by Christianity, 386-392.
Poison's theory of differently warmed spaces, 98, 99.
Poisons, little known of their chemical combination and action, 87.
Polycarp, letter of, 288.
Political life, as influenced by Christianity, 370-373.
Positivists, so the negative thinkers in Paris style themselves, 308.
Presensé, on significance of Jesus' resurrection, 241.
Ptolemy, a disciple of Valentine, 290.

Quietism, the Lyellian: opposed to biblical account of creation, 91-95; disproved (1) by fact of its confounding creation with preservation, 95, 96; (2) by fact of incidental circumstances controlling geological changes, 96, 97; (3) by probability of forces operating in times past which are not now recognizable, 97, 98; (4) by astronomical probabilities and postulates respecting a higher degree of heat obtain-ing anciently than now, 98, 99; (5) by fact that historical traditions of oldest nations do not go back farther than from 2500 to 2700 B. C., 99.

Racine, "Esther" and "Athalie," 390.
Rationalistic view of God, 26, 27; protest against, 30-32; truth in, 35, 36.
Rebmann, an African explorer, 79.
Renan: his conception of Jesus, 189; his theory of Jesus' resurrection, 221.
RESURRECTION OF CHRIST, THE, AS A SOTERIOLOGICO-HISTORICAL FACT, 211-248.
REVELATION, REASON, CONSCIENCE, AND, 109-142.
Ritter, Karl, on influence of Christian missions, 376.
Ritualists, tendency of appearing in Germany, 315.
Rokatanski, head of a medical school at Vienna, 87.
Ross, John, Arctic explorer, 78.
Rosse, Lord, nebulæ resolved by, 80.
Ruscher, proved that the cochineal is an insect, 82.

Sabbath, The, what Christianity does for it, 373.
Salpæ generate by alternation, 82.
Salamander, mistaken by Scheüzer for a man who perished in the flood, 90
Schaaffhausen, Prof., on date of oldest human fossil, 91.
Schelling: his definition of God, 39; approaches very closely the Christian view of the Trinity, 61.
Schenkel: his theory of resurrection of Christ, 239, 240, 245; says that conscience alone relates to Deity, 313.
Schiller, his notion of culture, 394-396.
Schlagintweit, Rob. v. in Andreë's "Globus," 79.
Schleiden, remarks on nature of superstition, 75.
Schleiermacher: on miracles, 150, 151; on lust in Greek popular life, 357; theory of resurrection of Jesus, 217; letters about F. Schlegel's "Luzinde," 369.
Scholten, *Die ältesten Zeugnisse*, 294.

GENERAL INDEX   405

Schmidt, calculations of, on the earth's oblateness, 85.
Schnaase, on painting as connected with ecclesiastical themes, 383.
Schubert, investigations touching the earth's oblateness, 85.
Schwalb, *Der alte und der neue Glaube*, 328.
Science, its indebtedness to Christianity, 378–380.
Sculpture, as influenced by Christianity, 383, 384.
Sebaldus Monument, The, 384.
"Seefarht," building in Bremen where these lectures were delivered, 306.
Shakespeare: speaks powerfully of sin as a law controlling the subject, 264; his poetry inconceivable without biblical Christianity, 389.
Siedler, *De Skepticismo Commentatio*, 77.
Sin, only biblical Christianity makes no compromise with, 360.
Skull, The Engis, discovered by Schmerling, 90, 91.
Socialist unions, the avowed aims of many of them atheistic, 22.
Socrates: what is narrated of him by Plato in his "Charmidas," 357; his δαιμόνιον, 312.
Spallanzani, gives description of internal state of Stromboli, 89.
Speke, an African explorer, 79.
Spiegel, *Zeitschrift*, etc., 93.
Spinoza: the father of Occidental pantheism, 25; genesis of his conception of the Deity, 56.
Spontaneous generation, a disputed doctrine until recently, 87.
Stein, minister, his indignation at abuses inflicted on hymnology by unbelief, 391.
Steitz, Ulrich, *Die Schöpfungsgeschichte nach Geologie und Bibel*, 101.
Stephens, "Hist. of Methodist Church in America," 83.
Stones, showers of, near L'Aigle, 80, 81.
Strabo, disbelieved the testimony of Megasthenes and Daimachus regarding India, 77.
Strauss: on the theory of Jesus being only apparently dead, 218; felt the impossibility of so great a change in the disciples in only three days, 230; his delusion theory of Jesus' resurrection, 233; on significance of Jesus' resurrection, 241.
Suffrage Universel, 332.
Suidas, 93.
Swammerdam and Leeuwenhoeck, Dutch naturalists, their microscopical discoveries discredited a century after made, 81.

Tertullian, accused of falsely attributing to Marcion a knowledge of the Gospels, 291.
Testaments of the Twelve Patriarchs, 292.
Theism biblical, 28–50.
Theseus, temple of, at Athens, 382.
Tholuck, on fatherhood of God, 42.
Thorwaldsen, his "Christ and the Twelve Apostles," 384.
Thucydides, on elements of decomposition in highest Greek life, 352.
Tiberius, Roman emperor, heathen writers tell of Jesus' crucifixion during his reign, 185.
Tischendorf, Constantin, his lecture, 281.
Trinitarian Conception of the Divine Nature, 50–63; supports of doctrine from history, 55–57; advantages derived from doctrine, 57, 58; collateral arguments from speculative theology, 58, 59; reflections of the idea in human nature and in creation generally, 59–61; proved also by philosophy, 61–63.
Tractarians, among recent appearances in Germany, 315.
Truth, the Greek word for, 121.
Turkish Empire and the Chinese, remain the only non-Christian States, 374.
Tyndall, paper of, before British natural science gathering at Norwich, 86.

Ulrici, *Gott und die Natur*, 83, 86, 87.
Ulrick von Würtemberg, Duke, delusions respecting, 233.
Ukerwi, lake in Equatorial Africa, 79.

Valentine, ancient heretical teacher, 289.
Vaccination, discovery of, 83.
Venus, The Medicean, beautiful form concealing a corrupt cultural life, 355.
Vespucius, Americus, geographical discoveries of discredited, 78.
Victoria Nyanza, lake in Equatorial Africa, 79.
Vilmar, *Pastoral theol.*, 90.
Vischer, Peter, his statues and reliefs on the Sebaldus Monument, 384.
Vogt, C.: a noted materialist, 24; draws weapons from the Lyellian quietism, 94.
Voltaire, his "Zaire" and "Alzire" pervaded by Christian life-emotions, 390.
Von Der Decken, his expedition ascended Mount Kilimanjaro in Africa, 80.
Von Auberlen, 85.
Von Baer, R. E., does not agree wholly with the long-time view of the world's creation, 99.
Von Chamisso, discovered peculiarities respecting the Salpæ, 82.
Von Daldorff, testimony respecting the *Perca Scandens*, 82.
Von Eschenbach, Wolfram, author of "Percival," 387.
Von Haller, Albrecht, on disbelief of African king, 84, 85.
Vulcanist, one who believes in formation of earth by the action of fire, 89.

Wagner, R., needed faith, 73.

Wagner, Andr., *Die Berufung*, etc., 98.
Wagner, A., and the Lyellian quietism, 98.
Walther von der Vogelweide and his song, 387, 388.
Wann wurden unsere Evangelien verfasst? 294.
Wappäus, Dr., statistics regarding crime, 262.
Webb, a Himalaya explorer, 78.
Wellingtonians (Sequoias), trees in California, 81, 82.
Werner, Abraham, one of the first scientific geologists, 88.
Wieland, conversation of, with Napoleon, 184.
Winkelmann, indignant at abuses inflicted on the hymn by unbelief, 391.
Woodward, C., on trinity in unity of light, 60.
Wundt, W., *Die physikalischen Axiome*, etc., 86.

Xenophanes, a Greek philosopher, 24, 25.

Young, T. R., "Modern Skepticism Viewed in Relation to Modern Science," 77.

Zambesi, river in Africa, 79.
Zedlitz, his lines on Byron, 392.
Zöckler, Otto, his lecture, 69.
Zollman, on chance as creator of the world, 157.
Zöllner, J., *Ueber die universelle Bedeutung der mechanischen Principien*, 86.